The Synoptic Problem

Steven M. Sheeley: "It will be a good resource for anyone who desires either an introduction to the Synoptic problem or a refresher course in Synoptic studies. It will also be useful for those whose students have been inoculated against rather than introduced to Source, Form, and Redaction criticism." *(Review and Expositor)*

Harold W. Hoehner: "The real value of the book lies in the last two parts. Stein helps Bible students understand and evaluate form criticism and redaction criticism. He is fair to those with whom he disagrees. The student of the Scriptures will be able to understand better the discussion in the more recent commentaries on the Gospels." *(Bibliotheca Sacra)*

Fred W. Burnett: "Expertly introduces the student to the synoptic problem and to the methodologies which it entails. With its glossary, scriptural and topical indices, its workbook format, and its reasonable price, it is an excellent textbook for one of almost any theological persuasion." *(Christian Scholar's Review)*

Richard B. Vinson: "A clear, readable, evangelical introduction to certain aspects of Gospel criticism, one which presupposes the Two-source Hypothesis. For those who share those points of view, it would be an excellent introductory text; for those who don't, it would make an excellent 'op-ed' parallel reading representative for another perspective." *(Perspectives in Religious Studies)*

The Synoptic Problem

An Introduction

Robert H. Stein

Baker Books

A Division of Baker Book House Co
Grand Rapids, Michigan 49516

©1987 by Baker Book House Company

Published by Baker Books
a division of Baker Book House Company
P.O. Box 6287, Grand Rapids, MI 49516-6287

First paperback edition, 1994
Second printing, 1998

Printed in the United States of America

ISBN 0-8010-2019-0

Unless otherwise noted, all Scripture references are taken from the Revised Standard Version of the Bible, copyright 1946, 1952, 1971, 1973 by the Division of Christian Education of the National Council of Churches of Christ in the United States of America.

For information about academic books, resources for Christian leaders, and all new releases available from Baker Book House, visit our web site:
http://www.bakerbooks.com

To

Julie and **Bruce**

And

Keith and **Barbara**

" . . . from the beginning of creation, God made them male and female. For this reason a man shall leave his father and mother and be joined to his wife, and the two shall become one flesh. So they are no longer two but one flesh. What therefore God has joined together, let not man put asunder."

Mark 10:6–9

Contents

Preface

During my years of teaching it has been my privilege to teach at least one course a year on either "The Life and Teachings of Jesus" or "The Gospels." More often than not, I have taught at least two courses on this subject each year. Despite the myriads of relevant texts available, I have never found the particular kind of text that I thought was needed for introducing students to the study of the synoptic Gospels. Although there are many excellent and valuable works on the subject, what seemed to be lacking was an introduction that would help students work their way, step by step, through the Gospels disciplines. The plan of this text is to do just that. As a result, it serves both as an introduction and a work manual. It is hoped that students will proceed systematically through the text and underline the numerous parallel passages included, using the suggested color code. The importance of underlining the texts cannot be overestimated, for it is only by analyzing the texts in this manner that students can become familiar with the various disciplines and work their own way through them.

The order of the major sections of this work (Literary Criticism, Form Criticism, Redaction Criticism) is based less on exegetical considerations than on historical ones. The development of Gospel studies over time has proceeded in this manner. In reality, however, these disciplines overlap and are interrelated, so that we are involved in a kind of hermeneutical circle. It seemed best to begin in the same way that gospel studies have developed historically, for in so doing students will not only proceed with greater facility through the various disciplines but will also develop at the same time a sense for the historical development of these disciplines in other areas of biblical studies as well.

There are a number of people who have been especially helpful in the publication of this work. I am indebted to Gloria Metz, the faculty secretary, for all her help in the preparation of this manuscript and for rescuing me time and time again from various disagreements with my word processor. Thanks also needs to be expressed to Bonnie Goding, for her careful checking of the manuscript for errors and for her suggestions as to how something confusing or esoteric could be better worded for students. I would like to thank my colleague Marvin W. Anderson, professor of church history, for his kind and helpful assistance in researching the material involving the early harmonies and synopses of the Gospels. To my wife I express my deep appreciation, for without her support this work would never have been completed. I would also like to mention my gratitude to the European Nazarene Bible College in Büsingen in the Federal Republic of Germany, for all the kindness shown me during my sabbatical leave in 1984, when much of this manuscript was written. A special word of thanks is extended to the United Bible Societies for permission to use the *Synopsis of the Four Gospels*, edited by Kurt Aland, for the parallel passages included in the text. All quotations, both from this synopsis and elsewhere from the Bible, are from the Revised Standard Version.

Abbreviations

Bib	*Biblica*
BZ	*Biblische Zeitschrift*
CBQ	*Catholic Biblical Quarterly*
EQ	*Evangelical Quarterly*
ET	*Expository Times*
Interp	*Interpretation*
JBL	*Journal of Biblical Literature*
JETS	*Journal of the Evangelical Theological Society*
JQR	*Jewish Quarterly Review*
JSNT	*Journal for the Study of the New Testament*
JTS	*Journal of Theological Studies*
L	Material unique to the Gospel of Luke
Loeb	The Loeb Classical Library
M	Material unique to the Gospel of Matthew
NT	*Novum Testamentum*
NTS	*New Testament Studies*
Q	A hypothetical source (or sources) used by Matthew and Luke in writing their Gospels, i.e., the material common to Matthew and Luke but not found in Mark
TDNT	*Theological Dictionary of the New Testament*
TZ	*Theologische Zeitschrift*
ZNW	*Zeitschrift für die neutestamentliche Wissenschaft*

Introduction

Within the New Testament there exist four works that bear the name *Gospel*. Although all four of these books are anonymous, early tradition has ascribed to them the following titles: The Gospel of Matthew; The Gospel of Mark; The Gospel of Luke; and The Gospel of John.[1] From the beginning it has been apparent that these four works possess both similarities and differences. The similarities are, of course, most evident. All four works deal with the life of Jesus of Nazareth. All four portray him as one who was uniquely sent from God, worked numerous miracles, taught a noble ethic, associated with the outcasts of society, drew upon himself the hatred of the Jewish religious leaders, was by the design and plan of God crucified and raised from the dead, and so on. All clearly claim that this Jesus is the Son of God, the Savior of the world. At times all four Gospels record the same events—for example, the coming on the scene of John the Baptist as the forerunner of Jesus; the anointing of Jesus by the Spirit; the cleansing of the temple; the feeding of the five thousand; Jesus' triumphal entry into Jerusalem; the denial of Peter. Yet it is likewise obvious from even a cursory reading that there are also differences between these four Gospels. Matthew and Luke speak of a virgin birth, whereas Mark and John do not. Each Gospel also seems to emphasize different aspects and themes with regard to the life of Jesus. Occasionally

---

1. The anonymity of the canonical Gospels is all the more striking when compared to the apocryphal gospels and the rest of the books of the New Testament.

the order of the events and sayings in the Gospels deviates from one Gospel to another, as does the wording of Jesus' sayings.

It has also become clear that three of these four Gospels resemble each other to a great extent, both in their wording and their ordering of the material. Matthew, Mark, and Luke obviously have more in common with each other than with John. A quick glance through a fourfold Gospel parallel in any language will immediately reveal this. As early as the second century, Christian scholars have wrestled with the issue of the similarity and diversity of the Gospels. Why are they both alike and different? If we say they are "alike" because they all deal with the life of Jesus, we must also wonder why at times they are different. If we say they are "different" because they were written by four different people, then we must ask why three of them are so very much alike in certain instances. The obvious similarities of the first three Gospels—the Synoptics—have raised many questions and given rise to much scholarly investigation. In fact it may well be that more time and effort has been spent on this "Synoptic Problem" than on any other biblical issue.

Early Comparisons of the Gospels

The earliest serious attempt to resolve the problem of unity and diversity, i.e., the similarities and differences, in the canonical Gospels was by Tatian (c. 110–172). Tatian, a pupil of Justin Martyr, wrote his famous *Diatesseron* around A.D. 150. In this work Tatian sought to go "through the four" (*dia tesseron*) individual Gospels in order to produce a single comprehensive text. Using a separate manuscript for each Gospel, he interwove the various gospel accounts. Beginning with the Johannine prologue, he followed the order of the Jewish festivals in the Gospel of John. As he proceeded, he crossed out phrases in the manuscripts as he used them.[2] When he was finished, Tatian had reduced the 3,780 verses of the four Gospels to 2,769. Tatian's work became quite popular. Although it may very well have been originally written in Greek, its greatest influence came through the Syriac version. Even after the appearance of one of the Syriac translations of the Bible (the Peshitta [411]), Theodoret (393–458) was able to find over two hundred copies of the *Diatesseron* still in use.

Tatian's *Diatesseron* is the earliest example of what has been called a "harmony of the Gospels." This term is most generally used to describe works that seek to establish the correct historical order of the

---

2. So Bruce M. Metzger, *The Early Versions of the New Testament* (Oxford: Clarendon, 1977), pp. 11–12.

various events found in the four Gospels and/or try to explain or "har-monize" the apparent discrepancies in them. Tatian was concerned primarily with the former, or "historical," issue. Later on, harmonists such as Augustine and Osiander, while interested in chronology, were even more concerned with the latter, or "apologetical," issue.

The work of the rather unknown Ammonius of Alexandria (c. 220) is probably the earliest forerunner of our modern "Synopsis." Ironically, Ammonius was apparently the first person to use the term *harmonia* ("harmony") to describe his work, although technically his work is more accurately classified as a synopsis, since its main purpose is not to arrange the accounts in historical order but to list the parallel pas-sages in the Gospels for the sake of comparison. We know of Ammo-nius primarily through the work of Eusebius of Caesarea (265–339).[3] Eusebius himself built upon the work of Ammonius in order to pro-duce his famous "Canons of Eusebius." In this list of canons Eusebius provides a useful table that enables the reader to find parallel materials in the various Gospels. It found extensive use in different Greek manu-scripts of the New Testament and in numerous printed editions of the Greek New Testament as well. It is still found in the "Explanations" section of the Nestle editions of the Greek New Testament. Eusebius' table contains ten "canons," or lists. To compile these canons, Euse-bius first divided each of the Gospels into sections beginning with the number one. Matthew was divided into 355 sections; Mark into 233; Luke into 342; and John into 232. The first table lists the material that was common to all four Gospels. Thus the first entry—Mt-8; Mc-2; Lc-7; Ioh (John)-10—indicates that the eighth section of Matthew, the second section of Mark, the seventh section of Luke, and the tenth section of John contain parallel material, i.e., the baptism of Jesus. The second canon deals with material common to Matthew, Mark, and Luke; the third with material common to Matthew, Luke, and John; and the fourth with material common to Matthew, Mark, and John. The fifth canon lists material common to Matthew and Luke; the sixth, material common to Matthew and Mark; the seventh, material common to Matthew and John; the eighth, material common to Luke and Mark; and the ninth, material common to Luke and John. The tenth and last canon contains four subsections and lists what is unique to Matthew, to Mark, to Luke, and to John.

A third important work dealing with the similarities and differences found in the Gospels is Augustine's *De Consensu Evangelistarum*. In

---

3. See his *Letter to Carpianus*. A copy of the letter in Greek can be found in a *Nestle Greek New Testament*. For an English translation see Harold H. Oliver, "The Epistle of Eusebius to Carpianus: Textual Tradition and Translation," *NT* 3 (1959): 144–45.

Book One of this work Augustine gives a general apology for the
Gospels and the Christian faith. Then, in Books Two, Three, and Four,
he discusses the various Gospels, using Matthew for his basic outline
of Jesus' life. His purpose is clearly harmonistic, for he seeks to demonstrate that the accounts do not conflict with or contradict each other.
Two examples help illustrate this. In Augustine's discussion of the
ministry of John the Baptist he points out the differences that exist in
the words that John is reported to have said. He concludes, however,
that such differences should not cause any great difficulty, in that we
are able to know the truth of what was said even if we do not know the
precise words.[4] For Augustine, the truthfulness of the gospel accounts
is not so much dependent on reproducing the exact words (*ipsissima
verba*) of John the Baptist (or, in other instances, of Jesus) as much as in
truly presenting their words without falsehood.

The second example of how Augustine handles the variations in the
Gospels involves the Sermon on the Mount. After pointing out some of
the differences that exist between Matthew's Sermon on the Mount
and Luke's Sermon on the Plain, Augustine seeks to explain why they
are so much alike. He acknowledges that perhaps one approach would
be to see the differences as due to Luke's omission of certain material
and his addition of other material omitted by Matthew, and he states
that the Evangelists may have expressed "these utterances in somewhat different terms, but without detriment to the integrity of the
truth."[5] What stands in his way of accepting this view, however, is
that Matthew portrays the sermon as being presented on a mountain
while Jesus was sitting, whereas Luke portrays the sermon as being
presented on a plain while Jesus was standing.[6] Thus Augustine suggests that we have, in the two accounts, reports of two separate events
that contain sayings spoken by Jesus on two different occasions. Matthew happened to record the one and Luke the other.

It is clear from these two examples that Augustine sought to harmonize many of the apparent discrepancies found in the parallel accounts. No doubt this was due to his view that the Gospels were
written by men through the agency of the Holy Spirit.[7] Not all of
Augustine's explanations are convincing, but his *De Consensu Evangelistarum* is still worthwhile reading for conservative and liberal scholars
alike. For the former, it is valuable to see how a great defender of the
faith handled problematic passages in the Gospels and to note the
freedom he granted the Evangelists in the wording and arrangement of

4. See 2.12.27.
5. 2.19.44. The translation comes from *The Nicene and Post-Nicene Fathers*, vol. 6.
6. 2.19.45.
7. 1.1.2.

their Gospels. For the latter, it is helpful to see that "harmonizing" the Gospels has a noble history and that many of the greatest minds of the church have been involved in this task.[8]

During the following centuries, numerous harmonies of the Gospels were produced, and the influence of Tatian can be seen in many of them. One of the most important was John Gerson's *Monotesseron Sive Unum Ex Quattuor Evangeliis*.[9] In this work Gerson, chancellor of the University of Paris, divides the life of Jesus into 151 Rubricae or chapters. (Actually there are 150, because number 136 is omitted for some reason.) To these 151 chapters, which are divided into three parts, are appended four additional sections dealing with various issues. Gerson's work is essentially a harmony, but at the end of each of the Rubricae he gives the references to the parallel accounts, although the parallels are not listed. The sixteenth century witnessed a dramatic increase in the number of harmonies that were produced. The exact number of new harmonies that appeared is not known. It was probably well over thirty, ". . . but on any rational reckoning it is safe to say that the sixteenth century produced more harmonies than the combined fourteen centuries that preceded it."[10] It also appears that new Roman Catholic harmonies outnumbered Protestant ones. The exact reason why this flowering of harmonies took place is uncertain. The invention of a printing press with movable type no doubt brought about an increase in publication in general. Even more significant may be the increased interest in history and the concomitant need of a Christian '"harmonizing" of some of the historical problems found in the Gospels.

8. Two other attempts, one ancient and one modern, to "harmonize" the gospel accounts should be mentioned. Origen sought such a harmony, but in a way distinctly his own. In contrast to Augustine, Origen believed that there exist historical and chronological errors, i.e., "material falsehood," in the accounts. Nevertheless harmony is to be found in the anagogical or allegorical interpretation of the accounts. (See his *Commentary on John*, 10:2–4.) Note his comment: "The spiritual truth was often preserved, as one might say, in material falsehood" (10:4). Recently Brevard S. Childs has sought by his "canonical criticism" to steer a middle road between the attempts of the ancient harmonists, such as Augustine, and the modern approach of historical criticism. By his "canonical harmonization" Childs attempts to do justice to the distinct meanings of the Evangelists and demonstrate their related and complementary interpretations despite their lack of historical consistency (*The New Testament as Canon: An Introduction* [Philadelphia: Fortress, 1984], pp. 154–209).

9. The most available edition of this is in Johannes Gersonii, *Opera Omnia* (Antwerpiae: Sumptibus Societatis, 1706), pp. 83–202, but the editio princeps was published in four volumes in Cologne in 1483–84.

10. Harvey K. McArthur, *The Quest Through the Centuries* (Philadelphia: Fortress, 1966), p. 86. See also pp. 157–64 for a listing of these harmonies.

One of the most famous harmonies of all time is Andreas Osiander's *Harmoniae Evangelicae,* which was published in Basel in 1537. Again we find a single harmonious account of the gospel materials without the printing of the parallel accounts. The Greek composite text is printed on the left page and the Latin text on the right. Osiander has a code in which, by using the letters A to P, he denotes whether the printed gospel material is found in a single Gospel or is a combination of various accounts. The text is then followed by his famous "Annotationum," in which he seeks to explain or harmonize the difficulties that exist between the gospel accounts. Due to his particular view of the inspiration of the Scriptures, Osiander tends to explain almost every variation in the narratives or the sayings of Jesus by claiming that the events or sayings occurred on more than one occasion. Thus he argues that Jairus' daughter was raised from the dead on two separate occasions, that there were four separate healings of blind men at Jericho, that there were two healings of the Gerasene maniac, that Jesus was crowned with thorns on two separate occasions during his trial, that Peter warmed himself at a fire four times, and so on. Both Luther and Calvin rejected such an approach.[11] Osiander's harmony provides a good example of how a holy reverence for the text can go astray when coupled with certain presuppositions of how the inspired Evangelists must have written their accounts. Still another important harmony of this period is that of Cornelius Jansen.[12] That interest in such harmonies has in no way waned but continues today is witnessed to by the continuous publication of such works.[13]

The Development of Gospel "Synopses"

In the earliest harmonies no attempt was made to place similar parallel materials side by side. As a result, these works were shorter than the total length of the four Gospels. Tatian, as has been noted, was

11. Cf. Calvin in his *Harmony* on Matthew 20:29–34 and parallels. Cf. also Jaroslav Pelikan, ed., *Luther's Works* (Saint Louis: Concordia Publishing, 1957), 22:218–19, where Luther almost certainly had Osiander in mind.

12. Cornelii Jansenii, *Commentariorum in suam concordiam* (Antwerpiae: Petrus Belleri, 1613).

13. Note, for instance, Manuel Komroff, *The One Story* (New York: Dutton, 1943), and Baird W. Whitlock, *The Gospel* (New York: Schocken, 1984). Most modern harmonies, however, tend to include all the parallel accounts as well. See, for example, Ralph Daniel Heim, *A Harmony of the Gospels for Students* (Philadelphia: Muhlenberg, 1947); John Franklin Carter, *A Layman's Harmony of the Gospels* (Nashville: Broadman, 1961); Robert L. Thomas and Stanley N. Gundry, *A Harmony of the Gospels* (Chicago: Moody, 1978); J. Dwight Pentecost, *A Harmony of the Words and Works of Jesus Christ* (Grand Rapids: Zondervan, 1981).

able to reduce the 3,780 verses of the Gospels down to 2,769, so that the *Diatesseron* was approximately 27 percent shorter than the individual Gospels. This was actually one of the values of such a harmony, in that the four Gospels could be condensed into a kind of "Reader's Digest Abridged Version." In a time of expensive paper and hand transcription, this served a valuable purpose. With the advent of printing, however, these considerations became less important, and it is therefore not surprising that after the invention of the printing press greater interest was shown in the production of harmonies that contained the parallel accounts for the sake of comparison. Along with the increase in the number of harmonies produced in the sixteenth century, a new format came on the scene. Whereas earlier harmonies were almost all "integrated harmonies"—like that of Tatian, in which all the parallel accounts in the four Gospels were integrated into a single narrative—now "parallel harmonies"[14] began to appear. These came in two main formats: horizontal parallel harmonies and vertical parallel harmonies.

The most famous of the horizontal parallel harmonies was John Calvin's *A Harmony of the Evangelists Matthew, Mark, and Luke*, which was published in Geneva simultaneously in both French and Latin in 1555.[15] In this work, which was dependent at least in part on Martin Bucer's earlier work,[16] Calvin places the parallel accounts under each other. He does not do this line by line, as in a modern horizontal line synopsis, but each entire passage is placed below the other. Calvin's harmony appears to have been the first harmony that used verse divisions. This was probably due to the fact that Robert Stephanus (also Robert Estienne), who introduced verse divisions into the Greek New Testament in 1551, was the publisher of Calvin's Latin harmony of the Gospels. The degree to which Calvin's harmony is devoted to commentary indicates that although Calvin was concerned with the question of historical order and "harmonizing" the gospel accounts, this was not his main concern. As a result, it is probably best to include this work under the designation "commentary" rather than "harmony." Some twenty years earlier, however, Robert Goullet, a Roman Catholic professor of theology in Paris, had produced a horizontal parallel harmony entitled *Tetramonon Evangeliorum*, and around 1300 Guido de

14. This terminology is found in McArthur, *The Quest*, p. 89.
15. The French edition is entitled *Concordance qu'on appelle Harmonie, Composee de trois Euangelistes ascavoir S. Matthieu, S. Marc, et. S. Luc* and was published by Conrad Badius, whereas the Latin is entitled *Harmonia ex tribus euangelistis composita, matthaeo, marco & luca* and was published by Robertus Stephanus.
16. Bucer's work was entitled *Enarrationum in evangelia Matthaei, Marci, & Lucae* (Strasbourg, 1527).

Perpignan in his *Quattuor Unum—Hoc Est Concordia Evangelica* used the same pattern.[17]

We also find appearing in the sixteenth century vertical parallel harmonies. Two of the earliest to appear were Charles Du Moulin's (Carolus Molinaeus) *Collatio et Unio Quatuor Evangelistarum Domini Nostri Jesu Christi* (1565) and Paul Crell's *Evangelion Unsers Herrn Jesu Christi . . . aus Allen Vier Evangelisten*, which was first published in Wittenberg in 1566.[18] To be sure, the primary purpose of these works was still "harmonistic," in that the great concern was to produce a chronological account of the gospel materials and to explain apparent discrepancies in order and wording, so that the transition from a "harmony" to a "synopsis" was a gradual one.

Another work that sought even more systematically to arrange the parallel material together was Martino Chemnitz's *Harmoniae Evangelicae*, which appeared in 1593.[19] Here the parallel accounts are placed in columns, in Greek on the left page and in Latin on the right. In this harmony, which also includes the Gospel of John, economy of space is attained by eliminating empty columns when a parallel is lacking in one or more of the other Gospels. Chemnitz also provided an extensive commentary after the synopsis of the material, so that each chapter consisted of the synopsis at the beginning and the following commentary. In 1644 there appeared a harmony in English by John Lightfoot entitled *The Harmony of the Four Evangelists*. Lightfoot, who was a member of the Westminster Assembly and later became vice-chancellor of Cambridge, places the parallel accounts in his harmony in column form. Due to his inclusion of the Gospel of John and his extensive commentary, this harmony goes only to Mark 2:14.[20] It was Johannes Clericus, also known as Le Clerc, who carried out the design and plan of Lightfoot to completion. In 1699 his *Harmonia Evangelica* was published.[21] In this work Le Clerc places the materials in parallel form, for the primary purpose of the work is not to provide a harmonious interweaving of a single chronological narrative but to place the parallel accounts side by side for comparison. Le Clerc's work became very popular and experienced several new editions. Some of the more popular were those of William Newcome in 1778 and Edward Robinson in 1834.

17. McArthur, *The Quest*, p. 91.

18. Ibid., pp. 89, 161.

19. This was published in Frankfurt by Iohannes Spies.

20. The best source for this work is found in *The Works of John Lightfoot* (London: 1684). In this work the harmony takes up 308 large 9" × 15" pages.

21. The work appears under the following name: Joanne Clerico, *Harmonia Evangelica* (Amstelodami: Sumptibus Huguetanorum, 1699).

The first "pure" synopsis must be credited to Johann Jacob Griesbach, who in 1776 published his *Synopsis Evangeliorum Matthaei, Marci
et Lucae*. Griesbach rejected all harmonistic concerns and sought to
produce a handy text by which interpreters could compare parallel
accounts. He states as his goal:

> The authors of harmonies have principally tried to determine the time
> and sequence in which the events written down by the Evangelists hap-
> pened; but this lies far outside my purpose. For I freely admit—and I
> wish to draw the reader's attention to this—that a "harmonia" in the
> literal sense of the word is not the aim of this book. For although I am
> not unaware of how much trouble very learned men have taken to build
> up a well-ordered harmony according to self-imposed rules, yet I still
> think not only that out of this minute care small advantage may be
> obtained, or even practically none at all that my synopsis would not also
> offer; but further I have serious doubts that a harmonious narrative can
> be put together from the books of the evangelists, one that adequately
> agrees with the truth in respect of the chronological arrangement of the
> pericopes and which stands on a solid basis. For what [is to be done], if
> none of the Evangelists followed chronological order exactly everywhere
> and if there are not enough indications from which could be deduced
> which one departed from the chronological order and in what places?
> Well, I confess to this heresy![22]

Because of this new purpose, Griesbach uses a different term in his
title. Instead of the term "harmony" he uses "synopsis." Whereas the
term was used in other areas and disciplines, this appears to be the
first time that it was used with regard to the arranging of the gospel
materials in parallel form.

Griesbach in his *Synopsis* ignores the Gospel of John almost completely and simply places together the parallel accounts of Matthew,
Mark, and Luke for the purpose of comparison. No attempt is made to
harmonize or reconcile the chronologies of John and the synoptic Gospels or, for that matter, that of the synoptic Gospels themselves. What
is sought is the production of a useful tool by which the parallel accounts in the synoptic Gospels can be compared. Although the results
of such investigation would no doubt raise questions with regard to
how the similarities and differences in the synoptic Gospels could be

---

22. The quotation comes from Heinrich Greeven, "The Gospel Synopsis from 1776 to
the Present Day," trans. Robert Althann in *J. J. Griesbach: Synoptic and Text-Critical Studies
1776–1976*, ed. Bernard Orchard and Thomas R. W. Longstaff (Cambridge: Cambridge
University, 1978), p. 27.

explained, Griesbach was careful not to construct his synopsis in order
to demonstrate or prove his own solution to the Synoptic Problem.[23]

In 1797 Griesbach published a second edition of his *Synopsis* in
which he included John 12:1–8 and 18:1–21:25. This was followed by a
third edition in 1809 and a fourth published posthumously in 1822.
Griesbach's *Synopsis* became the archetype of a whole family of synopses based on his work. In 1818 W. M. L. deWette and F. Lücke
published a synopsis based upon Griesbach's 1809 third edition. Even
the name of their work shows their dependence upon Griesbach for
they entitled it *Synopsis Evangeliorum Matthaei, Marci et Lucae*, and only
after these words do we find a difference in their title from Griesbach's.
In 1829 Moritz Roediger published a synopsis based upon those of
Griesbach and deWette/Lücke. His title also began *Synopsis Evangeliorum Matthaei, Marci et Lucae!* Other important synopses have followed.
It would be impossible to mention all of them, but some of the more
important ones are W. G. Rushbrooke's *Synopticon* in 1880; Albert
Huck's 1892 *Synopse der Drei Ersten Evangelien,* which contained no
references to the Gospel of John and went through new editions in
1898, 1906, 1910, 1916 (from that point on the parallels in John were
given), 1922, 1927, 1931, 1936, and 1950; E. D. Burton and E. J. Good-
speed's *A Harmony of the Synoptic Gospels in Greek* in 1920. Today there
exist two outstanding synopses in Greek that have found widespread
use. The most popular is Kurt Aland's *Synopsis Quattuor Evangeliorum,*
which was published in 1963 and has seen new editions in 1967, 1976,
and 1978. Its rich presentation of apocryphal and patristic material, its
inclusion of the Gospel of Thomas (in Latin, German, and English),
and the full incorporation of the Gospel of John make it a most useful
tool whose widespread use is fully deserved. A new edition of the
Huck synopsis came out in 1981, edited by Heinrich Greeven, which is
also entitled *Synopse der Drei Ersten Evangelien.* Both of these are excellent synopses and will prove most useful in gospel studies. The former
has the advantage of including greater parallel materials and arranging
them in less-confusing straight columns, but the latter has a better
textual apparatus.

For students without access to the original languages, Burton H.
Throckmorton, Jr., edited a fine synopsis in 1949 that has gone through
several editions. His work, *Gospel Parallels,* uses the text of the Revised
Standard Version and contains only the material found in the synoptic

23. Compare, for example, the criticism of Griesbach's format of placing the Gospel
of Mark in the middle by Bernard Orchard who holds Griesbach's solution to the Synoptic Problem in "Are All Gospel Synopses Biased?" *TZ* 34 (1978): 157–61. Cf. also David L.
Dungan, "Theory of Synopsis Construction," *Bib* 61 (1980): 305–29.

Gospels. In 1982, Kurt Aland edited an English version of his Greek synopsis under the title *Synopsis of the Four Gospels,* and this is clearly the best English synopsis now available. Although it does not include the apocryphal and patristic materials found in the Greek synopsis, it does include the Gospel of John and a helpful textual apparatus in which are listed variant readings of the King James Version, the Catholic edition of the Revised Standard Version of 1965, the English Revised Version of 1881, the American Standard Version of 1901, and the Revised Standard Version of 1946. Furthermore, although the size of Aland's synopsis is nearly twice that of Throckmorton's work (361 pages to 191), the cost is considerably less because of the subsidy of the United Bible Societies. As a result, it would be hard to recommend any better synopsis for English-reading students than this one by Aland.

PART **I**

The Literary Relationship of the Synoptic Gospels

1

The Literary Interdependence of the Synoptic Gospels

Despite the differences in size between Matthew (1,086 verses), Mark (661 verses), and Luke (1,149 verses), the use of a synopsis reveals that there exists a remarkable similarity between these three Gospels. This is especially evident when one compares the synoptic Gospels with the Gospel of John. This similarity is evident in several ways. For one, there is an obvious agreement in the wording of the individual accounts, or "pericopes," that these Gospels have in common. Second, this similarity manifests itself in the common order in which these individual pericopes are arranged. Third, we find a remarkable agreement in the synoptic Gospels in that these Gospels often contain exactly the same parenthetical material. Finally, it must be noted that in his opening prologue (1:1–4) Luke explicitly refers to other narratives that had been written before his Gospel and that he had investigated.

Agreement in Wording

The easiest way of observing the close similarity in the wording of the synoptic Gospels is to underline the agreements that exist between them in parallel passages. In order to facilitate not only the present discussion but later discussion as well, the following code is suggested. I suggest you underline carefully and word by word in one color (BLUE) the agreements that all three Gospels have in common. Use an unbroken line for exact agreements in order and wording and a broken line for agreements that are not exact but which are agreements nevertheless. Underline in another color (YELLOW or, if the yellow is hard to see, BLACK) the agreements that exist only between Matthew and Mark, using broken or unbroken line as just described. Underline in a third color (RED) the agreements that exist only between Matthew and Luke, and underline with still another color (GREEN) the agreements between Mark and Luke, using unbroken or broken lines according to the degree of exactness.[1]

1.1

Matthew 19:13–15	Mark 10:13–16	Luke 18:15–17
[13]Then children were brought to him that he might lay his hands on them and pray.	[13]And they were bringing children to him, that he might touch them;	[15]Now they were bringing even infants to him that he might touch them;
		and when the disciples saw it,
The disciples rebuked the people; [14]but Jesus said,	and the disciples rebuked them. [14]But when Jesus saw it he was indignant, and said to them,	they rebuked them. [16]But Jesus called them to him, saying,
"Let the children come to me, and do not hinder them; for to such belongs the kingdom of heaven."	"Let the children come to me, do not hinder them; for to such belongs the kingdom of God. [15]Truly, I say to you, whoever does not receive the kingdom of God like a child shall not enter it." [16]And he took them in his arms and blessed them, laying his hands upon them.	"Let the children come to me, and do not hinder them; for to such belongs the kingdom of God. [17]Truly, I say to you, whoever does not receive the kingdom of God like a child shall not enter it."
[15]And he laid his hands on them and went away.		

1.2

Matthew 22:23–33	Mark 12:18–27	Luke 20:27–40
[23]The same day Sadducees came to him, who	[18]And Sadducees came to him, who	[27]There came to him some Sadducees, those who
say that there is no resurrection;	say that there is no resurrection;	say that there is no resurrection.

1. Ideally such underlining should be done by using a Greek synopsis, but since many readers will not have access to this most basic tool, an English synopsis has been used for illustrative purposes. If the reader has access to a Greek synopsis, however, he or she is encouraged to compare these passages (as well as any others referred to) in the original language.

and they asked him a question, [24]saying, "Teacher, Moses said,	and they asked him a question, saying, [19]"Teacher, Moses wrote for us	[28]and they asked him a question, saying, "Teacher, Moses wrote for us
'If a man dies,	that if a man's brother dies and leaves a wife, but	that if a man's brother dies, having a wife but
having no children, his brother must marry the widow, and raise up children for his brother.' [25]Now there were seven brothers among us;	leaves no child, the man must take the wife, and raise up children for his brother. [20]There were seven brothers;	no children, the man must take the wife and raise up children for his brother. [29]Now there were seven brothers;
the first married, and died, and having no children left his wife to his brother. [26]So too the second	the first took a wife, and when he died left no children;	the first took a wife, and died without children;
and third, down to the seventh.	[21]and the second took her, and died, leaving no children; and the third likewise; [22]and the seven left no children.	[30]and the second [31]and the third took her, and likewise all seven left no children and died.
[27]After them all, the woman died. [28]In the resurrection, therefore, to which of the seven will she be wife? For they all had her."	Last of all the woman also died. [23]In the resurrection whose wife will she be? For the seven had her as wife."	[32]Afterward the woman also died. [33]In the resurrection, therefore, whose wife will the woman be? For the seven had her as wife."
[29]But Jesus answered them, "You are wrong, because you know neither the scriptures nor the power of God.	[24]Jesus said to them, "Is not this why you are wrong, that you know neither the scriptures nor the power of God?	[34]And Jesus said to them,
		"The sons of this age marry and are given in marriage; [35]but those who are accounted worthy to attain to that age and to the resurrection from the dead neither marry nor are given in marriage, [36]for they cannot die any more, because they are equal to angels and are sons of God, being sons of the resurrection.
[30]For in the resurrection they neither marry nor are given in marriage,	[25]For when they rise from the dead, they neither marry nor are given in marriage,	
but are like angels in heaven.	but are like angels in heaven.	
[31]And as for the resurrection of the dead, have you not read what was said to you	[26]And as for the dead being raised, have you not read in the book of Moses, in the passage	[37]But that the dead are raised, even Moses showed, in the passage

by God, ³²'I am the God of Abraham, and the God of Isaac, and the God of Jacob'? He is not God of the dead, but of the living." ³³And when the crowd heard it, they were astonished at his teaching.	about the bush, how God said to him, 'I am the God of Abraham, and the God of Isaac, and the God of Jacob'? ²⁷He is not God of the dead, but of the living; you are quite wrong."	about the bush, where he calls the Lord the God of Abraham and the God of Isaac and the God of Jacob. ³⁸Now he is not God of the dead, but of the living; for all live to him." ³⁹And some of the scribes answered, "Teacher, you have spoken well." ⁴⁰For they no longer dared to ask him any question.

1.3

Matthew 24:4–8	Mark 13:5–8	Luke 21:8–11
⁴And Jesus answered them, "Take heed that no one leads you astray. ⁵For many will come in my name, saying, 'I am the Christ.' and they will lead many astray. ⁶And you will hear of wars and rumors of wars; see that you are not alarmed; for this must take place, but the end is not yet. ⁷For nation will rise against nation, and kingdom against kingdom, and there will be famines and earthquakes in various places: ⁸all this is but the beginning of the birth-pangs.	⁵And Jesus began to say to them, "Take heed that no one leads you astray. ⁶Many will come in my name, saying, 'I am he!' and they will lead many astray. ⁷And when you hear of wars and rumors of wars, do not be alarmed; this must take place, but the end is not yet. ⁸For nation will rise against nation, and kingdom against kingdom; there will be earthquakes in various places, there will be famines; this is but the beginning of the birth-pangs.	⁸And he said, "Take heed that you are not led astray; for many will come in my name, saying, 'I am he!' and, 'The time is at hand!' Do not go after them. ⁹And when you hear of wars and tumults, do not be terrified; for this must first take place, but the end will not be at once." ¹⁰Then he said to them, "Nation will rise against nation, and kingdom against kingdom; ¹¹there will be great earthquakes and in various places famines and pestilences; and there will be terrors and great signs from heaven.

If you have done the color-coded underlining as suggested, the different colors present in the underlining of the above texts may be somewhat confusing, but for the present the differences in color can be ignored, for what is important to note at this point is the degree of underlining present. The presence of numerous unbroken lines reveals repeated exact agreements between two and often all three of these Gospels.[2] The degree to which these Gospels agree in wording naturally gives rise to the question of *why* they agree so closely. How are we to explain the obvious similarities in wording that we find in these passages? One possible explanation is that they all deal with the same incidents or sayings of Jesus. In other words, they agree because they are dealing with history! They are reporting exactly what happened and what was said. However, this explanation is less than satisfactory for several reasons. For one, it does not explain why at times the accounts do not agree exactly, unless we assume that perfect agreement means exact historical reproduction and that imperfect agreement or lack of agreement means that we do not have exact historical reproduction, i.e., that we are talking about different sayings and actions of Jesus. A second problem that this explanation encounters is that whereas Jesus spoke and taught primarily in Aramaic, these agreements in wording are in Greek! It is rather unlikely that each writer would have translated the sayings and actions of Jesus from Aramaic into Greek in exactly the same manner. A third problem raised is the question of why, when John reports a similar incident or saying in the life of Jesus, there is little or no exactness present in the wording.

A second explanation that has sometimes been proposed as to why such similarities exist in the synoptic Gospels is that these writers were guided by the Holy Spirit in their writing. Whereas the present writer believes this, it is apparent upon reflection that this is likewise an insufficient explanation for the presence of such agreements. Was not John also guided by the Spirit in the writing of his Gospel? Yet few such agreements are found there! Furthermore, if the Spirit's inspiration caused these agreements, why are there also differences? If the Spirit is the cause of the similarities, who is the cause of the differences? Only by means of dictation-type inspiration can such an explanation for the look-alike quality of the synoptic Gospels be accepted, and such a theory of inspiration has never been the dominant understanding among Christians with regard to how the Gospels came into

---

2. Some other passages that can be used to demonstrate the close agreement in wording between the synoptic Gospels are (1) Matthew 8:2–4/Mark 1:40–45/Luke 5:12–16; (2) Matthew 9:1–8/Mark 2:1–12/Luke 5:17–26; (3) Matthew 16:24–28/Mark 8:34–9:1/Luke 9:23–27; (4) Matthew 21:23–27/Mark 11:27–33/Luke 20:1–8; (5) Matthew 21:33–46/Mark 12:1–12/Luke 20:9–19.

being. No, the exactness of wording seen in the passages just under-lined argues for some sort of a common source, either oral or written, that lies behind the similarities of the synoptic Gospels.

Agreement in Order

Another impressive area of agreement between the synoptic Gospels involves the common order of the events recorded in them. We shall look at three portions of these Gospels in order to observe the order of the individual pericopes found within them.[3]

In the first example given (table 1) the common agreement in order between Mark and Luke is most apparent. Only in the last two events listed is there any difference, and here one of the Evangelists has simply reversed the order of the two events. There is also a general agreement with the Matthean order, although the material in the "summaries" appears in different locations, and the choosing of the Twelve occurs considerably before, rather than after, the controversy of healing on the sabbath. In the second example (Table 2) we again see a common order. At times one Evangelist may omit an account[4] or insert one,[5] but the same order is maintained. It is apparent that although an Evangelist may at times depart from the common order of the ac-counts, he nevertheless always returns to the same order. For example, even after Luke adds his large insertion of teaching material in 9:51–18:14, he immediately then picks up the departed order at Luke 18:15! In the third example (table 3) we find once again that there exists a common order in the arrangement of the material. Some differences do exist. This is most clear in the Lukan placement of the parables of the mustard seed and the leaven (h. and i.) as well as his placement of the mother and brothers of Jesus (a.), and in Matthew's placements of Jesus' stilling the storm (o.), healing the Gerasene demoniac (p.), and healing Jairus' daughter (q.); but again, both return to the common order after these departures.

Whereas attention is sometimes focused upon the variations in the order of the gospel events, we must not lose sight of the rather impres-sive agreement in order as seen in the examples given above. This common order naturally raises the question of *why* such a common

3. In the following examples the order of Mark is followed since it stands in the middle position in most synopses. As a result, it is easier to compare Matthew and Luke to Mark.

4. Luke omits *e.*, the return of Elijah; *r.*, teachings on divorce; and *x.*, the request of the sons of Zebedee. Matthew omits *j.*, the use of Jesus' name. Mark omits *l.*, the parable of the lost sheep.

5. Matthew adds *h.*, the temple tax; *m.* through *p.*, teachings in 18:15–35; and *v.*, the parable of the laborers in the vineyard. Luke adds his major section of 9:51–18:14.

Table 1

	Matthew	Mark	Luke
a. Jesus' teaching in the synagogue in Capernaum		1:21–22	4:31–32
b. Jesus' healing of the demoniac in Capernaum		1:23–28	4:33–37
c. Jesus' healing of Peter's mother-in-law	8:14–15	1:29–31	4:38–39
d. Jesus' healing in the evening	8:16–17	1:32–34	4:40–41
e. Jesus leaves Capernaum		1:35–38	4:42–43
f. Jesus' preaching in Galilee—a summary	4:23	1:39	4:44
g. The miraculous catch of fish			5:1–11
h. Jesus' healing of the leper	8:1–4	1:40–45	5:12–16
i. Jesus' healing of the paralytic	9:1–8	2:1–12	5:17–26
j. The calling of Levi	9:9–13	2:13–17	5:27–32
k. Controversy over fasting	9:14–17	2:18–22	5:33–39
l. Controversy over plucking grain	12:1–8	2:23–28	6:1–5
m. Controversy over healing on the sabbath	12:9–14	3:1–6	6:6–11
n. Healing by the sea—a summary	4:24–25 12:15–16	3:7–12	6:17–19
o. The choosing of the Twelve	10:1–4	3:13–19	6:12–16

Table 2

	Matthew	Mark	Luke
a. Peter's confession of Christ	16:13–20	8:27–30	9:18–21
b. First passion prediction	16:21–23	8:31–33	9:22
c. Teachings on discipleship	16:24–28	8:34–9:1	9:23–27
d. The transfiguration	17:1–9	9:2–10	9:28–36
e. Concerning the return of Elijah	17:10–13	9:11–13	
f. Jesus' healing of the demon-possessed boy	17:14–21	9:14–29	9:37–43a
g. Second passion prediction	17:22–23	9:30–32	9:43b–45
h. The temple tax	17:24–27		
i. Teachings on true greatness	18:1–5	9:33–37	9:46–48
j. Concerning the use of Jesus' name		9:38–41	9:49–50
k. Teachings on temptations	18:6–9	9:42–50	17:1–2 14:34–35
l. Parable of the lost sheep	18:10–14		15:3–7
m. Teachings on reproving a brother	18:15–18		
n. Teachings on the presence of Jesus	18:19–20		
o. Teachings on reconciliation with a brother	18:21–22		17:4
p. Parable of the unforgiving servant	18:23–35		
q. Departure to Judea *Largest block of Lukan teaching material*	19:1–2	10:1	9:51 (9:51–18:14)
r. Teachings on divorce	19:3–12	10:2–12	
s. Jesus blesses the children	19:13–15	10:13–16	18:15–17
t. The rich young man	19:16–22	10:17–22	18:18–23
u. Teachings on the dangers of riches	19:23–30	10:23–31	18:24–30
v. Parable of the laborers in the vineyard	20:1–16		
w. Third passion prediction	20:17–19	10:32–34	18:31–34
x. The request of the sons of Zebedee	20:20–28	10:35–45	
y. The healing of the blind man	20:29–34	10:46–52	18:35–43

Table 3

	Matthew	Mark	Luke
a. The mother and brothers of Jesus	12:46–50	3:31–35	8:19–21
b. Parable of the sower	13:1–9	4:1–9	8:4–8
c. Why Jesus taught in parables	13:10–17	4:10–12	8:9–10
d. The interpretation of the parable of the sower	13:18–23	4:13–20	8:11–15
e. Parables of lamp on a stand and "measure upon measure"		4:21–25	8:16–18
f. Parable of the growing seed		4:26–29	
g. Parable of the weeds	13:24–30		
h. Parable of the mustard seed	13:31–32	4:30–32	13:18–19
i. Parable of the leaven	13:33		13:20–21
j. Jesus' use of parables	13:34–35	4:33–34	
k. The interpretation of the parable of the weeds	13:36–43		
l. Parables of hidden treasure and pearl	13:44–46		
m. Parable of the net	13:47–50		
n. Parable of the householder	13:51–52		
o. Jesus stills the storm	8:23–27	4:35–41	8:22–25
p. Jesus heals the Gerasene demoniac	8:28–34	5:1–20	8:26–39
q. Jesus heals Jairus' daughter	9:18–26	5:21–43	8:40–56
r. Jesus rejected at Nazareth	13:53–58	6:1–6a	(4:16–30)

order exists. If it is argued that this is due to the fact that this was the chronology in which the events occurred in the life of Jesus, it must be mentioned that the exceptions given above indicate that, at times at least, the Evangelists give a different "historical" order.[6] It is furthermore apparent that other than historical considerations have governed this common ordering of materials. The parables listed in table 3 are not a chronological listing of the parables Jesus spoke all at once but a collection that someone made of Jesus' parables. Note how Mark refers to these parables: "With many such parables he spoke the word to them, as they were able to hear it; he did not speak to them without a parable, but privately to his own disciples he explained everything" (4:33–34). It is clear that Mark sees the parables of Mark 4:3–32 as a summary collection and not a chronology of consecutive parables that Jesus taught in a single day. Thus Matthew felt free to add to the collection, and Luke could place the parables of the mustard seed and the leaven in another location.[7] It is also clear that certain materials in

6. Note, for instance, in table 1 the placement of *o.* by Matthew and in table 3 Matthew's placement of *o.*, *p.*, and *q.*, as well as Luke's placement of *h.* and *i.*

7. There are other hints that Mark 4:1–32 is a collection of parables based on topical considerations. In Mark 4:10 the disciples ask Jesus concerning the "parables" (emphasis added). The plural seems to have the entire chapter in mind, not just Mark 4:3–8 (the parable of the sower). It is true that 2:21 and 3:23–26 are parables, but 4:10–12 seems to have chapter four in mind and not any previous parables. The changes in audience

the Gospels seem to be grouped together according to subject matter, for between Mark 1:23 and 2:12 we have five miracles of healing, interrupted at 1:35–39 by a summary; and from Mark 2:13 to 3:6 we have a collection of controversy stories. Matthew has furthermore arranged his entire Gospel so that collections of narratives alternate with collections of sayings.[8] All this indicates that some of the material in the Gospels was arranged due to topical rather than chronological considerations, and this makes the agreement in order seen above even more significant. As a result it would appear that some common source served as a pattern for this similarity. It would also appear that such a source would more likely be written than oral, for such lengthy and precise agreement is more difficult to explain on the basis of using a common oral tradition than on the basis of a common written source.

Agreement in Parenthetical Material

One of the most persuasive arguments for the literary interdependence of the synoptic Gospels is the presence of identical parenthetical material, for it is highly unlikely that two or three writers would by coincidence insert into their accounts exactly the same editorial comment at exactly the same place. It is furthermore evident in the example below that we can conclude that the common source of the material was *written*, for both Matthew and Mark refer to the "reader" in the comment.

1.4

Matthew 24:15–18	Mark 13:14–16	Luke 21:20–22
[author's italics]	[author's italics]	
[15]"So when you see	[14]"But when you see	[20]"But when you see Jerusalem surrounded by armies, then know that
the desolating sacrilege spoken of by the prophet Daniel,	the desolating sacrilege	its desolation has come near.
standing in the holy place	set up where it ought not to be	
(*let the reader understand*),	(*let the reader understand*),	

found within the chapter (4:1, crowd; 4:10, alone with the twelve; 4:13, 21, "them" = the disciples; 4:33, "them" = crowds + disciples) also seem to indicate that this chapter consists of a collection of Jesus' parables rather than a specific historical incident. This does not mean, however, that an incident in the life of Jesus could not have served as the core around which this collection was built.

8. Note his arrangement of Narratives (N) and Sayings (S): N, chapters 1–4; S, chapters 5–7; N, chapters 8–9; S, chapter 10; N, chapters 11–12; S, chapter 13; N, chapters 14–17; S, chapter 18; N, chapters 19–22 (or 23); S, chapter 23 (or 24)–25; N, chapters 26–28.

[16]then let those who are in Judea flee to the mountains;	then let those who are in Judea flee to the mountains;	[21]Then let those who are in Judea flee to the mountains, and let those who are inside the city depart, and let not those who are out in the country enter it; [22]for these are days of vengeance, to fulfil all that is written."
[17]let him who is on the housetop not go down	[15]let him who is on the housetop not go down, nor enter his house,	
to take what is in his house; [18]and let him who is in the field not turn back to take his mantle."	to take anything away; [16]and let him who is in the field not turn back to take his mantle."	

The comment—"(let the reader understand)"—is a most impressive agreement between Matthew and Mark. That such a comment is not "necessary" in this eschatological discourse is evident in that Luke does not have it. Furthermore, that such a comment could not be due to a common oral tradition is obvious, for it does not refer to the "hearer" but rather to the "reader."

Another good example of a common parenthetical comment is found in Jesus' healing of the paralytic.

1.5

Matthew 9:1–8 [author's italics]	Mark 2:1–12 [author's italics)	Luke 5:17–26 [author's italics]
[1]And getting into a boat he crossed over and came to his own city.	[1]And when he returned to Capernaum after some days, it was reported that he was at home. [2]And many were gathered together, so that there was no longer room for them, not even about the door; and he was preaching the word to them.	[17]On one of those days, as he was teaching, there were Pharisees and teachers of the law sitting by, who had come from every village of Galilee and Judea and from Jerusalem; and the power of the Lord was with him to heal.

²And behold, they
brought
to him a paralytic,
lying on his bed;

and when Jesus saw their
faith he said
to the paralytic,
"Take heart, my son;
your sins are forgiven."

³And behold, some of
the scribes

said to themselves,

"This man is
  blaspheming."

⁴But Jesus,
knowing their thoughts,

said,
"Why do you think evil
in your hearts?
⁵For which is easier,
to say,
'Your sins are forgiven,'

or to say, 'Rise
and walk'?
⁶But that you may know
that the Son of man has
authority on earth to
forgive sins"—*he then
said to the paralytic—*

"Rise, take up your bed
and go home."

---

³And they came,
bringing
to him a paralytic
carried by four men.

⁴And when they could not
get near him
because of the crowd,
they removed the roof
above him; and when they
had made an opening,
they let down the pallet
on which the paralytic lay.

⁵And when Jesus saw their
faith, he said
to the paralytic,
"My son,
your sins are forgiven."

⁶Now some of
the scribes

were sitting there,
questioning in their hearts,
⁷"Why does this man
    speak
thus?
It is blasphemy!

Who can forgive sins but
God alone?"
⁸And immediately Jesus,
perceiving in his spirit
that they thus questioned
within themselves,
said to them,
"Why do you question
thus in your hearts?
⁹Which is easier,
to say to the paralytic,
'Your sins are forgiven,'

or to say, 'Rise, take up
your pallet and walk'?
¹⁰But that you may know
that the Son of man has
authority on earth to
forgive sins"—*he
said to the paralytic—*

¹¹"I say to you,
rise, take up your pallet
and go home."

---

¹⁸And behold, men were
bringing on a bed
a man who was paralyzed,

and they sought to bring
him in and lay him before
Jesus;
¹⁹but finding no way to
bring him in
because of the crowd,
they went up on the roof

and let him down
with his bed through the
tiles into the midst before
Jesus.
²⁰And when he saw their
faith he said,

"Man,
your sins are forgiven
you."

²¹And the scribes
and the Pharisees

began to question, saying,
"Who is this

that speaks blasphemies?

Who can forgive sins but
God only?"
²²When Jesus
perceived
their questionings

he answered them,
"Why do you question
in your hearts?
²³Which is easier,
to say,
'Your sins are forgiven
you,'
or to say, 'Rise
and walk'?
²⁴But that you may know
that the Son of man has
authority on earth to
forgive sins"—*he
said to the man who
was paralyzed—*
"I say to you,
rise, take up your bed
and go home."

[7]And he rose	[12]And he rose,	[25]And immediately he rose before them,
	and immediately took up the pallet	and took up that on which he lay,
and went home.	and went out before them all;	and went home, glorifying God.
[8]When the crowds saw it, they were afraid,	so that they were all amazed	[26]And amazement seized them all,
and they glorified God, who had given such authority to men.	and glorified God,	and they glorified God
		and were filled with awe,
	saying, "We never saw anything like this!"	saying, "We have seen strange things today."

In this account, just before he heals the paralytic, Jesus states: "But that you may know that the Son of man has authority on earth to forgive sins" (Mark 2:10), and then each Evangelist places in the same location the following editorial comment for his readers: "—he said to the paralytic—." This comment reminds one of editorial directions in a play production, such as "—now turn away from the Pharisees, look at the paralytic, and say—." The fact that each of the Evangelists has the same comment (Matthew's and Mark's are exactly the same) at the same place argues strongly for their having used a common written source.

Two additional examples of common parenthetical material are found below.

1.6

Matthew 8:28–29	Mark 5:1–8 [author's italics]	Luke 8:26–29 [author's italics]
[28]And when he came to the other side, to the country of the Gadarenes,	[1]They came to the other side of the sea, to the country of the Gerasenes.	[26]Then they arrived at the country of the Gerasenes, which is opposite Galilee.
	[2]And when he had come out of the boat,	[27]And as he stepped out on land,
two demoniacs met him, coming out of the tombs,	there met him out of the tombs a man with an unclean spirit,	there met him a man from the city who had demons; for a long time he had worn
	[3]who lived	no clothes, and he lived not in a house but
	among the tombs;	among the tombs.

	and no one could bind him any more, even with a chain; ⁴for he had often been bound with fetters and	
so fierce	chains, but the chains he wrenched apart, and the fetters he broke in pieces;	
that no one could pass that way.	and no one had the strength to subdue him.	
	⁵Night and day among the tombs and on the mountains he was always crying out, and bruising himself with stones.	
²⁹And behold,	⁶And when he saw Jesus from afar, he ran and worshiped him;	²⁸When he saw Jesus,
they cried out,	⁷and crying out	he cried out and fell before him,
	with a loud voice, he said,	and said with a loud voice,
"What have you to do with us, O Son of God? Have you come here to torment us before the time?"	"What have you to do with me, Jesus, Son of the Most High God? I adjure you by God, do not torment me."	"What have you to do with me, Jesus, Son of the Most High God? I beseech you, do not torment me."
	⁸*For he had said to him,*	²⁹*For he had commanded the unclean spirit*
	"Come out of the man, you unclean spirit!"	*to come out of the man.*

1.7

Matthew 27:15–18 [author's italics]	**Mark 15:6–10** [author's italics]
¹⁵Now at the feast the governor was accustomed to release for the crowd any one prisoner whom they wanted. ¹⁶And they had then	⁶Now at the feast he used to release for them one prisoner for whom they asked. ⁷And among the rebels in prison, who had committed murder in the insurrection, there was a man
a notorious prisoner, called Barabbas. ¹⁷So when they had gathered,	called Barabbas. ⁸And the crowd came up and began to ask Pilate to do as he was wont to do for them.
Pilate said to them, "Whom do you want me to release for you, Barabbas or Jesus who is called Christ?"	⁹And he answered them, "Do you want me to release for you the King of the Jews?"

¹⁸*For he knew that it was out of*
envy that they had
delivered him up.

¹⁰*For he perceived that it was out of*
envy that the chief priests had
delivered him up.

Other examples that can be referred to in this regard are Matthew 26:5/Mark 14:2/Luke 22:2; Matthew 26:14/Mark 14:10/Luke 22:3; Matthew 26:47/Mark 14:43/Luke 22:47; and Matthew 9:21/Mark 5:28.

Luke 1:1–4

Along with the synoptic Gospels' frequent agreement in wording, in order, and in parenthetical material, the Lukan prologue argues for the fact that Luke, at least, used written materials in the composition of his Gospel. In Luke 1:1–4 we read:

> Inasmuch as many have undertaken to compile a narrative of the things which have been accomplished among us, just as they were delivered to us by those who from the beginning were eyewitnesses and ministers of the word, it seemed good to me also, having followed all things closely for some time past, to write an orderly account for you, most excellent Theophilus, that you may know the truth concerning the things of which you have been informed.

Later we shall look more closely at this extremely important passage,[9] but at this point it need only be noted that Luke refers to early written accounts that existed before his Gospel. He states, "Inasmuch as many have undertaken to compile a narrative. . . ." Although there is debate as to whether this includes written material used in the composition of the Book of Acts, it is clear that it refers at least to such material in regard to the Gospel of Luke. Others wrote before Luke concerning Jesus' acts and teachings. Luke does not tell us how many others had written, and the term "many" is rather ambiguous, but Luke clearly had available written materials on the life and teachings of Jesus. We should also note that Luke made use of these materials in that he "followed all [these] things closely." If Luke was not an eyewitness of Jesus' life—and tradition as well as the statement about the eyewitnesses in Luke 1:2 that distinguishes Luke from the eyewitnesses indicates this—then Luke no doubt "followed" these things via these written narratives as well as the oral traditions available to him. The common agreement in Luke's "narrative of the things which have been

---

9. See below pp. 194–96.

accomplished among us" with the other synoptic Gospels strongly suggests the use of a common source.

Conclusion

In the history of investigating the Synoptic Problem a number of attempts have been made to explain the various similarities by means of a common oral tradition. As early as 1796, J. G. von Herder brought forth such a proposal, which was then developed more fully by J. K. L. Gieseler in 1818. Gieseler argued that behind the synoptic Gospels lay an oral tradition, which was originally created by the apostles for the purpose of preaching. This soon received a fixed form and was then translated from Aramaic into Greek, and it was in this form that the tradition came to and was used by the Evangelists. The agreements of the synoptic Gospels were therefore due to this fixed oral tradition.

We shall see later that before the Gospels were written there did exist a period in which the gospel materials were passed on orally,[10] and it is clear that this oral tradition influenced not only the first of our synoptic Gospels but the subsequent ones as well. As an explanation for the general agreement between Matthew–Mark–Luke, however, such an explanation is quite inadequate. There are several reasons for this. For one, the exactness of the wording between the synoptic Gospels is better explained by the use of written sources than oral ones. Second, the parenthetical comments that these Gospels have in common are hardly explainable by means of oral tradition. This is especially true of Matthew 24:15 and Mark 13:14, which address the *readers* of these works! Third and most important, the extensive agreement in the order of material cannot be explained by any other means than a common written tradition. Whereas the memorization of the gospel traditions by both missionary preachers and laypeople is conceded by all, it is most doubtful that this involved the memorization of a whole gospel account in a specific order. Memorizing individual pericopes, parables, and sayings, and even small collections of such material, is one thing, but memorizing a whole Gospel of such material is something else. The large extensive agreement in order between the synoptic Gospels is best explained by the use of a common literary source. Finally, as has already been pointed out, whereas Luke 1:2 does refer to an oral period in which the gospel materials were transmitted, Luke explicitly mentions his own investigation of written sources.

10. See below pp. 161–228, especially 163–65, 211–16.

If the best explanation of the various agreements in wording, order, and parenthetical material, as well as the Lukan prologue, points to the use of a common written source by Matthew, Mark, and Luke—or the use of one of these Gospels by the other two—the next question that must be investigated involves the question of what literary sources were involved in the writing of these Gospels. It is to this issue that we must now turn.

2

The Priority of Mark

Once it was recognized that a literary relationship exists between the synoptic Gospels, the next question that was raised concerned the nature of that relationship. The various theories that arose can be divided into three types. One type involves the use of various written gospel fragments. F. Schleiermacher (1817) suggested that the apostles had written down brief recollections (*memorabilia*) of Jesus' activities and sayings. As the apostles began to die off, these *memorabilia* began to be collected and arranged according to such topics as miracle stories, the passion narrative, various discourses, and so on. Out of these collections the synoptic Gospels originated. This "fragmentary hypothesis" has never achieved much popularity because, like the "oral hypothesis," it is unable to explain the large agreement in order that exists between the synoptic Gospels. It can explain a certain degree of order, as for instance in a collection of parables (Mark 4:1–32) or a collection of miracle stories (Mark 2:1–3:6), but the agreement in order found in the synoptic Gospels goes far beyond individual fragments.[1]

Another theory, which was suggested even earlier than the fragmentary theory and received much greater support, is the theory of an Ur-gospel. According to G. E. Lessing (1776) and J. G. Eichhorn (1796), there existed before Matthew, Mark, and Luke a primitive Aramaic Gospel that was translated into Greek. Various revisions were made of the translation, and the synoptic writers used different revisions of this

---

1. Compare the examples of such agreement given above on pp. 34–37.

Ur-gospel in the composition of their own works. This purportedly explains why the synoptic Gospels are both alike (the use of a common Ur-gospel) and at the same time different (the use of different revisions of the Ur-gospel). One argument raised against such a theory is the fact that no trace of such an Ur-gospel exists. However, such an "argument from silence" is always dangerous, and it is certainly not an argument that followers of the Q hypothesis can raise, for there exists no trace of Q either! The main problem with the Ur-gospel theory is that, as scholars began to reconstruct the configuration of the Ur-gospel from the common agreements in Matthew, Mark, and Luke, it began to look more and more like an Ur-Mark, i.e., it began to look more and more like Mark. In fact the Ur-gospel was soon simply called Ur-Mark. Yet, as Ur-Mark was constructed, it continued to look more and more like our present Gospel of Mark. It therefore appeared that instead of postulating an Ur-gospel, the relationship between the synoptic Gospels could be better and more simply explained by some sort of an interdependence between them.

The third theory that arose to explain the Synoptic Problem is the theory of interdependence or utilization. Here, in theory at least, there exist "eighteen fundamental ways in which three documents, among which there exists some kind of direct literary dependence, may be related to each other."[2] If A = Matthew, B = Mark, and C = Luke, we have then the possibilities represented in figure 1. Of these eighteen possibilities, only three have commended themselves over the years: 1(a), 4(b), and 3(b). These are also illustrated in figures 2–4, respectively.

The first solution (see figure 2), which states that Matthew wrote first and was used by Mark, who in turn was used by Luke, dates back to Augustine.

The second solution (see figure 3) is commonly called the Griesbach Hypothesis, since it was J. J. Griesbach who suggested this in 1776. According to this theory, Matthew wrote first and was used by Luke. Mark in turn wrote last and used both Matthew and Luke. This solution has experienced a revival of interest of late due to the influence of W. R. Farmer.

The third solution (see figure 4) is the most popular one by far and has been associated with H. J. Holtzmann (1863) and B. H. Streeter (1924). According to this theory, Mark wrote first and was used independently by Matthew and Luke. In this chapter we shall look at a number of arguments that have led the majority of scholars to argue in favor of solution 3(b), or the priority of Mark.

---

2. William R. Farmer, *The Synoptic Problem: A Critical Analysis* (New York: Macmillan, 1964), pp. 208–9.

Figure 1

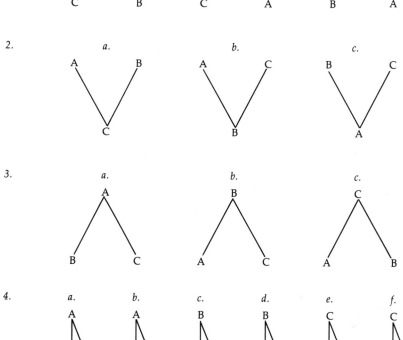

Figure 2

Matthew

Mark

Luke

Figure 3

Figure 4

Mark's Shortness: The Argument from Length

As compared to Matthew and Luke, the Gospel of Mark is much shorter. It consists of only 661 verses, whereas Matthew contains 1,068 verses and Luke 1,149. When broken down into words we find that Mark contains 11,025 words, Matthew 18,293, and Luke 19,376.[3] Of the words found in Mark, 132 have no parallel in Matthew or Luke; of the words found in Matthew, 3,102 have no parallel in Mark or Luke; and of the words found in Luke, 6,700 have no parallel in Matthew or Mark. Of the 11,025 words found in Mark, only 304 have no parallel in Matthew and 1,282 have no parallel in Luke.[4] This means that 97.2 percent of the words in Mark have a parallel in Matthew and 88.4 percent have a parallel in Luke. Assuming an interdependence among the three synoptic Gospels, scholars raised the question as to whether it was more likely that Mark used either Matthew or Luke (or both) or that Matthew and/or Luke used Mark.

The use of Matthew and/or Luke by Mark seems least likely, for a number of reasons. For one, why would Mark omit so much material if Matthew or Luke were his source? Of the 18,293 words that appear in Matthew, 7,392 (40.4%) have no parallel in Mark, and of the 19,376 words that appear in Luke, 10,259 (52.9%) have no parallel in Mark.[5]

---

3. These word statistics come from Joseph B. Tyson and Thomas R. W. Longstaff, *Synoptic Abstract*, The Computer Bible, vol. 15 (Wooster, Ohio: College of Wooster, 1978), pp. 169–71.

4. Ibid.

5. Ibid.

Why would Mark omit so much material from his Gospel? Why would he omit everything concerning Jesus' birth, the birth of John the Baptist, the Sermon on the Mount, so much teaching material, the Lord's Prayer, all the resurrection narratives (if Mark originally ended at 16:8), and so on? It is hard to conceive of any reason why Mark would want to omit so much material from his Gospel, if it all lay before him as he copied Matthew and/or Luke. Some scholars, however, have argued that a reason does in fact exist as to why Mark would do this and that was to provide a shorter Gospel for use in the church. This explanation postulates that it was for the purpose of providing an abridged Gospel (a *Reader's Digest*-like condensed version) that Mark omitted so much of Matthew and/or Luke when he "copied" them.

There are, however, some weighty reasons why the attempt to see Mark as an abridgement of Matthew and/or Luke is unconvincing. The most important reason is that whereas Mark is considerably shorter in total length than Matthew and Luke, when we compare the individual pericopes that they have in common, time and time again we find that Mark is the longest! Note the comparisons in table 4, in which the total number of words appears in parentheses.[6]

It can be seen that in the fifty-one examples listed in table 4 Mark is the longest twenty-one times, Matthew is the longest eleven times, and Luke is the longest ten times.[7] In the other nine instances, where there was a difference of at most three words between the two longest accounts, one of the two longest accounts was always Mark's. From the above it is clear that—far from being an abridgement—Mark is usually the longest of the parallel accounts.[8] It would therefore appear that one can only call Mark an abridgement of Matthew and Luke if one compares the size of the total Gospels rather than the size of the individual accounts. If one compares the individual accounts, Mark is generally not an abridgement but rather the opposite, i.e., an enlargement. It is

6. The examples listed are the clearest parallel accounts in the triple tradition after the baptism of Jesus and up to the passion narrative.

7. These statistics come from Tyson and Longstaff, *Synoptic Abstract*, pp. 109–19. E. P. Sanders (*The Tendencies of the Synoptic Tradition* [Cambridge: Cambridge University, 1969], pp. 85–86) refers to eighty-three pericopes in the triple tradition, of which Matthew is longer than Mark in thirty-seven and Mark longer than Matthew in forty-four. I do not know, however, where he obtained these statistics.

8. In this regard it should also be noted that in a number of instances where Matthew is the longest account, this is due to his adding an Old Testament quotation (cf. Matt. 12:1–8; 13:10–17), a reference to the "church" and the famous rock quotation, which is not found in the parallels (Matt. 16:13–20); and the Matthean theme of the kingdom being taken away from the people of Israel and given to others (Matt. 21:33–46). In Luke 9:28–36 the explanation of what Jesus, Moses, and Elijah were talking about likewise appears to be an addition to the triple tradition.

Table 4

		Matthew		Mark		Luke	
1	Simon's mother-in-law	8:14–15	(30)	**1:29–31**	(44)	4:38–39	(38)
2	Sick healed in evening	8:16–17	(36)	1:32–34	(46)	**4:40–41**	(52)
3	Cleansing of leper	8:1–4	(62)	1:40–45	(98)	5:12–16	(98)
4	Healing of paralytic	9:1–8	(126)	2:1–12	(196)	**5:17–26**	(213)
5	Calling of Levi	9:9–13	(71)	**2:13–17**	(109)	5:27–32	(94)
6	Question about fasting	9:14–17	(104)	2:18–22	(129)	**5:33–39**	(142)
7	Picking grain on sabbath	**12:1–8**	(136)	2:23–28	(108)	6:1–5	(92)
8	Man with withered hand	12:9–14	(90)	3:1–6	(94)	**6:6–11**	(115)
9	Choosing of the Twelve	10:1–4	(74)	**3:13–19**	(90)	6:12–16	(76)
10	Parable of sower	13:1–9	(131)	**4:1–9**	(151)	8:4–8	(90)
11	Why Jesus used parables	**13:10–17**	(154)	4:10–12	(52)	8:9–10	(36)
12	Interpretation of sower	13:18–23	(128)	**4:13–20**	(146)	8:11–15	(109)
13	Parable of mustard seed	13:31–32	(50)	**4:30–32**	(57)	13:18–19	(40)
14	Stilling the storm	8:23–27	(73)	**4:35–41**	(120)	8:22–25	(94)
15	Gerasene demoniac	8:28–34	(135)	**5:1–20**	(325)	8:26–39	(293)
16	Jairus' daughter and woman with hemorrhage	9:18–26	(138)	**5:21–43**	(374)	8:40–56	(280)
17	Opinions concerning Jesus	14:1–2	(34)	**6:14–16**	(54)	9:7–9	(53)
18	Death of John the Baptist	14:3–12	(136)	**6:17–29**	(248)	3:19–20	(33)
19	Feeding five thousand	14:13–21	(158)	**6:32–44**	(194)	9:10–17	(156)
20	Teachings on defilement	15:1–20	(280)	**7:1–23**	(359)	11:37–41	(73)
21	Confession of Peter	**16:13–20**	(207)	8:27–30	(75)	9:18–21	(66)
22	First passion prediction	16:21–23	(72)	8:31–33	(69)	9:22	(25)
23	Teachings on discipleship	16:24–28	(117)	**8:34–9:1**	(135)	9:23–27	(106)
24	The transfiguration	17:1–9	(168)	9:2–10	(157)	**9:28–36**	(178)
25	Demon-possessed boy	17:14–21	(133)	**9:14–29**	(270)	9:37–43a	(124)
26	Second passion prediction	17:22–23	(30)	9:30–32	(47)	**9:43b–45**	(54)
27	Teachings on true greatness	18:1–5	(78)	**9:33–37**	(85)	9:46–48	(60)
28	Jesus blesses children	19:13–15	(45)	**10:13–16**	(64)	18:15–17	(57)
29	Rich young man	**19:16–22**	(116)	10:17–22	(110)	18:18–23	(92)
30	On riches and rewards	19:23–30	(154)	**10:23–31**	(171)	18:24–30	(120)
31	Third passion prediction	20:17–19	(53)	**10:32–34**	(73)	18:31–34	(61)
32	Healing the blind man	20:29–34	(79)	**10:46–52**	(123)	18:35–43	(108)
33	The triumphal entry	21:1–9	(163)	11:1–10	(164)	**19:28–40**	(193)
34	Cleansing the temple	21:12–13	(45)	**11:15–17**	(65)	19:45–46	(25)
35	Question of authority	21:23–27	(116)	**11:27–33**	(125)	20:1–8	(118)
36	Parable of tenants	**21:33–46**	(223)	12:1–12	(181)	20:9–19	(198)
37	Paying taxes to Caesar	**22:15–22**	(114)	12:13–17	(106)	20:20–26	(104)
38	On the resurrection	22:23–33	(163)	12:18–27	(167)	**20:27–40**	(185)
39	Concerning David's son	**22:41–46**	(78)	12:35–37a	(56)	20:41–44	(47)
40	On destruction of temple	24:1–2	(41)	13:1–2	(39)	21:5–6	(28)
41	Signs before the end	24:3–8	(96)	13:3–8	(93)	21:7–11	(88)
42	Coming persecution	24:9–14	(75)	13:9–13	(97)	21:12–19	(98)
43	Desolating sacrilege	24:15–22	(115)	13:14–20	(115)	21:20–24	(93)
44	Coming of Son of man	**24:29–31**	(92)	13:24–27	(71)	21:25–28	(67)
45	Parable of fig tree	24:32–36	(86)	13:28–32	(86)	21:29–33	(66)
46	Conspiracy against Jesus	**26:1–5**	(70)	14:1–2	(34)	22:1–2	(24)
47	The betrayal of Judas	26:14–16	(35)	14:10–11	(30)	**22:3–6**	(44)
48	Preparation for Passover	26:17–20	(69)	14:12–17	(106)	22:7–14	(106)
49	The last supper	26:26–29	(79)	14:22–25	(69)	**22:15–20**	(111)
50	Peter's denial foretold	**26:30–35**	(95)	14:26–31	(87)	22:31–34	(63)
51	Gethsemane	**26:36–46**	(194)	14:32–42	(181)	22:39–46	(88)

The longest Gospel version is indicated by boldface type.

difficult to understand why, if Mark had Matthew and/or Luke before
him, he would choose to omit so much material. To claim that he
wanted to create a shorter gospel account for some reason or other
simply runs counter to the fact that Mark is not an abridgement of the
triple tradition. It is, on the contrary, an expansion!

A second problem with the view that Mark is an abridgement of
Matthew and/or Luke is his omission of so much teaching material.
This is especially surprising in that one of the strong redactional emphases of Mark is upon the teaching ministry of Jesus. We see this
emphasis in the introductory **seams** by which he joins his pericopes—
1:21–22 (the noun or verb for "teach" is found three times); 2:13; 4:1–2
(the noun or verb for "teach" is again found three times); 6:2; 8:31;
12:35; 12:38; cf. also 6:30 and 13:1–2. This is also seen in his **insertions**
and **explanatory notes**—6:34: 9:31; 11:17, 18—as well as in his **summaries**—6:6b and 10:1. It is clear from the above that Mark in his
Gospel is seeking to emphasize Jesus' role as a teacher.[9] Yet, the majority of the material that Matthew and Luke have in common and that
Mark has omitted consists of teaching material, such as Matthew's
Sermon on the Mount (5:1–7:29) or Luke 6:20–8:3 and 9:51–18:14. It is
difficult to understand why, if Mark used Matthew and/or Luke, he
would at the same time make a great effort on the one hand to emphasize Jesus' teaching ministry and then on the other hand eliminate
the majority of the teachings of Jesus found in his source(s). Furthermore, if one would argue that he did so because he sought to compose
an abbreviated or abridged version of Matthew and/or Luke, then the
fact that he lengthened the material he did use becomes even less
understandable. An abridged work becomes shorter by both eliminating various materials and abbreviating the accounts retained. The fact
that the common material in Matthew–Mark–Luke is usually longer in
Mark reveals that Mark is not an abridgement of the other synoptic
Gospels. Only when one compares the total size of the Synoptics can
one argue that Mark is an abridgement; once one compares the individual accounts it becomes immediately clear that it is not.

Faced with the observation that Mark is the shortest of the synoptic
Gospels, what theory of interdependence can best explain this? As
mentioned above, the attempt to explain this fact by the theory that
Mark sought to abridge Matthew and/or Luke is unconvincing because
Mark is simply not an abridgement of one or both of the other Gospels.
As early as 1786, G. C. Storr recognized that it was impossible to
explain a Markan omission of so much of the material in Matthew and

---

9. To these one could also add those editorial passages in Mark that speak of Jesus
"preaching" (1:14–15, 39; 3:14) or "speaking the word" (2:2; 4:33–34; 8:32).

Luke.[10] On the other hand, the use of Mark by Matthew and Luke makes perfectly good sense. Their adding such additional material as birth narratives, resurrection accounts, teaching material, and so on, is exactly what one would expect if they used Mark. And their abbreviation of the parallel accounts in Mark and their omission of certain Markan material—such as Mark 3:20–21 (Jesus is thought to be "beside himself") and 8:22–26 (the "two-stage" healing of the blind man at Bethsaida)—is far more understandable than Mark's lengthening of the accounts found in Matthew and/or Luke, his adding of Mark 3:20–21 and 8:22–26, and his omitting the birth narratives, the Sermon on the Mount, the resurrection narratives, and so on. To add their common material (Q) and their special material (M [Matthew] and L [Luke]), Matthew and Luke would have had to shorten their Markan source if they wanted to remain within the limits of their scrolls. Their use of Mark is therefore understandable; the reverse (Mark's supposed use of Matthew and/or Luke) is not. As one writer has aptly put it, "given Mk, it is easy to see why Matt. was written; given Matt., it is hard to see why Mk was needed."[11]

Mark's Poorer Writing Style: The Argument from Grammar

A second argument frequently brought forward in favor of the priority of Mark involves the inferior quality of the Markan grammar. The term "grammar" is used broadly here to include matters of vocabulary, style, idiom, and sentence construction. When compared to Matthew and Luke, it quickly becomes apparent that Mark possessed lesser literary skills. In numerous situations the Matthean and Lukan parallels contain a more polished and improved literary form. This is evident in a number of areas.

Colloquialisms and Incorrect Grammar

In several instances we find in the Markan account incorrect grammar or a colloquial expression not contained in Matthew or Luke. In Mark 10:20 the rich young man replies to the question of Jesus concerning the commandments, "All these I have observed [*ephylazamēn*] from my youth." The parallels in Matthew 19:20 and Luke 18:21 change the

10. See Werner Georg Kümmel, *The New Testament: The History of the Investigation of Its Problems*, trans. S. McLean Gilmour and Howard C. Kee (Nashville: Abingdon, 1972), pp. 75–76.

11. G. M. Styler, "The Priority of Mark," in C. F. D. Moule, *The Birth of the New Testament* (New York: Harper, 1962), p. 231. See also Joseph A. Fitzmyer, *To Advance the Gospel* (New York: Crossroad, 1981), p. 6.

verb to *ephylaza*. Although this is not evident in the English translations, Mark has used an incorrect form of the verb. He has used an
aorist middle, which Matthew and Luke have changed to the correct
aorist active. Such a change by Matthew and Luke is quite understandable, but an intentional change by Mark from correct grammar to incorrect grammar is not.

A second example is found in Mark 2:4, where the paralytic is described as lying on a "pallet" (*krabatton*). This term is a slang expression
for "bed." We could perhaps get a sense of the term's meaning if we
were to have Jesus command the paralytic to take up his "pad" and
follow him. Matthew and Luke change this term to the more-
acceptable "bed" (*klinēs*) and "bed" (*klinidiō*). Again, this change of
their Markan source is far more understandable than the reverse.
Another example of an improvement in style in Matthew and Luke is
their change of Mark 1:12, where we read that after Jesus' baptism the
Spirit "drove" (*ekballei*) him into the wilderness to be tempted. Matthew 4:1 has "Jesus was led up [*anēchthē*] by the Spirit," and Luke 4:1
states that Jesus "was led [*ēgeto*] by the Spirit." In the case of both
Matthew and Luke we see a refinement of style that is more easily
understandable than the reverse, i.e., that Mark willingly chose to
forsake the good Greek of Matthew and/or Luke for a cruder and more
confusing term. In Mark 4:41 we find still another example of incorrect
grammar in Mark's use of the singular verb "obey[s]" with the preceding
compound subject—"wind and sea." Both Matthew and Luke correctly
use a plural verb.[12] Another example of incorrect grammar on the part
of Mark that is corrected by Matthew and Luke is found in Mark 16:6.
Here the angel tells the women, " 'See the place where they laid
him.' " In English the grammatical errors by Mark are not evident, but
in the Greek text we find two of them. The first involves the verb
"see." This is singular in Greek even though the angel is addressing
the women (plural). It should be *idete* as we find it in Matthew, and not
ide as it is in Mark. Also in Mark the term "the place" is in the nomina-
tive instead of the accusative case, i.e., it has a case ending that desig-
nates it as the subject of the sentence rather than as the object! Mat-

12. In Greek it is normal to have the verb agree with the first part of a compound
subject when the compound subject follows the verb. In such instances, if the first of the
compound subject is singular, the verb will be singular. In Mark 4:41, however, the
compound subject does not follow the verb but precedes it. There are few other examples of a singular verb following a compound subject. In Matthew 5:18 we have such
an example, but the reason for this is obvious. The singular verb [*parelthē*] is used earlier
in the sentence and the later use of the singular is no doubt due to attraction to its earlier
use. In two other examples (Matt. 6:19; 1 Cor. 15:50) the compound subjects are an-
arthrous and no doubt considered as a unity. In Mark 4:41 there are articles present with
each of the compound subjects.

thew correctly converts this to the accusative and has *ton topon* instead of Mark's incorrect *ho topos*.

A final example that will be mentioned is found in Mark 5:9–10:

2.1

Mark 5:9–10	Luke 8:30–31
[9]And Jesus asked him, "What is your name?"	[30]Jesus then asked him, "What is your name?"
He replied, "My name is Legion;	And he said, "Legion";
for we are many."	for many demons had entered him.
[10]And he begged him eagerly not to send them	[31]And they begged him not to command them
out of the country.	to depart into the abyss.

In this example we find that after the plural "for *we are* many," Mark uses the singular, "And *he begged* him eagerly," and then the plural once again, "not to send *them* out of the country." Luke, on the other hand, has after the statement "for *many demons had entered* him" the more consistent "And *they begged* him not to command *them* to depart. . . ." (Italics are author's.) Luke's correction of Mark's grammatical fluctuations is more easily understood than Mark's changing Luke's consistent use of the plural.[13]

In the above examples the most likely direction of change would be for the later writers to improve upon the grammar and style of their source. This would then argue for the priority of Mark. It is, of course, not impossible for a later writer to worsen the grammar of his source, but in such an instance one must ask "Why?" Two possible explanations suggest themselves. One is that such a "disimprovement" was unintentional and that the writer was incompetent. That Mark was not a Greek literary giant has always been acknowledged, but to claim that he was so incompetent that he could not see the difference between the good Greek of his source(s) and his own poor Greek goes much too far in the other direction. The Gospel of Mark was clearly not written by an incompetent! A second possible explanation is that all or most of such changes are intentional, but no really convincing argument has been put forward as to why Mark would intentionally change the better grammar and style of his source(s) for the worse. The poorer style and grammar of Mark are therefore best explained on the basis of a Markan priority.

---

13. Two additional examples of how the later synoptic writers improve on Mark's grammar are: (1) the Greek of Matthew 16:26 and Luke 9:25 is a clear improvement of Mark 8:36; (2) Matthew 18:6, "fastened around" (*kremasthē*), is an improvement of Mark 9:42 (and Luke 17:2), "were hung round' (*perikeitai*).

Aramaic Expressions

The priority of Mark has frequently been argued for on the basis of its being a more Semitic or "Hebraizing" Gospel.[14] We shall not deal with this issue here, but we shall look instead at seven clear Aramaic expressions found in Mark.[15]

2.2

Matthew 10:1-2	Mark 3:14-17 [author's italics]	Luke 6:13-14
[1]And he called to him his twelve disciples	[14]And he appointed twelve, to be with him, and to be sent out to preach	[13]And when it was day, he called his disciples, and chose from them twelve,
and gave them authority over unclean spirits, to cast them out, and to heal every disease and every infirmity. [2]The names of the twelve apostles are these: first,	[15]and have authority to cast out demons:	whom he named apostles;
Simon, who is called Peter,	[16]Simon whom he surnamed Peter;	[14]Simon, whom he named Peter,
and Andrew his brother; James the son of Zebedee, and John his brother;	[17]James the son of Zebedee and John the brother of James, whom he surnamed *Boanerges*, that is, sons of thunder;	and Andrew his brother, and James and John,

2.3

Matthew 9:25	Mark 5:40-41 [author's italics]	Luke 8:54
[25]But when the crowd had been put outside,	But he put them all outside, and took the child's father and mother and those who were with him, and	[54]But
he went in	went in where the child was.	
and took her by the hand,	[41]Taking her by the hand, he said to her,	taking her by the hand he called, saying,

14. C. H. Weisse argued this way in 1838. See Kümmel, *The New Testament: Problems,* pp. 149–51. For a more recent argument along these lines, see Vincent Taylor, *The Gospel According to St. Mark* (London: Macmillan, 1952), pp. 55–66.
15. Mark 11:9–10 is not included in this list, since *Hosanna* is a transliteration of the Old Testament text found in Psalm 118:25.

"*Talitha cumi*"; which
     means,
"Little girl,   "Child,
I say to you

and
the girl arose.   arise."   arise."

2.4

Matthew 15:3–6   ### Mark 7:9–13
                                                      [author's italics]

[3]He answered them,   [9]And he said to them,
"And why do you transgress   "You have a fine way of rejecting
the commandment of God   the commandment of God
for the sake of your tradition?   in order to keep your tradition!
[4]For God commanded,   [10]For Moses said:
'Honor your father and your mother,'   'Honor your father and your mother';
and, 'He who speaks evil of father or   and, 'He who speaks evil of father or
mother, let him surely die.' [5]But you   mother, let him surely die'; [11]but you
say, 'If any one   say, 'If a man
tells his father or his mother,   tells his father or his mother,
What you would have gained from me is   What you would have gained from me is
given to God,   *Corban*' (that is, given to God)—
he need not honor his father.'   [12]then you no longer permit him to do
[6]So, for the sake of your tradition,   anything for his father or mother,
you have made void the word of God.   [13]thus making void the word of God
                                              through your tradition which you hand
                                              on. And many such things you do."

2.5

Matthew 15:30   ### Mark 7:32–35
                                                      [author's italics]

[30]And great crowds came to him,   [32]And they
bringing with them   brought to him
the lame, the maimed, the blind, the
dumb, and many others,   a man who was deaf and had an
                                                  impediment
                                              in his speech;
and they put them at his feet,   and they besought him to lay his hand
                                              upon him. [33]And taking him aside from
                                              the multitude privately, he put his
                                              fingers into his ears, and he spat and
                                              touched his tongue; [34]and looking up to
                                              heaven, he sighed, and said to him,
                                              "*Ephphatha*, that is, "Be opened."
and he healed them,   [35]And his ears were opened, his tongue
                                              was released, and he spoke plainly.

2.6

Matthew 26:39	Mark 14:35–36 [author's italics]	Luke 22:41–42
[39]And going	[35]And going	[41]And he withdrew from them
a little farther he fell on his face and prayed,	a little farther, he fell on the ground and prayed that, if it were possible, the hour might pass from him. [36]And he said,	about a stone's throw, and knelt down and prayed,
"My Father, if it be possible,	"*Abba*, Father, all things are possible to thee;	[42]"Father, if thou art willing,
let this cup pass from me; nevertheless, not as I will, but as thou wilt."	remove this cup from me; yet not what I will, but what thou wilt."	remove this cup from me; nevertheless not my will, but thine, be done."

2.7

Matthew 27:33–34	Mark 15:22–23 [author's italics]	Luke 23:33
[33]And when they came to a place called Golgotha (which means the place of a skull), [34]they offered him wine to drink, mingled with gall; but when he tasted it, he would not drink it.	[22]And they brought him to the place called *Golgotha* (which means the place of a skull). [23]And they offered him wine mingled with myrrh; but he did not take it.	[33]And when they came to the place which is called The Skull, there they crucified him,

2.8

Matthew 27:46	Mark 15:34 [author's italics]

[46]And about the ninth hour Jesus cried
with a loud voice,
"Eli, Eli,
lama sabachthani?" that is,
"My God, my God, why hast thou
  forsaken
me?"
	[34]And at the ninth hour Jesus cried
	with a loud voice,
	"*Eloi, Eloi*,
	lama sabachthani?" which means,
	"My God, my God, why hast thou
	  forsaken
	me?"

In these seven illustrations the Aramaic expression is missing in all five parallel accounts in Luke and in at least five of the seven parallel accounts in Matthew. In only Matthew 27:33 do we find the same Aramaic expression as found in Mark. Matthew's "*Eli, Eli*" in 27:46 is really not a second example, for this is Hebrew and a direct quotation of Psalm 22:1.

The omission of the Aramaic expressions by Matthew and Luke in their parallel accounts would make good sense from their point of view. Since Matthew's and Luke's audiences were Greek-speaking, the inclusion of Aramaic expressions would serve no major purpose, especially if they each had to abbreviate the material they shared in common with Mark in order to include their additional material (Q, M, or L). The elimination of Mark's Aramaisms is thus quite understandable. On the other hand, for Mark to have added into his Gospel all these Aramaisms, which were not in his source(s), is unexplainable. If Mark were a gnostic, perhaps such foreign terms might have had some mystical and esoteric value, but Mark was not a gnostic and in his Gospel absolutely nothing is made over these Aramaic expressions. Furthermore, if Mark sought to abridge a Matthean and/or Lukan source, why would he lengthen his narratives by including expressions unintelligible to his Greek, non-Aramaic Roman audience? Cadbury has furthermore pointed out that careful writers of Greek avoided foreign words, which might explain why such better writers of Greek as Matthew and Luke would tend to omit the Aramaisms found in their Markan source.[16] The lack of any convincing argument for Mark's adding these Aramaisms to his source(s) and the presence of a most logical explanation for their omission by Matthew and Luke argue in favor of the priority of Mark.

Redundancy

A third argument in favor of the priority of Mark is the fact that in numerous instances we find a rather clumsy redundancy in Mark that is not found in Matthew or Luke. Some examples of this are illustrated below.

16. See Henry J. Cadbury, *The Making of Luke-Acts* (London: SPCK, 1958), pp. 123–26, and *The Style and Literary Method of Luke* (Cambridge: Harvard University, 1920), pp. 154–58. Sanders (*Synoptic Tradition*, pp. 187–88) disagrees with Cadbury but is not convincing.

2.9

Matthew 8:16	Mark 1:32	Luke 4:40
[16]That evening	[32]That evening, at sundown,	[40]Now when the sun was setting, all those who had any that were sick with various diseases
they	they	
brought to him many who were possessed with demons;	brought to him all who were sick or possessed with demons.	brought them to him;
		and he laid his hands on every one of them and healed them.

2.10

Matthew 9:14	Mark 2:18	Luke 5:33
[14]Then the disciples of John	[18]Now John's disciples and the Pharisees were fasting; and people	
came to him, saying, "Why do we and the Pharisees fast,	came and said to him, "Why do John's disciples and the disciples of the Pharisees fast,	[33]And they said to him, "The disciples of John fast often, and offer prayers, and so do the disciples of the Pharisees,
but your disciples do not fast?"	but your disciples do not fast?"	but yours eat and drink."

2.11

Matthew 12:3–4	Mark 2:25–26	Luke 6:3–4
[3]He said to them, "Have you not read what	[25]And he said to them, "Have you never read what	[3]And Jesus answered, "Have you not read what
David did, when	David did, when he was in need and	David did when
he was hungry, and those who were with him; [4]how he entered	was hungry, he and those who were with him; [26]how he entered	he was hungry, he and those who were with him; [4]how he entered
the house of God	the house of God, when Abiathar was high priest,	the house of God,

		and took
and ate the bread	and ate the bread	and ate the bread
of the Presence,	of the Presence,	of the Presence,
which it was not lawful	which it is not lawful	which it is not lawful
for him to eat nor for		
those who were with him,		
but only for the priests?	for any but the priests	for any but the priests
	to eat, and also gave it to	to eat, and also gave it to
	those who were with	those with him?"
	him?"	

2.12

Matthew 27:35	Mark 15:24	Luke 23:33–34
[35]And when	[24]And	[33]And when
		they came to the
		place which is called
		The Skull,
they had crucified him,	they crucified him,	there they crucified him,
		and the criminals, one on
		the right and one on the
		left. [34]And Jesus said,
		"Father, forgive them; for
		they know not what they
		do."
		And they cast lots
they divided his garments	and divided his garments	to divide his garments.
among them	among them,	
by casting lots;	casting lots for them,	
	to decide what each	
	should	
	take.	

It is evident from the above that the Markan parallels tend to be wordy and contain unnecessary material. From the number of examples of such redundancy in Mark it is clear that this is a feature of Mark's style.[17] It has been suggested that such a redundancy as in 2.9—where Mark has both "evening" and "at sundown"—may be an example of a Markan conflation of Matthew (which has "evening") and Luke (which has "When the sun was setting").[18] Since there are numerous examples of later scribal tendencies to harmonize two or more sources by including all the variants, some have proposed that Mark's redundancy is due to his conflation of Matthew and Luke. In this regard it has been pointed out that there are 213 examples of redundancy or duplicate expressions in Mark. These are broken down as follows:

---

17. C. M. Tuckett, *The Revival of the Griesbach Hypothesis* (New York: Cambridge University, 1983), pp. 16–21.

18. Thomas R. W. Longstaff, *Evidence of Conflation in Mark?* (Missoula: Scholars, 1977), pp. 140–52.

Matthew has one half, Luke the other half 17 times

Matthew has one half, Luke has both halves 11 times

Matthew has one half, Luke has no parallel 46 times

Luke has one half, Matthew has both halves 17 times

Luke has one half, Matthew has no parallel 25 times

Both omit the same half 39 times

Both have Mark's duplicate expression 6 times

Matthew has both halves, Luke has no parallel 14 times

Luke has both halves, Matthew has no parallel 1 time

Matthew and Luke both have no parallel 37 times[19]

From the above list it is evident that redundancy is a clearly Markan stylistic feature. However, the argument that such redundancy is a result of conflation by Mark of Matthew and Luke is difficult to accept, for in only 17 of the 213 examples could Mark be said to conflate the redundant expression found in Matthew but not found in Luke or the redundant expression found in Luke but not found in Matthew. As a result "Mark's pleonastic style can only be explained by his conflating of his two sources in 17 out of 213 cases."[20]

An even greater argument against the view that Mark's redundancy can be explained by his conflation of Matthew and Luke is the fact that Mark, if he used Matthew and Luke, is supposedly an abridged edition of these other two Gospels. His purpose would then be to shorten not lengthen his sources by conflating them. It is difficult to think that Mark chose to eliminate such material as the Beatitudes, the Lord's Prayer, and the birth narratives but chose in the examples above to enlarge his accounts by the use of redundant expressions. Such a use of Matthew and Luke by Mark is much more difficult to accept than to believe that Matthew and Luke tended to make such redundant ex-

19. Tuckett, Griesbach Hypothesis, p. 20.

20. Ibid., p. 21. Contrast, on the other hand, David Laird Dungan, who states that the phenomenon of Matthew's having one-half of the Markan redundancy and Luke the other occurs "time after time" ("Mark—The Abridgement of Matthew and Luke," in Jesus and Man's Hope [Pittsburgh: Pittsburgh Theological Seminary, 1970], p. 67). Certainly seventeen instances out of 213 occurrences is not "time after time." Tuckett points out that in only fifty-six instances out of the 213 do Matthew and Luke at the same time omit one of Mark's redundant expressions, and in seventeen of them do they choose the opposite one. Actually, one would expect that in twenty-eight instances (one-half of the time) they would do this.

pressions shorter. The redundancy of Mark is best explained on the basis of a Markan priority.[21]

Mark's Harder Readings

Another important argument often raised in favor of the priority of Mark is the presence of various kinds of difficulties in Mark that are not found in Matthew and/or Luke. These "harder readings," at least at first glance, appear contrary to the generally accepted portrait of Jesus held by the early church and therefore were likely to be modified in order to be made less difficult for their readers. There are a number of such examples in Mark.

The Apparent Limitation of Jesus' Power or Influence

2.13

Matthew 8:16	Mark 1:32–34a	Luke 4:40
[16]That evening	[32]That evening, at sundown,	[40]Now when the sun was setting,
they	they	all those who had any that were sick with various diseases
brought to him	brought to him	brought them to him;
many who were possessed with demons;	all who were sick or possessed with demons. [33]And the whole city was gathered together about the door.	
		and he laid his hands on every one of them and healed them.
	[34]And he healed many who were sick with various diseases,	
and he cast out the spirits	and cast out many demons;	
with a word, and healed all who were sick.		

21. Longstaff uses as an example of conflation Tatian's *Diatesseron* (*Conflation in Mark?*, pp. 10–42), but it should be noted that Tatian omitted very little material from the Gospels that lay before him. Furthermore, even if we eliminated the material from the *Diatesseron* that comes from the Gospel of John, this work would be considerably longer than any one of the Gospels he used. Mark's conflation would be very much unlike that of Tatian, for he would have omitted vast amounts of source material (Q, M, and L), which Tatian included in his and is considerably shorter than any of the Gospels he supposedly used.

2.14

Matthew 12:15	Mark 3:9–10	Luke 6:19
[15]Jesus, aware of this, withdrew from there. And many followed him,		
	[9]And he told his disciples to have a boat ready for him because of the crowd, lest they should crush him; [10]for he had healed many, so that	
	all who had diseases pressed upon him to touch him.	[19]And all the crowd sought to touch him, for power came forth from him
and he healed them all. . .		and healed them all.

2.15

Matthew 13:58	Mark 6:5–6
[58]And he did not do many mighty works there,	[5]And he could do no mighty work there, except that he laid his hands upon a few sick people and healed them. [6]And he marveled
because of their unbelief.	because of their unbelief.

In the first two examples (2.13 and 2.14) it appears as if Mark might be interpreted as meaning that Jesus lacked sufficient power to heal "all" and could only heal "many." Upon closer examination such a conclusion is not necessary, for "many" is clearly a synonym in Mark 1:34 for the "all" in 1:32. (Note also the use of "many" in Isaiah 53:12 for "all." "Many" is a semiticism for "all.") It is not surprising, however, why Matthew and Luke would change Mark's "many" to "all," for (at least at first glance) Mark's "many" could be misunderstood as implying a certain inability on the part of Jesus to heal. Both Matthew and Luke also modify the reference in Mark 6:5 to Jesus' not being able to work miracles in Nazareth. Luke does so by eliminating the reference altogether, and Matthew qualifies the statement by pointing out that this was due to the "unbelief" in Nazareth.

In all three of the above examples it is evident that Mark possesses the "harder" reading. In textual criticism the presence of a harder reading in a manuscript is usually seen as evidence for its being more primitive or authentic, since the scribal tendencies were to make harder readings less difficult. In a similar way it is easier to understand why Matthew and Luke might have changed their Markan source by making the account easier for their readers than to think of any reason why Mark would have changed his source(s) and made the readings more difficult.

Negative Descriptions of the Disciples

Another area of harder readings found in Mark involves his description of the disciples. In a number of instances Mark refers to the dullness and hardness of heart of the disciples.

2.16

Matthew 13:18	Mark 4:13	Luke 8:11
	[13]And he said to them, "Do you not understand	
[18]"Hear then the parable	this parable? How then will you understand all the parables?	[11]Now the parable is this:
of the sower.		The seed is the word of God.

2.17

Matthew 14:32–33	Mark 6:51–52
[32]And when they got into the boat,	[51]And he got into the boat with them and
the wind ceased.	the wind ceased.
[33]And those in the boat worshiped him, saying, "Truly you are the Son of God."	And they were utterly astounded,
	[52]for they did not understand about the loaves, but their hearts were hardened.

2.18

Matthew 19:14	Mark 10:14	Luke 18:16
[14]but	[14]But when Jesus saw it he was indignant, and said to them,	[16]But Jesus called them to him, saying,
Jesus said, "Let the children come to me, and do not hinder them;	"Let the children come to me, do not hinder them;	"Let the children come to me, and do not hinder them;
for to such belongs the kingdom of heaven."	for to such belongs the kingdom of God.	for to such belongs the kingdom of God.

2.19

Matthew 20:20–21	Mark 10:35–37
[20]Then the mother of the sons of Zebedee came up to him, with her sons, and kneeling before him she asked him for something	[35]And James and John, the sons of Zebedee, came forward to him,
	and said to him, "Teacher, we want you to do for us whatever we ask of you."
[21]And he said to her,	[36]And he said to them,

"What do you want?" She said to him, "Command that these two sons of mine may sit, one at your right hand and one at your left, in your kingdom."	"What do you want me to do for you?" [37]And they said to him, "Grant us to sit, one at your right hand and one at your left, in your glory."

In the above four examples[22] it is clear that the disciples are portrayed less favorably in Mark than in Matthew and Luke. In the past this fact has been interpreted as indicating that Mark is more primitive and historical than Matthew and Luke, for the tendency in the church was to canonize the disciples and to minimize their failures. Recently, among certain redaction critics, these references have been interpreted as a Markan attempt to vilify the disciples and their theological understanding of Jesus as found in the Gospel of Mark.[23] Yet, if Mark had sought to do this, he was singularly inept, for not until the 1960s did anyone ever interpret Mark in this way.[24] Certainly such a view is contradicted by the Markan insertion in Mark 16:7, which must be read as an affectionate and forgiving promise of a reunion of the disciples and Peter with Jesus. If Mark was not interested in vilifying the disciples, in which direction is it easier to understand the later writers to have moved? Surely Matthew's and Luke's handling of the Markan text, with its harder reading, is far more understandable than a Markan change of Matthew and/or Luke.

Miscellaneous Theological Issues

Along with the areas mentioned above there are a number of other difficulties that appear in the Markan parallels but are not found in the Matthean and/or Lukan accounts.

2.20

Matthew 19:16–17	Mark 10:17–18	Luke 18:18–19
[16]And behold,	[17]And as he was setting out on his journey,	[18]And

22. Cf. also Matthew 16:8–9/Mark 8:17–18/Luke 12:1.
23. Cf. Theodore J. Weeden, *Mark—Traditions in Conflict* (Philadelphia: Fortress, 1971).
24. Cf. Raymond E. Brown's comment in a book review of this approach: "If these four essays are right, Mark was one of the most incompetent writers of all times, since almost all his readers have interpreted him to say the opposite of what he intended about the Eucharist, about Peter [and the disciples], and about the resurrection" (*CBQ* 39[1977]:285).

one	a man	a ruler
came up	ran up	
to him,	and knelt before him, and	
saying,	asked him,	asked him,
"Teacher,	"Good Teacher,	"Good Teacher,
what good deed must I do,	what must I do	what shall I do
to have eternal life?"	to inherit eternal life?"	to inherit eternal life?"
[17]And he said to him,	[18]And Jesus said to him,	[19]And Jesus said to him,
"Why do you ask me		
about what is good?	"Why do you call me good?	"Why do you call me good?
One there is who is good.	No one is good	No one is good
	but God alone.	but God alone.
If you would enter life, keep the commandments."		

2.21

Matthew 12:12b–13	Mark 3:4–5	Luke 6:9–10
	[4]And he said to them,	[9]And Jesus said to them, "I ask you,
So it is lawful to do good on the sabbath."	"Is it lawful on the sabbath to do good	is it lawful on the sabbath to do good
	or to do harm, to save life or to kill?" But they were silent.	or to do harm, to save life or to destroy it?"
	[5]And he looked around at them with anger, grieved at their hardness of heart,	[10]And he looked around on them all,
[13]Then he said to the man, "Stretch out your hand." And the man stretched it out, and it was restored, whole like the other.	and said to the man, "Stretch out your hand." He stretched it out, and his hand was restored.	and said to him, "Stretch out your hand." And he did so, and his hand was restored.

2.22

Matthew 12:3–4	Mark 2:25–26	Luke 6:3–4
[3]He said to them, "Have you not read what	[25]And he said to them, "Have you never read what	[3]And Jesus answered, "Have you not read what
David did, when	David did, when he was in need and	David did when
he was hungry, and those who were with him; [4]how he entered	was hungry, he and those who were with him; [26]how he entered	he was hungry, he and those who were with him; [4]how he entered
the house of God	the house of God, when Abiathar was high priest,	the house of God,
		and took
and ate the bread of the Presence, which it was not lawful	and ate the bread of the Presence, which it is not lawful	and ate the bread of the Presence, which it is not lawful

for him to eat nor for those who were with him, but only for the priests?	for any but the priests to eat, and also gave it to those who were with him?"	for any but the priests to eat, and also gave it to those with him?"

In the first example it is clear that the words of Jesus in Mark 10:18 and Luke 18:19 ("Why do you call me good? No one is good but God alone") are considerably more difficult than what we find in Matthew 19:17 ("Why do you ask me about what is good?"). Throughout the history of the church, Mark 10:18/Luke 18:19 have been difficult passages to interpret and have raised numerous problems. It is inconceivable to think that if Mark used Matthew, he (and Luke) would have changed the Matthean text, which causes no problems, to his problem-plagued version. On the other hand, Matthew's changing of Mark is most understandable.

As to the omission of the expression "with anger" in Mark 3:5 by Matthew and Luke, this is again perfectly understandable. On the other hand, Mark's addition of this to a Matthean and/or Lukan source is more difficult to explain. The same can also be said about the Abiathar reference in Mark 2:26, since it, too, causes difficulties in that it was actually Ahimelech, the father of Abiathar, who held office at the time of the incident.

The various examples listed in this section[25] all demonstrate that on numerous occasions Mark possesses a reading that is "harder" than the one found in one or both of the parallel accounts in Matthew and Luke. Advocates of a Markan priority see this as strong support for their view, since the process of changing the more difficult reading in Mark by Matthew and/or Luke is far more likely than Mark's changing of an easier reading in Matthew and/or Luke into his more (at times "*much* more"!) difficult reading. This furthermore accords well with the harmonistic tendencies that we find in the early church.

The Lack of Matthew–Luke Agreements Against Mark: The Argument from Verbal Agreements

In underlining the parallel passages in the triple tradition it becomes apparent that, of the four colors used, one color occurs far less frequently. Whereas the most common color is BLUE (agreements between

25. Two other examples that could be mentioned are Matthew 12:8/Mark 2:27–28/Luke 6:5 and Matthew 16:28/Mark 9:1/Luke 9:27.

all three Gospels), and whereas there are present goodly amounts of YELLOW or BLACK (agreements between Matthew and Mark) and GREEN (agreements between Mark and Luke), there is a notable lack of RED (agreements between Matthew and Luke). It is an undeniable fact that if one were to underline all the material of the triple tradition, very little use would be made of the red pencil, for Matthew–Luke agreements against Mark are considerably less frequent than any of the other forms of agreement. If one limits oneself to the possibility of one Gospel having served as the basis of the other two, we possess only three possibilities (figure 5). These options are identical to 3(a), 3(b), and 3(c), respectively, in figure 1.

Of the three options in figure 5, it is clear that only (b) can explain the following:

1. Why at times Matthew and Mark agree against Luke—Luke diverges from his Markan source whereas Matthew does not.
2. Why at times Mark and Luke agree against Matthew—Matthew diverges from his Markan source whereas Luke does not.
3. Why Matthew and Luke seldom agree against Mark—this would require a coincidental change on the part of Matthew and Luke of their Markan source in exactly the same manner.

Yet certain other possibilities could also explain this kind of agreement. These are 1(a) and 1(f) in figure 1, also illustrated below in figure 6; and 4(a–f) in figure 1, illustrated again in figure 7. Concerning the six possibilities in figure 7, it should be noted that they presume a Matthean knowledge of Luke or a Lukan knowledge of Matthew, and this possibility will be challenged later.[26]

Figure 5

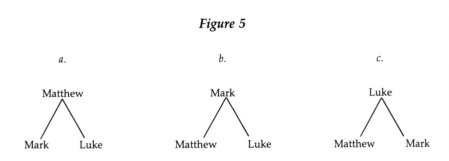

26. See below pp. 91–103.

Figure 6

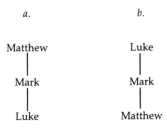

Figure 7

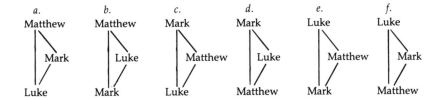

The Lack of Matthew—Luke Agreements Against Mark: The Argument from Order

In 1835 an observation was made by Lachmann that has played an important role in the discussion of the Synoptic Problem. Lachmann observed that in the triple tradition the order of Matthew and Luke resemble each other a great deal, whereas in the non-triple tradition they do not agree. Lachmann furthermore observed that Matthew and Luke never agree in order against Mark, whereas at times Matthew and Mark agree in order against Luke and at times Mark and Luke agree in order against Matthew.[27] Lachmann went on to argue that the reasons for Matthew's and Luke's having changed the order of Mark were plausible, whereas the changes Mark would have had to make to Matthew and/or Luke were not.[28] From this, Lachmann argued that Mark was closer to an original Ur-gospel than Matthew or Luke. Since the time of Lachmann, his name has been associated with "the argument from order," and it has often been stated that Lachmann—on the basis of the lack of agreements in order between Matthew and Luke against Mark—"proved" that Mark was the source of the other two

27. See above pp. 34–37. Note especially *f.* and *o.* in table 1; *q.* in table 2; *h.* and *i.* in table 3.

28. See C. M. Tuckett, "The Argument from Order and the Synoptic Problem," *TZ* 36 (1980): 340–41.

Gospels. Butler in 1951, however, pointed out that there was an error in this reasoning and referred to a "Lachmann Fallacy," since a number of other possibilities could also explain this fact.[29]

It is therefore common today for the opponents of the theory of Markan priority to speak of the "Lachmann Fallacy." It is clear that the argument from order cannot by itself prove any particular solution of the Synoptic Problem for, at least hypothetically, solutions 1(a), 1(f), 3(b), and 4(a–f) (see figure 1) could explain this. Yet Lachmann's argument involved not only the observation of a lack of Matthew–Luke agreements against Mark but also an explanation of why Matthew's and Luke's divergences from the Markan order are more understandable than a Markan divergence from Matthew and/or Luke.[30] One major problem that other solutions encounter in seeking to explain the phenomenon of order is that they ultimately must postulate Matthew's use of Luke or Luke's use of Matthew. This drawback is found in the Griesbach Hypothesis and possibilities 4(a–f). As to 1(a) or 1(f) ([a] and [b] in figure 6), how can this explain the large amount of material Matthew and Luke have in common but which is not found in Mark? Did they have another major source in common? Did they have a Q? If we once accept Matthew's and Luke's use of a major common source other than Mark to explain this common material, there seems little reason to reject the theory of Markan priority. On the other hand, the view that Matthew knew (in the sense of "used") Luke or that Luke knew Matthew encounters insurmountable problems.[31] The fact that Matthew and Luke never agree in order against Mark and that they only agree in order in the material of the triple tradition is a strong argument against their having known each other's work.

Far from being tossed away on a junk heap, as some critics suggest, the observations and argumentation of Lachmann argue strongly for the theory of Markan priority. And, even after the discussion of the "Lachmann Fallacy," the full Lachmann argument is still seen by many scholars as "an irrefutable argument for the priority of Mark. . . ."[32]

Literary Agreements

There exist in the synoptic Gospels a number of literary agreements that can best be explained on the basis of a Markan priority. These

29. B. C. Butler, *The Originality of St. Matthew* (Cambridge: Cambridge University, 1951), pp. 62–71.

30. For an explanation of these Matthean and Lukan divergences see Werner Georg Kümmel, *Introduction to the New Testament*, trans. Howard Clark Kee (Nashville: Abingdon, 1975), pp. 57–60.

31. See below pp. 91–103.

32. Kümmel, *Introduction to the New Testament*, p. 148.

involve certain omissions and wordings that make much more sense
on the basis of Matthew and/or Luke having changed their Markan
source than vice versa.

2.23

Matthew 9:1–2	Mark 2:1–5	Luke 5:17–20
[1]And getting into a boat he crossed over and came to his own city.	[1]And when he returned to Capernaum after some days, it was reported that he was at home. [2]And many were gathered together, so that there was no longer room for them, not even about the door; and he was preaching the word to them.	[17]On one of those days, as he was teaching, there were Pharisees and teachers of the law sitting by, who had come from every village of Galilee and Judea and from Jerusalem; and the power of the Lord was with him to heal.
[2]And behold, they brought to him a paralytic, lying on his bed;	[3]And they came, bringing to him a paralytic carried by four men.	[18]And behold, men were bringing on a bed a man who was paralyzed, and they sought to bring him in and lay him before Jesus;
	[4]And when they could not get near him because of the crowd, they removed the roof above him; and when they had made an opening, they let down the pallet on which the paralytic lay.	[19]but finding no way to bring him in because of the crowd, they went up on the roof and let him down with his bed through the tiles into the midst before Jesus.
and when Jesus saw their faith he said to the paralytic, "Take heart, my son; your sins are forgiven."	[5]And when Jesus saw their faith, he said to the paralytic, "My son, your sins are forgiven."	[20]And when he saw their faith he said, "Man, your sins are forgiven you."

2.24

Matthew 27:15–22	Mark 15:6–13	Luke 23:18–21
[15]Now at the feast the governor was accustomed to release for the crowd any one prisoner whom they wanted. [16]And they had then	[6]Now at the feast he used to release for them one prisoner for whom they asked. [7]And among the rebels in prison, who had committed murder in the insurrection,	
a notorious prisoner, called Barabbas. [17]So when they had gathered,	there was a man called Barabbas. [8]And the crowd came up and began to ask Pilate to do as he was wont to do for them.	
Pilate said to them, "Whom do you want me to release for you, Barabbas or Jesus who is called Christ?" [18]For he knew that it was out of envy that they had delivered him up. [19]Besides, while he was sitting on the judgment seat, his wife sent word to him, "Have nothing to do with that righteous man, for I have suffered much over him today in a dream."	[9]And he answered them, "Do you want me to release for you the King of the Jews?" [10]For he perceived that it was out of envy that the chief priests had delivered him up.	
[20]Now the chief priests and the elders persuaded the people to ask for	[11]But the chief priests stirred up the crowd to have him release for them	
Barabbas and destroy Jesus. [21]The governor again said to them, "Which of the two do you want me to release for you?" And they said,	Barabbas instead. [12]And Pilate again said to them,	
"Barabbas."		[18]But they all cried out together, "Away with this man, and release to us Barabbas"— [19]a man who had been thrown into prison for an insurrection started in the city, and for murder.

[22]Pilate said to them,		[20]Pilate addressed them once more, desiring to release Jesus;
"Then what shall I do with Jesus who is called	"Then what shall I do with the man whom you call the King of the Jews?"	
Christ?" They all said, "Let him be crucified."	[13]And they cried out again, "Crucify him."	[21]but they shouted out, "Crucify, crucify him!"

In the first example we find that Matthew lacks the parallel in Mark 2:4/Luke 5:19 that explains why Jesus saw the faith of the paralytic and his four friends. Mark and Luke explain this as due to their having removed the roof. Matthew's treatment of the account here agrees well with his practice elsewhere. It is not untypical of Matthew to abbreviate the gospel accounts[33] and to leave out important, although not absolutely essential, information. In Matthew 8:5–13 he omits the reference to the Jewish elders and friends that Luke includes in 7:3–5 and 6; in Matthew 9:18–26 he omits much of the material found in Mark 5:29–33 and 35–37. In the second example given above Luke refers to the crowd as crying for the release of Barabbas, but he never mentions the custom of why the crowd was able to choose that someone be released! The difficulty of Luke's omission is witnessed to by the many textual variants that include such a reference. In both these instances such omissions can best be explained by the omission of this explanatory material by Matthew and Luke from their source—Mark.

In the next three examples the wording found in the triple tradition can best be explained by Matthew's and Luke's use of Mark.

2.25

Matthew 3:13–16	Mark 1:9–10	Luke 3:21–22a
[13]Then Jesus came from Galilee to the Jordan to John, to be baptized by him. [14]John would have prevented him, saying, "I need to be baptized by you, and do you	[9]In those days Jesus came from Nazareth of Galilee	

---

33. This was observed already by Augustine in his *De Consensu Evangelistarum*. See 2.28.66. The view that Matthew tends to abbreviate his sources has been challenged by Sanders (*Synoptic Tradition*, pp. 46–87), but in the examples given this seems undeniable.

               The Literary Relationship of the Synoptic Gospels

come to me?" 15But Jesus answered him, "Let it be so now; for thus it is fitting for us to fulfil all righteousness." Then he consented. 16And when Jesus was baptized,

and was baptized by John in the Jordan.

21Now when all the people were baptized, and when Jesus also had been baptized

and was praying,

he went up immediately from the water, and behold, the heavens were opened and he saw the Spirit of God descending

10And when he came up out of the water, immediately he saw the heavens opened and the Spirit descending upon him

the heaven was opened, 22and the Holy Spirit descended upon him in bodily form,

like a dove and alighting on him;

like a dove;

as a dove,

2.26

Matthew 19:16–17b

16And behold,

one came up to him, saying, "Teacher, what good deed must I do, to have eternal life?" 17And he said to him, "Why do you ask me about what is good?

One there is who is good.

Mark 10:17–18

17And as he was setting out on his journey, a man ran up and knelt before him, and asked him, "Good Teacher, what must I do to inherit eternal life?" 18And Jesus said to him,

"Why do you call me good? No one is good but God alone.

Luke 18:18–19

18And

a ruler

asked him, "Good Teacher, what shall I do to inherit eternal life?" 19And Jesus said to him,

"Why do you call me good? No one is good but God alone.

2.27

Matthew 20:20–23

20Then the mother of the sons of Zebedee came up to him, with her sons, and kneeling before him she asked him for something.

21And he said to her, "What do you want?" She said to him, "Command that these two sons of mine may sit, one at your right hand and one

Mark 10:35–40

35And James and John, the sons of Zebedee, came forward to him,

and said to him, "Teacher, we want you to do for us whatever we ask of you." 36And he said to them, "What do you want me to do for you?" 37And they said to him, "Grant us to sit, one at your right hand and one

at your left, in your
kingdom."
[22]But Jesus answered, "You do not
know what you are asking. Are you able
to drink the cup that I am to drink?"

They said to him, "We are able."
[23]He said to them,
"You will drink my cup,

but to sit at my right hand and at my
left is not mine to grant, but it is for
those for whom it has been prepared
by my Father."

at your left, in your
glory."
[38]But Jesus said to them, "You do not
know what you are asking. Are you able
to drink the cup that I drink,
or to be baptized with the baptism with
which I am baptized?"
[39]And they said to him, "We are able."
And Jesus said to them,
"The cup that I drink you will drink;
and with the baptism with which I am
baptized, you will be baptized;
[40]but to sit at my right hand or at my
left is not mine to grant, but it is for
those for whom it has been prepared."

In the first example the term "immediately" in Matthew 3:16 appears to make a good literary agreement with Mark against Luke, but its use in Matthew is confusing. According to Mark 1:10, upon coming up out of the water Jesus *immediately saw the heavens being opened;* but according to Matthew after Jesus was baptized he *immediately came out of the water.* This is best explained by Matthew having changed Mark's "Jesus was baptized (verb) and having come out (participle) . . . immediately he saw . . ." to "Jesus having been baptized (participle) came out (verb) immediately. . . ." In so doing, Matthew has followed the Markan order without being careful of the grammatical consequences in changing Mark's "baptized" to a participle and his "having come out" to a verb.[34]

In the other two accounts it appears that Matthew has changed his Markan source to remove a possible misunderstanding, but he retains the Markan wording elsewhere and thus reveals his dependence upon Mark. In Matthew 19:16–17 the Evangelist has as the reply of Jesus to the rich young man the much less difficult "Why do you ask me about what is good?" The Matthean statement clearly does not involve the christological problem that the Markan and Lukan parallels raise. Yet, in the very next statement ("One there is who is good"), Matthew has in the same order the same reply that we find in Mark and Luke, and this involves Jesus' question "Why do you call me good?" It is apparent that, although the statements following Jesus' question agree in all three of the synoptic Gospels and are similar (Mark and Luke are exactly the same), the question in Matthew that precedes the statement is different and does not fit nearly as well. The most reasonable explanation of this is that Matthew changed his Markan source in Matthew

34. For two other examples of how Matthew places Mark's "immediately" with a different and less suitable verb, see Mark 1:20/Matthew 4:22 and Mark 11:2/Matthew 21:2.

19:17 to eliminate the difficult question—but, after eliminating the difficult expression in his source ("Why do you call me good?"), he immediately returns to it even though it involves a switch from *good thing* to *good one.* In so doing, Matthew unintentionally betrays the fact that he is using Mark.

In the last example we again have an instance in which Matthew has apparently sought to modify a harsher-looking parallel in Mark. In Mark 10:35 it is the apostles James and John who present the selfish request for privileged positions in the kingdom of God. In Matthew 20:20–21, however, it is not James and John but their mother who brings the request. Yet the reply in Matthew 20:22, as in Mark, is directed not to their mother but to James and John. (The "you" in Matt. 20:22 is plural.) Again, this is easy to explain on the basis of a Markan priority. Matthew, in seeking to mollify the negative impression of James and John found in his source, placed the request on the lips of their mother.[35] After doing this, however, Matthew returned to and followed his Markan source and had Jesus address not the mother but James and John.

In the five examples shown above, other hypothetical explanations might be offered to explain the phenomena, but it appears that they are far better explained on the basis of a Markan priority.[36]

The Argument from Redaction

Probably the most weighty argument used today in favor of a Markan priority involves the comparison of the synoptic Gospels in order to note their respective theological emphases. There is little fear of contradiction in saying that most work in redaction criticism has assumed the priority of Mark and that not a great deal has been done on the basis of a Matthean priority. In general it would appear that a Matthean use of Mark provides a clear and consistent redactional emphasis. The same can also be said of Luke's handling of Mark. On the other hand, from the viewpoint of a Markan redaction criticism, a Markan use of Matthew (and/or Luke) seems most unlikely. In this

35. Whether or not this is a historical reminiscence is not important. It may well be that James and John presented this request to Jesus through their mother. This, however, does not change the fact that the use of the plural "you" in Matthew 20:22 indicates that Matthew's source had James and John asking the question. It is interesting to note in this regard that in the story of the healing of the centurion's servant (Matt. 8:5–13/Luke 7:1–10) it is Matthew who omits the intermediary messengers and has the centurion directly speak to Jesus, while Luke refers to the intermediary role of the Jewish elders.

36. For additional examples see G. M. Styler, "The Priority of Mark," in C. F. D. Moule, *The Birth of the New Testament*, 3d. ed. (New York: Harper, 1982), pp. 293–98.

section we shall investigate the vocabulary, style, and theological traits
of both Matthew and Mark and see how they fare in the other Synoptics. What we shall do first is to look at two clear Matthean theological
emphases and see if, on the basis of a Matthean priority, Mark's and
Luke's treatment of this material makes more sense or if, on the basis
of a Markan priority, Matthew's use of Mark seems a more reasonable
assumption. Then we shall look at two stylistic and verbal tendencies
in Mark and see if, assuming the priority of Mark, Matthew's and
Luke's treatment of this material makes more sense than if Mark added
this to a Matthean and/or Lukan source.

Matthean Redactional Emphases Compared with Mark and Luke

One theological title for Jesus that is a favorite of Matthew is "Son of
David." It appears eleven times in Matthew: 1:1, 20 (used of Joseph);
9:27; 12:23; 15:22; 20:30, 31; 21:9, 15; 22:42, 45. The last two references
differ somewhat in form but the concept is the same. In Mark, however, the title appears only four times: 10:47, 48; 12:35, 37. The last
reference again differs somewhat in form but the concept is the same.
The title also appears four times in Luke: 18:38, 39; 20:41, 44. As in the
case of Matthew and Mark, the last reference differs in form but the
concept is the same. That this title is a strong Matthean emphasis is
especially evidenced by its appearance in the introductory verse of this
Gospel: "The book of the genealogy of Jesus Christ, the son of David,
the son of Abraham." But it is when one compares the appearance of
this title in Matthew with the parallel accounts that it becomes apparent how strong a Matthean redactional emphasis this really is.

2.28

Matthew 12:22b–24	Mark 3:22	Luke 11:14b–15
[22]Then a blind and dumb demoniac was brought to him, and he healed him,		[14]Now he was casting out a demon that was dumb;
so that the dumb man spoke and saw.		when the demon had gone out, the dumb man spoke,
[23]And all the people were amazed, and said, "Can this be the Son of David?"		and the people marveled.
[24]But when the Pharisees heard it they	[22]And the scribes who came down from Jerusalem	[15]But some of them
said,	said,	said,

"It is only	"He is possessed	"He casts out demons
by Beelzebul,	by Beelzebul,	by Beelzebul,
	and by	
the prince of demons,	the prince of demons	the prince of demons;" . . .
that this man	he	
casts out demons."	casts out the demons."	

2.29

Matthew 15:21–25	Mark 7:24–26
[21]And Jesus went away from there and withdrew to the district of Tyre and Sidon.	[24]And from there he arose and went away to the region of Tyre and Sidon. And he entered a house, and would not have any one know it; yet he could not be hid.
[22]And behold, a Canaanite woman from that region came out and cried, "Have mercy on me, O Lord, Son of David; my daughter is severely possessed by a demon."	[25]But immediately a woman, whose little daughter was possessed by an unclean spirit, heard of him,
[23]But he did not answer her a word. And his disciples came and begged him, saying, "Send her away, for she is crying after us." [24]He answered, "I was sent only to the lost sheep of the house of Israel." [25]But she came and knelt before him,	and came and fell down at his feet. [26]Now the woman was a Greek, a Syrophoenician by birth. And she begged him
saying, "Lord, help me."	to cast the demon out of her daughter.

2.30

Matthew 21:9	Mark 11:9–10	Luke 19:37b–38
[9]And the crowds	[9]And those	. . . the whole multitude of the disciples began to rejoice and praise God with a loud voice for all the mighty works that they had seen,
that went before him and that followed him	who went before and those who followed	
shouted, "Hosanna to the Son of David! Blessed is he who comes in the name of the Lord!	cried out, "Hosanna! Blessed is he who comes in the name of the Lord! [10]Blessed is the kingdom of our father David that is coming!	[38]saying, "Blessed is the King who comes in the name of the Lord!

| | | Peace in heaven and |
| Hosanna in the highest!" | Hosanna in the highest!" | glory in the highest!" |

2.31

Matthew 21:12–15	Mark 11:15–17	Luke 19:45–46
	¹⁵And they came to Jerusalem.	
¹²And Jesus	And he	⁴⁵And he
entered the temple of God	entered the temple	entered the temple
and drove out	and began to drive out	and began to drive out
all who sold	those who sold	those who sold,
and bought	and those who bought	
in the temple,	in the temple,	
and he overturned the	and he overturned the	
tables of the money-	tables of the money-	
changers and the seats of	changers and the seats of	
those who sold pigeons.	those who sold pigeons;	
	¹⁶and he would not allow	
	any one to carry anything	
	through the temple.	
	¹⁷And he taught, and	
¹³He said to them,	said to them,	⁴⁶saying to them,
"It is written,	"Is it not written,	"It is written,
'My house shall be called	'My house shall be called	'My house shall be
a house of prayer';	a house of prayer	a house of prayer';
	for all the nations'?	
but you make it	But you have made it	but you have made it
a den of robbers."	a den of robbers."	a den of robbers."
¹⁴And the blind and the		
lame came to him in the		
temple, and he healed		
them.		
¹⁵But when the chief		
priests and the scribes saw		
the wonderful things that		
he did, and the children		
crying out in the temple,		
"Hosanna to the Son of		
David!" . . .		

In each of the examples given above it is evident that there is a strong Matthean emphasis on the title "Son of David." The question must then be raised as to which explanation appears more likely—that Mark and Luke chose to *omit* this title from their Matthean source or that Matthew *added* it to his Markan source. The former suggestion does not seem convincing, for both Mark and Luke use this title four times and are apparently not in the least seeking to avoid its use as a description for Jesus. Luke in fact clearly emphasizes the Davidic line-age of Jesus in his opening chapters (cf. 1:27, 32, 69; 2:4, 11). The agreement of Mark and Luke in omitting the references to the "Son of David" found in Matthew 12:23; 15:22; 21:9 and 15 argues rather that they did not have the Gospel of Matthew as a source before them. On the other hand, seeing the above references as additions by Matthew to his Markan source makes good sense. It is easy to see how Matthew in his construction of the seam for the Beelzebul account (12:23) could have added this title. The addition of the title upon the lips of a Canaanite woman (15:22) seems somewhat strange and looks like an insertion by someone for whom this title was especially significant. The appearance of this title in Matthew 21:9 and 15 also looks more like Matthean additions to the Markan narrative than Markan and Lukan omissions of this material in Matthew. As we look at this Matthean theological emphasis, the appearance of the title "Son of David" in Matthew 9:27; 12:23; 15:22; 21:9 and 15 is best explained by Matthew's having added these references to his Markan source in order to emphasize that Jesus was the fulfillment of the Old Testament hopes concerning the promised "Son of David" rather than by seeing them as omissions on the part of Mark and Luke. Luke's use of Mark also provides the best explanation of the fact that the four uses of this title in his Gospel correspond to the exact same four uses of this title in Mark.

The second Matthean theological emphasis that we shall look at involves the formula quotation "this was to fulfil . . . ." This occurs in Matthew 1:22; 2:15, 17, 23; 4:14; 8:17; 12:17; 13:35; 21:4; and 27:9. Closely related to these formula quotations are four additional references in Matthew—5:17 (Jesus came not to abolish the law and the prophets but "to fulfil" them); 13:14 (the term here is *anaplērountai* instead of *plērountai*); 26:54 ("But how then should the scriptures be fulfilled"?); and 26:56. That this prophecy-fulfillment scheme is a strong Matthean emphasis is acknowledged by all. But if we compare the appearance of these formula quotations in Matthew with the parallel passages in Mark and Luke, we observe something quite interesting. With regard to Matthew 1:22; 2:15, 17, 23; 27:9, there are no parallel passages in either Mark or Luke. In Matthew 5:17 we may have a possible parallel in Luke 16:16, for Matthew 5:18 and Luke 16:17 are quite similar. The formula quotation, however, is not found in the Lukan passage. In Matthew 4:14 possibly, but clearly in 8:17; 12:17; 13:14; 21:4; and 26:54, we have parallel accounts in Mark and Luke; and in Matthew 13:35 we have a parallel in Mark. Yet in *none* of these instances is this Matthean theological emphasis found in either Mark or Luke. In only one instance do we find something of a parallel, and that is the similar *but not exact* use of "to fulfill" in Matthew 26:56 and Mark 14:49, where both read that "the scriptures . . . be fulfilled."

In looking at this data, how are we to explain the omission of these formula quotations of Matthew in Mark and Luke? If Luke and Mark used Matthew, why did they totally omit this material except for the

Matthew 26:56/Mark 14:49 parallel? That they were not adverse to such an emphasis—but on the contrary had a similar theological conviction—is evident from Mark 14:49 and Luke 4:21; 24:44, where the same expression is used. It is also evident from the frequent appearance of "it is written" (*gegraptai*) in these works that they acknowledged that Jesus' coming was the fulfillment of what the Scriptures said.[37] If Matthew was their source, the almost-total omission of the formula quotations by Mark and Luke is most difficult to explain. On the other hand, if Matthew used Mark, the phenomenon becomes quite explainable as "Matthean additions to the Markan narrative." On that basis, what Matthew did in his copying of Mark was to add these passages to his text in order to show his readers, who were no doubt Jewish Christians, that Jesus of Nazareth was the Christ and the fulfillment of the Old Testament hopes of the Jewish people. Such a use of Mark by Matthew makes good sense, for it is easier to see Matthew as adding these formula quotations to his text[38] than to conceive of Mark and Luke coincidentally being in perfect agreement and for some reason omitting all these references.

Markan Stylistic Features Compared with Matthew

One of the better-known stylistic features of the Gospel of Mark is its frequent use of "immediately" (*euthys*).[39] Once one notes the frequency of this term in Mark and how it is used, it becomes apparent that the term "and immediately" functions less as a chronological determination than as a conjunction used to join passages.[40] Yet, when we compare the appearance of the term *euthys* in Mark and its appearance in Matthew, it becomes clear that Mark must have served as the source for Matthew. Within the Gospel of Mark the term appears forty-one times. Within Matthew *euthys* and its alternately spelled form

---

37. *Gegraptai* is found in Mark 1:2/Luke 3:4; Mark 7:6; 9:12, 13; 11:17/Luke 19:46 (= Matt. 21:13); 14:21 (= Matt. 26:24); 14:27 (= Matt. 26:31); in Luke 2:23; 4:4, 8, 10 (= Matthew 4:4, 6, 10); 4:17; 7:27 (= Matt. 11:10); 10:26; 18:31; 21:22; 22:37, 24:44, 46.

38. That the formula quotations are secondary additions to the text is evident in Matthew 1:22; 2:15, 17, 23; 4:14; 8:17; 12:17; 13:35; 21:4; and 27:9. These passages could all be simply excised from their context, and although we would be much poorer as a result, their omission would never be noticed.

39. It is interesting to note that in those passages, such as Mark 12:13–37, the Markan apocalypse, and the passion narrative, where scholars are convinced that Mark has used a source, "immediately" is seldom found. In Mark 12:13–17 and 13:1–37 it is not found at all, and in Mark 14:1–16:8 it is found only four times.

40. See E. J. Pryke, *Redactional Style in the Markan Gospel* (Cambridge: Cambridge University, 1978), p. 87.

eutheōs occur five and thirteen times respectively. In regard to the former, all five occurrences have Markan parallels—3:16 (= Mark 1:10); 13:20 (= Mark 4:16); 13:21 (= Mark 4:17); 14:27 (= Mark 6:50); and 21:3 (= Mark 11:3). With regard to the alternately spelled *eutheōs,* in nine of the thirteen instances we find a Markan parallel with *euthys*—4:20 (= Mark 1:18); 4:22 (= Mark 1:20); 8:3 (= Mark 1:42); 13:5 (= Mark 4:5); 14:22 (= Mark 6:45); 20:34 (= Mark 10:52); 21:2 (= Mark 11:2); 26:49 (= Mark 14:45); and 26:74 (= Mark 14:72). Of the other four instances, two (24:29 and 27:48) occur in accounts that have Markan parallels but lack the term; one (14:31) occurs in a "Matthean addition to the Markan narrative"; and one (25:15) has no parallel at all in Mark. Of the eighteen times that "immediately" appears in Matthew, fourteen have Markan parallels. Only four times does the term appear elsewhere in Matthew, and only one of these occurs in non-Markan material. This means that whereas seventeen usages of "immediately" in Matthew occur in material parallel in some way to Mark, only once does it appear in Matthew's other material. Of the 18,293 words found in Matthew, 10,901 have Markan parallels. In these 10,901 words, "immediately" occurs seventeen times, but in the 7,392 words in Matthew that do not have a Markan parallel, it occurs only once.[41] If Matthew were not using a major written source (or sources), but composing his Gospel from small units of oral or written traditions, one would expect that "immediately" would appear in the non-Markan parallels approximately twelve times. Again the question must be raised as to which hypothesis best explains the phenomenon. It is evident that Mark tends to add "immediately" to his sources (whether oral or written). His use of Matthew could explain the forty-one appearances in Mark, for Mark could have copied the instances he found in his Matthean source and added others. *BUT* the theory of Matthean priority would not explain why the material not having a Markan parallel (Q and M) lacks the term. To postulate that Matthew used such sources and that one major source contained "immediately," whereas the others did not, results in an Ur-source that looks a lot like Mark! On the other hand, if we assume that Matthew used Mark, we have a much more satisfactory solution: the appearance of "immediately" in Matthew results from its frequent occurrence in Mark. Although Matthew eliminates over half of the references in his Markan source, he still follows Mark fifteen times. On the other hand this favorite Markan term did not appear in Matthew's other sources (Q and M), so that he did not copy them into the non-Markan section of his Gospel. Once again the

---

41. These statistics come from Tyson and Longstaff, *Synoptic Abstract,* p. 169.

theory of Markan priority seems the best way to explain this particular redactional activity of Matthew.

The second Markan stylistic feature that we shall observe involves his use of a "for" (*gar*) explanatory clause to provide relevant information for his readers. Within the Gospel of Mark there are sixty-six *gar* clauses. Thirty-four of these are editorial comments by the Evangelist and were probably not part of the tradition Mark used.[42] In contrast Matthew contains one hundred and twenty-three *gar* clauses, but only eleven of these are editorial explanatory clauses. Of these eleven examples, ten have Markan parallels: 4:18 (= Mark 1:16); 7:29 (= Mark 1:22); 9:21 (= Mark 5:28); 14:3 (= Mark 6:17), 4 (= Mark 6:18), 24 (= Mark 6:48); 19:22 (= Mark 10:22); 21:26 (= Mark 11:32); 26:43 (= Mark 14:40); 27:18 (= Mark 15:10).[43] Only one (Matt. 7:12) has no Markan parallel. How can one explain the fact that ten of the eleven *gar* editorial explanations found in Matthew occur in material paralleled in Mark? On the basis of Matthean priority, it is difficult to think why there would exist in the 10,901 words of Matthew that have Markan parallels ten editorial *gar* clauses and in the 7,392 words that have *no* Markan parallels only one. Statistically one would expect approximately seven such clauses. On the other hand, on the basis of a Markan priority, one would expect a greater occurrence of the Markan stylistic feature in the sections of Matthew that have parallels to Mark than in the other sections, and this is exactly what we find.[44]

Whereas certain arguments for the priority of Mark may receive less emphasis today than in the past, the argument from redactional style and emphasis will take on greater and greater importance in the future. At the present time, however, the great majority of redaction critics believe in the priority of Mark because, having worked with the data, they believe that a Markan priority best explains such phenomena as discussed above.

---

42. These are Mark 1:16, 22; 2:15; 3:10, 21; 5:8, 28, 42; 6:14, 17, 18, 20, 31, 48, 50, 52; 7:3, 9:6 (two times), 31, 34; 10:22; 11:13, 18 (two times), 32; 12:12; 14:2, 40, 56; 15:10; 16:4, 8 (two times).

43. Matthew 27:43 and 28:2 are not included, for the former appears to be part of the scribal/Pharisaic charge against Jesus, and the latter, along with verses 3–6, is part of the account itself.

44. Another example of a Markan redactional style that is frequently used to argue for a Markan priority involves the use of the "historical present," i.e., the characteristically Markan use of the present tense ("and he com*es*, and s*ays*, and h*eals*, and g*oes*," etc.) in the narrative. According to Tuckett the historical present occurs approximately 2.36 times per page in Mark in the BFBS Greek text, compared to 0.80 and 0.10 per page in Matthew and Luke (*Griesbach Hypothesis*, p. 24). Tuckett points out that the phenomenon is more easily explained on the basis of a Markan priority than a Matthean one.

Mark's More Primitive Theology

Scholars in the past have referred to the more primitive and pictur-
esque nature of the Gospel of Mark in an attempt to prove not only its
priority but also its historicity. The vividness of such details as Mark
4:38 (Jesus "in the stern, asleep on the cushion") and 8:14 ("they had
only one loaf with them in the boat") was seen as evidence of eyewitness testimony and historical credence.[45] It should be remembered
in this regard that the investigation of the Synoptic Problem was not
simply an isolated piece of "pure research" but was from the beginning
intimately associated with the quest for the historical Jesus. The goal of
many investigators of the Synoptic Problem was to find the most primitive Gospel, which would then serve as the foundation for such a
quest. It is therefore not surprising that many scholars who wrote
about the literary problem of the sources also wrote about the problem
involving the "historical Jesus." As a result, indications of historical
and theological primitiveness were seen as strong evidence for priority.
It is now evident that the majority of such arguments no longer carry a
great deal of conviction.

Having acknowledged that the vividness or lack of vividness of an
account does not in itself demonstrate that one account is prior to the
other, it is nevertheless true that the more theologically developed an
account, the more likely it is to be secondary. One case in point involves the Christological title "Lord" and its appearances in the synoptic Gospels. If we limit ourselves to the triple tradition, we find that
Mark uses the term "Lord" (*kyrios*) with respect to Jesus six times:
Mark 1:3 (= Matt. 3:3/Luke 3:4); 2:28 (= Matt. 12:8/Luke 6:5); 7:28
(= Matt. 15:27; Luke omits the account); 11:3 (= Matt. 21:3/Luke 19:31);
12:36, 37 (= Matt. 22:44, 45/Luke 20:42, 44). On the other hand, only in
Matthew do we find *kyrios* used of Jesus in the following material of
the triple tradition: Matthew 8:2, 25; 14:28, 30; 15:22, 25; 16:22; 17:4, 15;
20:30 (there is a textual problem here), 31, 33; 22:43; 24:42 (here *kyrios* in
Matthew refers to the Lord Jesus, whereas in the parallel in Mark 13:35
it refers to the "master" of the house); and 26:22.[46] It seems reasonable,
simply on the basis of numbers, to understand the greater number of
instances in which Jesus is called *kyrios* in Matthew as a secondary
development in which this favorite title of the early church is read
more and more into the gospel accounts. This is especially evident
when we compare the following examples:

45. Cf. Taylor, *Mark*, pp. 135–40.
46. To these can be added the following references that are found in M or Q material:
Matthew 7:21 (Luke 6:46), 22; 8:6, 8 (Luke 7:6); 8:21 (probably Luke 9:59); 9:28; 18:21;
25:37, and 44.

2.32

Matthew 17:4	Mark 9:5–6	Luke 9:33
		[33]And as the men were parting from him,
[4]And Peter said to Jesus, "Lord,	[5]And Peter said to Jesus, "Master,	Peter said to Jesus, "Master,
it is well that we are here;	it is well that we are here;	it is well that we are here;
if you wish,		
I will make	let us make	let us make
three booths here,	three booths,	three booths,
one for you and one for Moses and one for Elijah."	one for you and one for Moses and one for Elijah."	one for you and one for Moses and one for Elijah"
	[6]For he did not know what to say, for they were exceedingly afraid.	—not knowing what he said.

2.33

Matthew 17:14–15	Mark 9:14–18a	Luke 9:37–39
[14]And when they came to	[14]And when they came to	[37]On the next day, when they had come down from the mountain,
	the disciples, they saw	
the crowd,	a great crowd about them, and scribes arguing with them. [15]And immediately all the crowd, when they saw him, were greatly amazed, and	a great crowd
	ran up to him and greeted him. [16]And he asked them, "What are you discussing with them?" [17]And	met him.
a man	one of the crowd	[38]And behold, a man from the crowd
came up to him and kneeling before him said, [15]"Lord, have mercy on my son,	answered him, "Teacher, I brought my son to you,	cried, "Teacher, I beg you to look upon my son, for he is my only child;"
for he is an epileptic and	for he has a dumb spirit; [18]and wherever it seizes him,	[39]and behold, a spirit seizes him, and he suddenly cries out;
he suffers terribly;	it dashes him down; and he foams and grinds his teeth and becomes rigid;	it convulses him till he foams, and shatters him, and will hardly leave him.
for often he falls into the fire, and often into the water.		

2.34

Matthew 24:42	Mark 13:35	Luke 12:40
[42]Watch therefore, for you do not know on what day	[35]Watch therefore— for you do not know when	[40]You also must be ready; for
your Lord is coming.	the master of the house will come, in the evening, or at midnight, or at cockcrow, or in the morning—	the Son of man is coming at an unexpected hour."

It is most difficult to give a convincing reason why Mark and Luke in the first two examples would have changed Matthew's *kyrios* to "rabbi," "master," or "teacher." On the other hand, Matthew's changing Mark's "rabbi" and "teacher" to the church's favorite designation, *kyrios* (or "Lord") is easily explained. And in the last example it seems evident that what Matthew has done is change the saying about the parable's "master of the house" to "Lord."

It is clear that the tendency of the church with regard to this title was to use it more and more in the gospel traditions. Not only does Luke heavily use this title for Jesus in his special material (Luke 1:43, 76; 2:11; 5:8; 9:54; 10:1, 17, 39, 40, 41; etc.) but he, too, adds the title to the triple tradition (Luke 7:6; 11:39; 19:34; 22:33, 49, 61; 24:3). More impressive still, however, is the way Luke uses the title "Lord" absolutely in his material some thirteen or fourteen times (Luke 7:13, 19; 10:1, 39, 41; 11:39; 12:42; 13:15; 17:5, 6; 18:6; 22:61; 24:3 [there is a textual problem here]). If Luke can be interpreted as revealing the general tendency of the tradition with regard to this title, we can conclude that generally the *omission* of this title in a parallel tradition indicates a more primitive form of the tradition than does its presence. As a result, it does seem legitimate to conclude with regard to this title that Mark witnesses to a more primitive tradition than Matthew or Luke, and that the phenomena concerning this title can best be explained on the basis of a Markan priority.

Conclusion

In this chapter we have looked at some of the evidence in favor of the theory of Markan priority. In any theory the issue at stake involves probability. If certainty were possible, one would no longer speak of a "theory." It is therefore important to remember that in light of the nature of the evidence any solution of the Synoptic Problem is and will always remain a theory. With regard to the evidence given, it should be pointed out that the theory of Markan priority is not based on any one single argument but rather on the cumulative weight of all the arguments presented. These arguments were:

1. *The argument from length.* Here we noted that the addition of material by Matthew and Luke to their Markan source appears far more understandable than to view Mark as an abridgement of Matthew and/or Luke, for in the individual pericopes Mark is clearly not an abridgement but tends to be the longest of the three accounts. The omission of so much valuable material by Mark from Matthew and/or Luke has furthermore never been explained convincingly.

2. *The argument from grammar.* The better quality of the Matthean and Lukan grammar can best be explained by their having improved upon Mark's literary skills.

3. *The argument from difficulty.* Here we noted that on numerous occasions in the triple tradition Mark has a "harder" reading that (at first glance at least) causes more problems than the Matthean and/or Lukan parallels. The removal of such difficulties by Matthew and Luke makes a great deal more sense than the view that Mark added such difficulties to his Matthean and/or Lukan source(s).

4. *The arguments from verbal agreements and order.* These two arguments are similar in that they both argue that within the triple tradition the Matthew–Mark agreements against Luke, the Mark–Luke agreements against Matthew, and the paucity of Matthew–Luke agreements against Mark both in wording and in order are best explained on the basis of a Markan priority. It is true that other explanations, such as 1(a) and (f) and 4(a–f) (see figure 1), can theoretically explain such agreements (although 4(a–f) presents a difficulty in explaining the paucity of Matthew–Luke agreements against Mark), when we couple these arguments with a reasonable explanation of why Matthew and Luke might have changed the wording or order of their Markan source, the theory of a Markan priority becomes quite convincing. Although the argument from order by itself does not prove a Markan priority (the "Lachmann Fallacy"), Lachmann's argument from order is still convincing when coupled with his and other explanations as to why Matthew and Luke changed the Markan order.

5. *The argument from literary agreements.* In this argument we observed certain verbal phenomena that were best explained by a Matthean abbreviation or rewording of Mark.

6. *The argument from redaction.* With the coming of redaction critical

studies in the Gospels, a "new" tool has become available in the study of the Synoptic Problem. In this section we observed the occurrence of certain Matthean and Markan redactional features in the other Gospels. With regard to the Matthean redactional features, we observed their frequency of occurrence in Mark and/ or Luke, for if Matthew served as their source, we would expect these emphases to appear in Mark and Luke. Since, with regard to the two emphases investigated we did *not* find this, a Markan and Lukan dependence upon Matthew seems unlikely. On the other hand, we also noted two redactional stylistic features characteristic of Mark and investigated Matthew to see if they appeared in his Gospel. We discovered that these features appear in the material Matthew has in common with Mark far more frequently than in the material found in Matthew but not in Mark. On the basis of a Markan priority, this is exactly what one would expect to find. It is clearly not what one would expect to find on the basis of a Matthean priority. No doubt this type of investigation will become more and more prominent in future discussions of the Synoptic Problem.

7. *The argument from Mark's more primitive theology.* In this final argument we noted that—if, as Luke demonstrates, there was a tendency in the church to use the title "Lord" or *kyrios* more and more for Jesus in the gospel traditions—Mark is more primitive than Matthew, and Matthew's use of Mark explains the greater occurrence of this term in Matthew.

The cumulative weight of the above arguments argues strongly for the priority of Mark as part of the basic solution of the Synoptic Problem.

3

The Existence of Q

$\mathbf{H}$aving demonstrated a literary dependence of Matthew and Luke on Mark, we discover another important fact. Within Matthew and Luke we find a considerable amount of common material not found in their Markan source. This material consists of approximately 235 verses. Using more exact statistics, Matthew has 4,290 words that have parallels in Luke but not in Mark, and Luke has 3,559 words that have parallels in Matthew but not in Mark.[1] Furthermore, the close similarity of this material is at times quite striking:

3.1

Matthew 6:24	Luke 16:13
[24]"No one can serve two masters; for either he will hate the one and love the other, or he will be devoted to the one and despise the other. You cannot serve God and mammon.	[13]"No servant can serve two masters; for either he will hate the one and love the other, or he will be devoted to the one and despise the other. You cannot serve God and mammon."

3.2

Matthew 7:7–11	Luke 11:9–13
[7]"Ask, and it will be given you; seek, and you will find; knock, and it will be opened to you. [8]For every one who asks	[9]"And I tell you, Ask, and it will be given you; seek, and you will find; knock, and it will be opened to you. [10]For every one who asks

1. Joseph B. Tyson and Thomas R. W. Longstaff, *Synoptic Abstract*, The Computer Bible, vol. 15 (Wooster, Ohio: College of Wooster, 1978), pp. 169, 171.

receives, and he who seeks finds, and to him who knocks it will be opened. [9]Or what man of you, if his son asks him for bread, will give him a stone? [10]Or if he asks for a fish,

will give him a serpent?

[11]If you then, who are evil, know how to give good gifts to your children, how much more will your Father who is in heaven give good things to those who ask him!

receives, and he who seeks finds, and to him who knocks it will be opened. [11]What father among you, if his son asks

for a fish, will instead of a fish give him a serpent; [12]or if he asks for an egg, will give him a scorpion? [13]If you then, who are evil, know how to give good gifts to your children, how much more will the heavenly Father give the Holy Spirit to those who ask him!"

3.3

Matthew 11:25–27

[25]At that time

Jesus declared, "I thank thee, Father, Lord of heaven and earth, that thou hast hidden these things from the wise and understanding and revealed them to babes; [26]yea, Father, for such was thy gracious will. [27]All things have been delivered to me by my Father; and no one knows the Son except the Father, and no one knows the Father except the Son and any one to whom the Son chooses to reveal him.

Luke 10:21–22

[21]In that same hour he rejoiced in the Holy Spirit and said, "I thank thee, Father, Lord of heaven and earth, that thou hast hidden these things from the wise and understanding and revealed them to babes; Father, for such was thy gracious will. [22]All things have been delivered to me by my Father; and no one knows who the Son is except the Father, or who the Father is except the Son and any one to whom the Son chooses to reveal him."

3.4

Matthew 23:37–39

[37]"O Jerusalem, Jerusalem, killing the prophets and stoning those who are sent to you! How often would I have gathered your children together as a hen gathers her brood under her wings, and you would not! [38]Behold, your house is forsaken and desolate. [39]For I tell you, you will not see me again, until you say, 'Blessed is he who comes in the name of the Lord.' "

Luke 13:34–35

[34]"O Jerusalem, Jerusalem, killing the prophets and stoning those who are sent to you! How often would I have gathered your children together as a hen gathers her brood under her wings, and you would not! [35]Behold, your house is forsaken. And I tell you, you will not see me until you say, 'Blessed is he who comes in the name of the Lord!' "

In seeking to explain why Matthew and Luke resemble each other in this material[2] there exist four possible explanations: (1) Luke may have

---

2. Some other passages which show a similar exactness in the double tradition are Matthew 3:7b–10/Luke 3:7b–9; Matthew 7:3–5/Luke 6:41–42; Matthew 11:4–6, 7b–11/Luke 7:22–23, 24b–28; Matthew 11:21–23/Luke 10:13–15; Matthew 12:43–45/Luke 11:24–26; and Matthew 24:45–51/Luke 12:42–46.

"known," i.e., used, Matthew; (2) Matthew may have known Luke; (3) Matthew and Luke may have used common oral material; or (4) Matthew and Luke may have used a common written source or sources. The second possibility is seldom argued today[3] and will not be discussed at length. The simplest of the remaining three explanations is that Luke knew Matthew (1), for such an explanation does not require the positing of any hypothetical sources. There are, however, several convincing reasons why it is probable that Luke did *not* know Matthew.

Did Luke Not Know Matthew?

Luke's Lack of Matthean Additions to the Triple Tradition

One of the strongest arguments against the use of Matthew by Luke is the fact that when Matthew has additional material in the triple tradition ("Matthean additions to the Markan narrative"), it is "never" found in Luke.[4] Note the following examples:

3.5

Matthew 8:16–17 [author's italics]	Mark 1:32–34	Luke 4:40–41
[16]That evening	[32]That evening, at sundown,	[40]Now when the sun was setting,
they	they	all those who had any that were sick with various diseases
brought to him many who were possessed with demons;	brought to him all who were sick or possessed with demons. [33]And the whole city was gathered together about the door.	brought them to him;
		and he laid his hands on every one of them
	[34]And he healed many who were sick with various diseases,	and healed them.

3. See Werner Georg Kümmel, *Introduction to the New Testament*, trans. Howard Clark Kee (Nashville: Abingdon, 1975), p. 64. It should also be pointed out that in the debate on the priority for the material in the triple tradition, the priority of Luke is seldom argued.

4. There are exceptions, such as the baptismal accounts (Matt. 3:7–10, 12/Luke 3:7–9, 17), the temptation (Matt. 4:3–11/Luke 4:3–13), the Beelzebul incident (Matt. 12:26–28, 30/Luke 11:18–20, 23), the parable of the mustard seed (Matt. 13:31–32/Luke 13:18–19), and the mission charge (Matt. 10:1, 7, 14, 16/Luke 9:1, 2, 5; 10:3).

and
he cast out the spirits
with a word, and healed
    all
who were sick

and
cast out many demons;

⁴¹And demons also
came out of many,

crying,
"You are the Son of God!"
But he rebuked them,
and would not allow
them to speak,
because they knew
that he was the Christ.

and he would not permit
the demons to speak,
because they knew
him.

¹⁷*This was to fulfil what
was spoken by the prophet
Isaiah, "He took our
infirmities, and bore our
diseases."*

3.6

Matthew 12:1–8	Mark 2:23–28	Luke 6:1–5
[author's italics] ¹At that time Jesus went through the grainfields on the sabbath;	²³One sabbath he was going through the grainfields;	¹⁰On a sabbath while he was going through the grainfields,
	and as they made their way	
his disciples were hungry, and they began to pluck	his disciples began to pluck	his disciples plucked
		and ate some
heads of grain and to eat.	heads of grain.	heads of grain, rubbing them in their hands.
²But when the Pharisees saw it, they said to him, "Look,	²⁴And the Pharisees said to him, "Look,	²But some of the Pharisees said,
your disciples are doing what is not lawful to do on the sabbath." ³He said to them, "Have you not read what	why are they doing what is not lawful on the sabbath?" ²⁵And he said to them, "Have you never read what	"Why are you doing what is not lawful to do on the sabbath?" ³And Jesus answered, "Have you not read what
David did, when	David did, when he was in need and	David did when
he was hungry, and those who were with him; ⁴how he entered	was hungry, he and those who were with him; ²⁶how he entered	he was hungry, he and those who were with him; ⁴how he entered
the house of God	the house of God, when Abiathar was high priest,	the house of God,
		and took
and ate the bread of the Presence, which it was not lawful	and ate the bread of the Presence, which it is not lawful	and ate the bread of the Presence, which it is not lawful

for him to eat nor for
those who were with him,
but only for the priests?

for any but the priests
to eat, and also gave it to
those who were with
him?"

for any but the priests
to eat, and also gave it to
those with him?"

*⁵Or have you not read in
the law how on the sabbath
the priests in the temple
profane the sabbath, and
are guiltless? ⁶I tell you,
something greater than the
temple is here. ⁷And if you
had known what this means,
'I desire mercy, and not
sacrifice,'' you would not
have condemned the
guiltless.*

²⁷And he said to them,
"The sabbath was made
      for
man, not man for the
sabbath;
²⁸so the Son of man
is lord
even of the sabbath."

⁵And he said to them,

"The Son of man
is lord
of the sabbath."

⁸For the Son of man
is lord
of the sabbath."

3.7

| **Matthew 13:10–15**
[author's italics] | **Mark 4:10–12** | **Luke 8:9–10** |

¹⁰And when he was alone,
those who were about him
with the twelve

⁹And when his disciples

¹⁰Then the disciples
came and
said to him,
"Why do you speak to
   them
in parables?"
¹¹And he answered them,
"To you it has been given

asked him
concerning the parables.

asked him
what this parable meant,

¹¹And he said to them,
"To you   has been
   given

¹⁰he said,
"To you it has been given

to know
the secrets of the kingdom
of heaven,
but to them
it has not been given.
¹²For to him who has will
more be given, and he will
have abundance; but from
him who has not, even
   what
he has will be taken away.
¹³This is why I speak to
them in parables,
because
seeing

the secret of the kingdom
of God,
but for those outside
everything is in parables;

to know
the secrets of the kingdom
of God;
but for others
they are in parables,

¹²so that
they may indeed see

so that
seeing

they do not see, and hearing they do not hear, nor do they understand.	but not perceive, and may indeed hear but not understand; lest they should turn again, and be forgiven."	they may not see, and hearing they may not understand.

[14]*With them indeed is fulfilled the prophecy of Isaiah which says: 'You shall indeed hear but never understand, and you shall indeed see but never perceive.* [15]*For this people's heart has grown dull, and their ears are heavy of hearing, and their eyes they have closed, lest they should perceive with their eyes, and hear with their ears, and understand with their heart, and turn for me to heal them.'*

How can one explain this "total" omission on the part of Luke of Matthew's additions to the Markan narrative? If we assume that Luke knew Matthew, an explanation is difficult to find. One attempted explanation for these omissions is that Luke preferred the simpler and more abbreviated Markan form of the accounts in all such instances, but the very fact that he would owe at least 3,559 words of his Gospel (18.4%) to Matthew (if we assume his use of Matthew for the Q material) argues against this. If, on the other hand, we argue on the basis of the Griesbach Hypothesis that when Mark used Matthew and Luke he always chose the shorter form and thus omitted these Matthean additions, we are confronted by the fact that Mark is usually the longest not the shortest account in the triple tradition!

A more convincing explanation of the omission of these "Matthean additions" by Luke is that Luke did not know Matthew and therefore was unacquainted with these additions. If Matthew and Luke both used Mark independently, we would expect that their editorial additions to the Markan account would seldom, if ever, agree with one another. Rather, they would appear as "Matthean additions" and "Lukan additions" to the Markan narratives. And this is exactly what we find. Along with the observation of this fact, we should also note the frequent redactional nature of these additions. It is not at all surprising that the "Matthean additions to the Markan narrative" possess a strongly Matthean theological emphasis. The same can also be said of the "Lukan additions." In the first and third examples given (Matt. 8:17; 13:14–15) the additions consist of a typical Matthean formula quotation. The second example consists of a small "midrash" from the Old Testament. In all these instances it is far easier to see these passages as Matthean additions to Mark and to understand Luke's omission of them as being due to the fact that he did not know Matthew.[5]

Luke's Different Context for the Q Material

Another factor that makes it difficult to believe that Luke used Matthew is the fact that Luke never places their common non-Markan material (Q) in the same context as it appears in Matthew. Within Matthew this material is found in five (or six) sections, all of which end with something like "And when Jesus finished these sayings" (7:28; cf. also 11:1; 13:53; 19:1; 26:1). These five sections (5–7; 10; 13; 18; 23–25 [or 23; 24–25]) are artistically arranged within Matthew's Gospel. In Luke, on the other hand, this material is found in 6:20–8:3 and 9:51–18:14. If Luke and Matthew were independently using a common source or sources, such a difference is easily explained. Usually it is explained by seeing Luke's arrangement as being the simple incorporation of his Q source into his Gospel in these two sections. Matthew's handling of his source, however, was far more thoroughgoing, for he has rearranged this material into five "books."[6] The result is a masterful organization whose artistry is well-recognized.

The thesis that Luke obtained the Q material from Matthew cannot explain why Luke would have rearranged this material in a totally different and "artistically inferior" format. Furthermore, if Luke obtained the material of the triple tradition from either Mark or Matthew and if he followed the narrative order of his source as carefully as he did in this area, why would he deliberately choose to make sure that all the sayings material that he obtained from Matthew would appear in a different order in his Gospel? No satisfactory answer to explain this fact has yet been found by those who argue that Luke knew Matthew.

Luke's More Primitive Context for the Q Material

Closely related to the preceding argument is the difficulty of explaining the more primitive context in which we find the common non-

5. Some other examples can be found in Matthew 10:5–8; 12:11; 14:28–31; 16:17–19; 17:6–7; 18:3–4; 19:9. The absence of "Lukan additions to the Markan narrative" in Matthew argues, of course, for the opposite, i.e., that Matthew did not know Luke. See Luke 4:14a; 5:17; 9:23, 31–32, 48.

6. Scholars have frequently seen in Matthew's treatment of this material an attempt to compose a "New Torah" of five books, but this is debated.

Markan material in Luke. The arrangement of the material in Matthew is extremely well done. The Sermon on the Mount (Matt. 5–7) ranks as one of the greatest works of literature ever written. Why would Luke, who was by no means an inept writer, choose to break up this masterpiece and scatter its material in a far less artistic fashion throughout his Gospel? (See table 5.) Explanations offered by those who maintain that Luke used Matthew, which seek to unscramble the mystery as to why Luke treated the material in Matthew in this fashion, have been far from convincing.[7]

The Form of the Q Material

If one assumes that Luke used Matthew as his source for the Q material, one would expect that this material would tend to be more primitive (theologically and/or tradition-wise) in the earlier source (Matthew) and more developed in the later source (Luke). An example of this was discussed with regard to the title "Lord" (*kyrios*) for Jesus.

Table 5

	Matthew	Luke
The Beatitudes	5:3–12	6:20b–23
The salt of the earth	5:13	14:34–35a
The light of the world	5:14–16	8:16
The law and the prophets	5:17–18	16:16–17
On reconciliation	5:25–26	12:58–59
On adultery and divorce	5:32	16:18
On retaliation	5:39–42	6:29–30
On love for one's enemies	5:43–48	6:27–28, 32–36
The Lord's Prayer	6:9–13	11:2–4
On treasures in heaven	6:20–21	12:33–34
Good eyes	6:22–23	11:34–35
On serving two masters	6:24	16:13
On anxiety	6:25–34	12:22–32
On judging others	7:1, 3–5	6:37, 41–42
On answers to prayer	7:7–11	11:9–13
The golden rule	7:12	6:31
The narrow way	7:13–14	13:23–24
A tree and its fruit	7:16–17	6:43–44
Saying, "Lord, Lord"	7:21–23	6:46; 13:25–27
Wise and foolish builders	7:24–27	6:47–49

Note: Verses in Matthew 5–7 without parallels in Luke have been omitted.

7. So Joseph A. Fitzmyer, *To Advance the Gospel* (New York: Crossroad, 1981), p. 18.

We found that this term was used far more frequently in a highly Christological sense in Luke than in his source (Mark). On the other hand, when we compare the Q material in Matthew and Luke, we sometimes find that the material is more primitive (i.e., less developed theologically) in Matthew and at other times we find it more primitive in Luke. This is exactly what we would expect if they both used a common source, but it is not what we would expect if Luke used Matthew or, for that matter, if Matthew used Luke.

We possess numerous examples in which the form of the material found in Matthew appears to be more primitive than in the Lukan parallel. Some of the clearest are:

3.8

Matthew 6:9–13	Luke 11:2–4
	[2]And he said to them,
[9]Pray then like this:	"When you pray, say:
Our Father who art in heaven,	"Father,
Hallowed be thy name.	hallowed be thy name.
[10]Thy kingdom come,	Thy kingdom come.
Thy will be done,	
On earth as it is in heaven.	
[11]Give us this day our daily bread;	[3]Give us each day our daily bread;
[12]And forgive us our debts,	[4]And forgive us our sins,
As we also have forgiven	for we ourselves forgive
our debtors;	every one who is indebted to us;
[13]And lead us not into temptation,	and lead us not into temptation."
But deliver us from evil.	

3.9

Matthew 7:9–11	Luke 11:11–13
[9]Or what man of you,	[11]What father among you,
if his son asks	if his son asks
him for bread, will give him a stone?	
[10]Or if he asks for a fish,	for a fish,
	will instead of a fish
will give him a serpent?	give him a serpent;
	[12]or if he asks for an egg, will give
	him a scorpion?
[11]If you then, who are evil, know how to	[13]If you then, who are evil, know how to
give good gifts to your children,	give good gifts to your children,
how much more	how much more
will your Father who is in heaven	will the heavenly Father
give good things	give the Holy Spirit
to those who ask him!	to those who ask him!"

3.10
Matthew 8:21–22

[21]Another of the disciples said to him,
"Lord, let me first go and bury my
father."
[22]But Jesus said to him,
"Follow me, and
leave the dead to bury their own dead."

Luke 9:59–60

[59]To another he said, "Follow me."
But he said,
"Lord, let me first go and bury my
father."
[60]But he said to him,

"Leave the dead to bury their own dead;
but as for you, go and proclaim the
kingdom of God."

3.11
Matthew 10:34–36
[34]"Do not think that I have come to
bring peace on earth;

I have not come to bring peace,
but a sword.

[35]For I have come to set

a man against his father,

and a daughter against her mother,

and a daughter-in-law against
her mother-in-law;
[36]and a man's foes will be those of his
own household.

Luke 12:51–53
[51]"Do you think that I have come to
give peace on earth?
No, I tell you,

but rather division;
[52]for henceforth in one house there will
be five divided, three against two and
two against three; [53]they will be
divided,

father against son and
son against father,
mother against daughter and
daughter against her mother,
mother-in-law against her
daughter-in-law and
daughter-in-law against
her mother-in-law."

It seems clear in the above examples that the Matthean expression
"forgive us our *debts*" (Matt. 6:12, emphasis added) (a common expression in Jesus' day for sins[8]) is more primitive (and probably closer to
the *ipsissima verba*) than Luke's "forgive us our sins." This is also true
of Matthew's "good gifts" (Matt. 7:11) in contrast to Luke's "Holy
Spirit," which looks like a post-Pentecost clarification of what God's
good gifts really are. Likewise, Matthew's "Follow me, and leave the
dead to bury their own dead" (Matt. 8:22) appears less developed
theologically than Luke's additional "but as for you, go and proclaim

8. See the Aramaic Targums on Genesis 18:20–26; Exodus 31:31; 34:7; Numbers
14:18–19; and Isaiah 53:4, 12, in which the Aramaic term for "debts" is used to translate
the Hebrew "sins." Cf. also Matthew 18:32–34; Luke 7:41–49.

the kingdom of God." Finally, Matthew's reference to the "sword" in Matthew 10:34 is a much harder reading than Luke's "division," and it is far easier to understand why a later writer might have switched from "sword" to "division" in order to avoid misunderstanding.[9]

In the examples given above it does appear that Matthew's version of these sayings is in each instance more primitive and less developed than the Lukan form. On the other hand, in the following examples it seems equally clear that the Lukan account appears to be more primitive than the corresponding Matthean version.

3.12

Matthew 5:3	Luke 6:20b
[3]"Blessed are the poor in spirit, for theirs is the kingdom of heaven.	[20]"Blessed are you poor, for yours is the kingdom of God.

3.13

Matthew 5:6	Luke 6:21
[6]Blessed are those who hunger and thirst for righteousness, for they shall be satisfied.	[21]Blessed are you that hunger now for you shall be satisfied.

3.14

Matthew 7:12	Luke 6:31
[12]"So whatever you wish that men would do to you, do so to them; for this is the law and the prophets.	[31]"And as you wish that men would do to you, do so to them.

3.15

Matthew 6:9–10	Luke 11:2
[9]Pray then like this: Our Father who art in heaven, Hallowed be thy name. [10]Thy kingdom come, Thy will be done, On earth as it is in heaven.	[2]And he said to them, "When you pray, say: "Father, hallowed be thy name. Thy kingdom come.

3.16

Matthew 10:37–38	Luke 14:26–27
[3]"He who loves father or mother more than me is not worthy of me;	[26]"If anyone comes to me and does not hate his own father and mother and wife

---

9. Some additional examples in which the Matthean account appears more primitive are Matthew 5:17–18/Luke 16:16–17; Matthew 5:44/Luke 6:27–28; Matthew 5:46–47/Luke 6:32–35; Matthew 7:1–2/Luke 6:37–38.

and he who loves son or daughter	and children and brothers and sisters, yes, and even his own life,
more than me is not worthy of me;	he cannot be my disciple.
[38]and he who	[27]Whoever
does not take his cross	does not bear his own cross
and follow me	and come after me,
is not worthy of me.	cannot be my disciple.

In each of the five examples given above it appears that Luke possesses a less developed form of the saying and that many times the Lukan form is "harder." In the first two examples the extra words found in Matthew appear to be material that the Evangelist has added to the tradition. The interpretive comments seek to make these particular Beatitudes clear and keep them from being misunderstood. In the third example the extra material is a typically Matthean theological comment concerning the fulfillment of the Scriptures. The Lukan version of the Lord's Prayer in the fourth example is likewise less developed than its Matthean counterpart with regard to the simple address "Father." Finally, in the last example Matthew has translated the "love/hate" idiom to a "love/love less" wording, which was less likely to be misunderstood.[10] Numerous other examples could be given.[11]

Whereas the examples in which Matthew appears more primitive than Luke pose no problem for the theory that Luke used Matthew, since this is what one would expect, the examples in which Luke is more primitive clearly pose a serious problem to such a view. How does one explain so many instances of the more primitive appearance of these sayings in Luke? In fact the examples of Lukan "primitiveness" are greater in number than those of Matthew. To claim that in all these instances Luke preferred an oral form of the tradition over his Matthean source runs into a number of difficulties. For one, this explanation seems too mechanical. Second, why is it that when Matthew (his alleged source) is more primitive, Luke chooses to use or write a more developed form of the tradition? One cannot explain the examples of Luke's more primitive form of the tradition as being due to his choosing the more primitive oral tradition over his Matthean source, without at the same time explaining why at other times Luke preferred a more developed form to Matthew's more primitive saying.

10. For a discussion of this idiom, see Robert H. Stein, *Difficult Passages in the Gospels: Jesus' Use of Overstatement and Hyperbole* (Grand Rapids: Baker, 1985), pp. 75–78.

11. Other additional examples in which the Lukan account appears more primitive are Luke 6:36/Matthew 5:48; Luke 11:20/Matthew 12:28; Luke 11:30/Matthew 12:40; Luke 11:49–51/Matthew 23:34–36; Luke 16:18/Matthew 19:9.

The most convincing explanation of the fact that neither Gospel consistently presents the more primitive form of the tradition is that *both* used a common source (or sources) and interpreted it as they were led of God to do so. As a result, at times Matthew presents certain theological reflections and interpretations that are more highly developed, and at times it is Luke who possesses the more developed form of the tradition. This does not, of course, exclude the possibility that their sources also possessed varying degrees of "primitiveness," but this cannot explain the extent of this phenomenon nor the fact that frequently the more developed form of the tradition betrays a highly redactional emphasis of the Evangelist.

Matthew's and Luke's Lack of Agreement in Order

We have already discussed the fact that Matthew and Luke never agree against Mark with regard to the question of order.[12] By itself this does not "prove" the priority of Mark, but along with the plausible reasons why Matthew and Luke would have changed the Markan order and the lack of such plausible explanations for Markan changes to the order of Matthew and/or Luke, this argument is quite convincing. If we assume a Markan priority, then this lack of agreement does argue for the independence of Matthew and Luke. Assuming the priority of Mark, only five of the eighteen possible literary relationships between the synoptic Gospels remain. These are 1(c), 1(d), 3(b), 4(c), and 4(d) in figure 1 (see chapter 2), represented as (a–e) in figure 8.

Of these five possibilities, (a.) and (b.) must be rejected since they do not explain the presence of Mark–Luke agreements against Matthew in (a.) and Mark–Matthew agreements against Luke in (b.). One would also expect in both of these instances many more Matthew–Luke agreements against Mark. Concerning (d.) and (e.), these two possibilities can explain the presence of both Mark–Matthew agreements against Luke and Mark–Luke agreements against Matthew, but the lack of Matthew–Luke agreements against Mark is again difficult to explain. One cannot help but expect that even if Matthew or Luke intended not to agree against Mark, simply on the basis of chance, a goodly number of such occurrences would have taken place by accident. And that they would not have been averse to using each other by this theory is clearly revealed by the material of the double tradition that they would have taken from the other. Again it would appear, assuming a Markan priority, that this lack of agreement is best explained by the theory that Matthew and Luke did not know each other's Gospels.

12. See above, pp. 69–70.

Figure 8

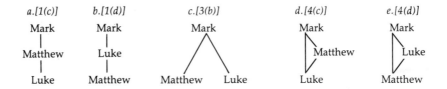

a.[1(c)]	b.[1(d)]	c.[3(b)]	d.[4(c)]	e.[4(d)]

Luke's Lack of M Material

One final argument that can be listed against the theory that Luke used the Gospel of Matthew as a source is the lack of M material in Luke. (The same type of argument can also be made for Matthew's not having used Luke, i.e., the lack of any L material in Matthew.) If we assume that Luke used Matthew, how are we to explain his great omission of all the narrative material outside of the triple tradition found in Matthew? Why would Luke have omitted such material as the coming of the wise men (Matt. 2:1–12)? Would not the presence of such Gentiles at the birth of Jesus been meaningful for Luke's Gentile-oriented Gospel? Why would he have omitted the flight to Egypt and return to Nazareth (Matt. 2:13–23); the story of the guards at the tomb (Matt. 27:62–66) and their report (Matt. 28:11–15); the unique Matthean material concerning the resurrection (Matt. 28:9–10, 16–20); and so on? Added to this is the observation that if Luke had before him Matthew's birth account and genealogy, one wonders if he would not have sought in some way to "harmonize" the one we have in his Gospel with the Matthean version.

It is, of course, impossible to know what was going through the mind of Luke when he wrote and why he might have omitted this or that account from his Gospel. Such mental acts are beyond the capacity of the exegete to reconstruct with any certainty.[13] Nevertheless, it is possible to discuss which procedure appears more probable in light of how an Evangelist handles the other material found in his Gospel. It would therefore appear that Luke's use of Matthew is improbable, due to the lack of his incorporation of the M material into his Gospel.

The various arguments presented above for the independence of Matthew and Luke are not, of course, equally weighty. Perhaps the most convincing are the lack of the Matthean additions to the triple

13. D. E. Nineham correctly points out that "arguments from what we should have done to what they [the Evangelists] 'must' have done have always to be treated with the greatest caution" ("Eyewitness Testimony and the Gospel Tradition," *JTS* 9 [1958]: 247).

tradition within Luke; the fact that Luke places the Q material in a totally different context than Matthew; and the fact that Matthew does not always contain the most primitive form of the double tradition, but that in fact Luke seems more often to contain the primitive form. Yet even the other arguments, though less convincing in themselves, add additional support to the thesis that Matthew and Luke did not know each other. When all the arguments are considered together, the conclusion seems reasonably certain that Matthew and Luke did not know each other. If Luke did not obtain the material from Matthew (or Matthew from Luke), then this information must have come to them from another source or sources. What was the nature of this source material? It is to this question that we must now turn.

Was "Q" a Written Source?

If Luke did not obtain the material of the double tradition from Matthew (nor Matthew from Luke), then some other source or sources must have provided this material for both of them. The designation Q has been used for the last one hundred years as the symbol for this source or sources. Whether Q was an abbreviation for *Quelle*, the German word for "source," is not certain,[14] and there is even some debate as to whether this symbol was first used in Great Britain or in Germany.[15] The question of the origin and even the appropriateness of this symbol as a designation for the double tradition is ultimately irrelevant, however, for Q is the symbol that has been used almost universally to designate this material and even suggesting a new symbol as a possible replacement would cause far more confusion than any such change would be worth.

As early as 1838, C. H. Weisse suggested that in the writing of their Gospels, Matthew and Luke used—along with an Ur-Markus—another source, which consisted of a collection of the sayings of Jesus.[16] In Germany G. H. A. Ewald in 1848 and H. J. Holtzmann in 1863 further developed this thesis and delineated more fully what this source looked like. In England Sir John C. Hawkins (1899) and B. H. Streeter (1924) became strong advocates for a written Q source. There have been, for the most part, four main arguments put forward for arguing

14. See John J. Schmitt, "In Search of the Origin of the SIGLUM Q," *JBL* 100 (1981): 609–11.

15. For the suggestion of a British origin of the symbol, see Robert Henry Lightfoot, *History and Interpretation in the Gospels* (London: Hodder and Stoughton, 1934), pp. 27–28.

16. E. Earle Ellis suggests that Herbert Marsh had, in fact, proposed this already in 1801 ("New Directions in Form Criticism," in *Jesus Christus in Historie und Theologie*, ed. G. Strecker [Tübingen: J. C. B. Mohr, 1975], p. 301).

that the Q material found in Matthew and Luke came to them in the form of a single written source.

The Exactness of the Wording

Examples of the exactness in wording of the Q material have already been given and need not be repeated.[17] It is frequently argued that the degree to which this material in the double tradition agrees can only be explained on the basis of a common written source. For example, in Matthew 6:24/Luke 16:13 twenty-seven of the twenty-eight Greek words are identical and the order is likewise identical. In Matthew 7:7–8/Luke 11:9–10 all twenty-four words in both passages are identical and again are in the same order. The similarity in other sayings in the double tradition is also impressive. Such exactness is striking, and scholars have seen this correspondence as evidence for a written common source in Greek. On the other hand, it must be pointed out that not all the Q material found in Matthew and Luke possesses a similar degree of exactness. One need only compare the following: Luke 6:29/Matthew 5:39–40; Luke 11:44/Matthew 23:27; Luke 12:2–9/Matthew 10:26–33; Luke 16:16–17/Matthew 11:12–13; 5:18; and so on.

The Order of the Material

If one seeks to prove the literary dependence of the Q material, a most important argument that must be dealt with involves the order of the material in the double tradition. We have already pointed out that the common order of the material in the triple tradition demonstrates a literary interdependence of the synoptic Gospels and argues for a common literary source.[18] Some scholars have sought to argue similarly with regard to the material in the double tradition. If a common order can be found, this will argue strongly for a common literary source, because when " . . . several pericopae, which have no apparent logical or chronological succession, are found in the same order, the natural inference is a literary connection."[19] It should be pointed out that such a common order could be equally explained on the basis of Matthew's and Luke's use of a common literary source (Q) or by Luke's use of Matthew. The lack of a common order argues likewise against Matthew's and Luke's use of Q or Luke's use of Matthew, even if it cannot absolutely disprove such a use.

Several attempts have been made to demonstrate the existence of

---

17. See above, pp. 89–90.
18. See above pp. 34–37.
19. J. W. Wenham, "Synoptic Independence and the Origin of Luke's Travel Narrative," *NTS* 27 (1981): 508.

Table 6

	Luke		Matthew	
1	3:7–9, 16f.	John the Baptist's Preaching	3:7–12	1
2	4:2–13	Temptation of Jesus	4:2–11	2
3	6:20–23, 27–30 32–36	Sermon on the Plain I	5:3–6, 11f., 39–42, 45–48	3
4	6:37f., 41–49	Sermon on the Plain II	7:1–5, 16–21 24–27	7
5	7:1–10	Centurion from Capernaum	8:5–13	9
6	7:18–35	John the Baptist's Sayings	11:2–19	13
7	9:57–60	Sayings on Discipleship	8:19–22	10
8	10:1–12	Missions Discourse	9:37–10:15	11
9	10:13–15, 21f.	Woes and Joys	11:21–23, 25f.	14
10	11:1–4	Lord's Prayer	6:9–13	5
11	11:9–13	On Prayer	7:7–11	8
12	11:14–23	Beelzebub Controversy	12:22–30	15
13	11:24–26	Saying on Backsliding	12:43–45	17
14	11:29–32	Against Request for Miracles	12:38–42	16
15	11:33–35	Sayings on Light	5:15; 6:22f.	4
16	11:39–52	Against the Pharisees	23:4, 23–25, 29–36	19
17	12:2–10	Summons to Confession	10:26–33	12
18	12:22–34	Cares and Treasures	6:19–21, 25–33	6
19	12:39–46	Watchfulness	24:43–51	22
20	13:18–21	Mustard Seed and Leaven	13:31–33	18
21	13:34f.	Predictions Concerning Jerusalem	23:37–39	20
22	17:22–37	Discourse on the Parousia	24:26–28, 37–41	21
23	19:11–27	Parable of the Talents	25:14–30	23

such a common order. One such attempt is found in table 6.[20] Kümmel points out that, despite various differences, there is nevertheless a significant correspondence in order. On the other hand, it must be acknowledged that the agreement demonstrated in table 6 does not necessarily demand that a common written source lies behind this Q material.

A more interesting argument from order has been made by Taylor, who compares the order of the Q material in Luke with each of the five major discourses in Matthew 5–7, 10, 13, 18, and 23–25 individually rather than as a whole. When this is done, an agreement in order does at times appear. In the Sermon on the Mount, for example, we have the correspondence indicated in table 7.[21] The correspondence in order between 1 to 9 is indeed impressive. On the other hand, the correspondence between 10 and 22 is far less striking.

20. Kümmel, *Introduction to the New Testament*, pp. 65–66.
21. Vincent Taylor, "The Original Order of Q," in *New Testament Essays*, ed. A. J. B. Higgins (Manchester: Manchester University, 1959), p. 249.

Table 7

	Luke	Matthew
1	6:20–23	5:3–6, 11f.
2	6:27–30	5:39b–42
3	6:31	(7:12)
4	6:32–36	5:44–48
5	6:37f.	7:1f.
6	6:41f.	7:3–5
7	6:43–45	7:16–20
8	6:46	7:21
9	6:47–49	7:24–27
10	11:2–4	6:9–13
11	11:9–13	(7:7–11)
12	11:33	(5:15)
13	11:34f.	6:22f.
14	12:22–31	6:25–33
15	12:33b, 34	(6:20f.)
16	12:57–59	(5:25f.)
17	13:23f.	7:13f.
18	13:25–27	7:22f., [25:10–12]
19	14:34f.	(5:13)
20	16:13	(6:24)
21	16:17	5:18
22	16:18	5:32

Another example Taylor gives, involving the mission charge found in Matthew 9:37–10:42, appears in table 8.[22] Here also the degree of correspondence in order is striking. Except for 1, 4, and 8, there is a marked agreement in order. Taylor has argued that these agreements in order (and the others he charts between Matthew 13, 18, 23–25, and the Lukan parallels) are not simply "by chance" but demonstrate that Matthew and Luke obtained the Q material from a common written source.

The argument from order has always been more convincing for some than for others. But we may well ask if the order that we have observed is as great as we might tend to expect if the Q material came to Matthew and Luke as a common *written* source. If Matthew's and Luke's use of Mark can serve as a pattern for how they used their sources, at least one of them did not use his Q source in the same way that he used Mark! Most scholars who believe in a written Q maintain that Luke was more faithful to the Q material both in his wording and his order than Matthew, who apparently reworked this material a great deal in order to fit it into his five discourses. This is undoubtedly true

22. Ibid., p. 254.

Table 8

	Luke	Matthew
1	6:40	(10:24f.)
2	10:2	9:37f.
3	10:3–12	10:9–16
4	10:16	(10:40)
5	12:2f.	10:26f.
6	12:4–7	10:28–31
7	12:8f.	10:32f.
8	12:11f.	(10:19f.)
9	12:51–53	10:34–36
10	14:26f.	10:37f.
11	17:33	10:39

with regard to Matthew, whether Q was written or not. In its present form the argument from order probably weighs slightly more favorably on the side of a written Q, or at least points to several common Q-like documents, but it is far from conclusive and convincing proof. It should be pointed out at this point that if one argues that the lack of a demonstrative order of the Q material in Matthew and Luke argues against the existence of a written Q, this likewise would argue against either the dependence of Luke for the Q material upon Matthew or of Matthew upon Luke! On the other hand, it is probably wiser to assume that whereas the demonstration of an agreement in order would confirm the use of a common written Q source, the lack of such an agreement does not deny the existence of such a source.

"Doublets" in Matthew and Luke

For some scholars, "the decisive proof" for a written Q is the existence of "doublets" in Matthew and Luke.[23] Sometimes there is a differentiation noted between "doublets" and "double traditions," but we shall not make such a fine distinction. For our purpose, a "doublet" refers to the appearance of the same account or text two times in a Gospel. In the case of Matthew and Luke one such account or text comes from the triple tradition, i.e., Mark, and the other comes from the double tradition or Q. Some examples are listed in table 9. Hawkins listed twenty-two separate examples of doublets in Matthew and eleven examples in Luke.[24] In contrast he gives only one such example for Mark—Mark 9:35 and 10:43–44.

---

23. So Kümmel, *Introduction to the New Testament*, p. 66.
24. John C. Hawkins, *Horae Synopticae* (Oxford: Clarendon, 1909), pp. 80–99 and 99–107, respectively.

Table 9

1	Luke 8:16	Mark 4:21
	Luke 11:33	Matthew 5:15
2	Luke 8:17	Mark 4:22
	Luke 12:2 (cf. also 3–9)	Matthew 10:26 (cf. also 27–33)
3	Matthew 19:9	Mark 10:11–12
	Matthew 5:32	Luke 16:18
4	Matthew 16:24	Mark 8:34 (cf. Luke 9:23)
	Matthew 10:37–38	Luke 14:26–27

In each of the examples given in table 9 the first source of the doublet comes from Mark. It is argued that the second part of the doublet must have come from a source that Matthew and Luke had in common. Yet do these "doublets" prove the existence of a written Q? Not really. Although the existence of such doublets does suggest and argue fairly strongly for the existence of a common source or sources used by Matthew and Luke in addition to Mark, the makeup of that source is uncertain. Matthew and Luke may have produced these doublets because they used a common written source, i.e., Q, but the presence of such doublets can also be explained by the use of written "fragments" of tradition or by the use of oral tradition. As a result, whereas on the basis of a Markan priority such doublets do argue for a common source(s), they do not and cannot prove that this was a single written source.

Attempts have also been made to prove the existence of a written Q by demonstrating that a common vocabulary and style is found in the Q material, but long ago it was shown that such a common and consistent vocabulary and style cannot be demonstrated.[25] A more recent attempt to demonstrate a common unity of literary forms is also not very convincing.[26] For if the Q material consists primarily of sayings of Jesus, one would expect a certain amount of unity in form. These and other attempts to prove the existence of a common literary source by means of a unified style and vocabulary have in general not been successful.[27]

25. Adolph Harnack, *The Sayings of Jesus: The Second Source of St. Matthew and St. Luke* (New York: Putnams, 1908), pp. 146–72.

26. Arland D. Jacobson, "The Literary Unity of Q," *JBL* 101 (1982): 365–89.

27. This should not be interpreted to mean that we are not able to detect the use of sources by means of vocabulary and style. It would appear fairly certain that the vocabulary and style of Luke 1–2 indicate that Luke is using a specific source(s) here.

Conclusion

The existence of Q is not an isolated hypothesis but has in practice been intimately associated with the argument for Markan priority.[28] This is due to the fact that most other hypotheses, whether that of a Matthean priority or the more-rare Lukan priority, assume that either Luke used Matthew or Matthew used Luke. If this were so, there would then be no need for Q, since Luke (or Matthew) could have obtained the material of the double tradition (the Q material) directly from Matthew (or Luke). Thus the Q hypothesis would be completely unnecessary if Matthew or Luke knew and used each other's work. Furthermore, why should one postulate a completely unnecessary hypothetical document if either Matthew or Luke will do? Once one assumes a Markan priority, however, we face the question of whether Luke knew Matthew (or *vice versa*), and for the majority of scholars such knowledge and dependence are most difficult to conceive. The Q hypothesis is clearly dependent upon the view that Luke did not use Matthew. If the arguments presented in the first section of this chapter are convincing, then one must assume some sort of Q hypothesis.

It has been argued (in the past more than in the present) that the Q hypothesis is impossible because such a document is inconceivable— that if Q existed, it would have to have been a document that began with the baptism and temptation of Jesus, omitted the birth, consisted almost exclusively of Jesus' sayings, and lacked a passion narrative. It was maintained that such a document could not have existed. Yet it is clear that the Gospel of Mark does not have a birth account and begins at the baptism of Jesus, as do a number of sermons in the Book of Acts (cf. 10:36f., 13:24f.). More important still, however, was the 1945 discovery of the Gospel of Thomas at Nag Hammadi, Egypt. This work, written in Coptic, consists entirely of 114 disconnected sayings of Jesus. For our present discussion, the relationship of the Gospel of Thomas to our Gospels, its date, and the gnostic character of this work are not important issues. What is important is the fact that the Gospel of Thomas demonstrates not only that a document of sayings of Jesus like the one hypothesized by the Q hypothesis could exist, but that something like Q did in fact exist. Although it is clear that the Gospel of Thomas is not Q, and knowledge of Q by the writer of this Coptic Gospel is not very likely, the existence of this work has once and for all refuted all objections to the possibility that a source like Q could have existed.

28. It should be noted that the hypothesis of the "priority of Mark" and the hypothesis of Q are two different hypotheses. They may be associated together in the views of various scholars, but the "priority of Mark" means Markan priority and not the two-document hypothesis.

Another objection sometimes raised against the Q hypothesis is that it requires a certain overlapping with the Markan materials in order to explain such Matthew–Luke agreements as we find in the baptismal accounts (Matt. 3:7–10, 12/Luke 3:7–9, 17); the temptation (Matt. 4:3–11/Luke 4:3–13); the Beelzebul incident (Matt. 12:26–28, 30/Luke 11:18–20, 23); the parable of the mustard seed (Matt. 13:31–32/Luke 13:18–19); and the mission charge (Matt. 10:1, 7, 14, 16/Luke 9:1, 2, 5; 10:3). The overlapping of the Q material with Mark has often been viewed as an embarrassment for the Q hypothesis and has even been sarcastically referred to as the "blessed overlap."[29] Yet, on a purely theoretical basis, it would be most unusual if two sources concerning Jesus, such as Mark and Q, did not overlap in some way. After all, they do deal with the same person, with incidents in his life and sayings that he uttered, so that some overlap would be expected. The issue of overlap serves as an embarrassment for the Q hypothesis only if the hypothesis requires an inordinate amount of such overlapping and is inherently "unlikely" in individual instances. Overlap in the baptism accounts, for example, is by no means that surprising. Furthermore, if one rejects the Q hypothesis and argues that Luke used Matthew, the fact remains that we still must deal with overlap, for Matthew possesses various doublets. Where did he find them? Within the sources he used, there apparently existed this same kind of "blessed overlap."

The Q hypothesis has its problems, but the alternative hypothesis— that Luke used Matthew (or *vice versa*)—has far greater problems still! The common agreements of the double tradition are best explained by Matthew's and Luke's use of a common source. That source we can simply call "Q." But the composition of that source is far from certain.[30] The arguments for a written Q are far from conclusive. Although the exactness of wording in certain instances is quite impressive, the lack of such exactness in other instances is also impressive. Furthermore, the exactness of certain sayings of Jesus could well be explained on other grounds in a society accustomed to the oral transmission of materials. It is clear today that one cannot deal with the Synoptic Problem on a purely literary basis, since the oral tradition had a significant influence on the writing of our Gospels. No doubt some of the Matthew–Luke agreements against Mark (see chapter 4) can best be explained by means of the continuing influence of the oral tradition. Concerning the argument from order, it must be acknowledged that the argument cuts two ways. When order is seen, it also raises the

29. David Laird Dungan, "Mark—The Abridgement of Matthew and Luke," in *Jesus and Man's Hope* (Pittsburgh: Pittsburgh Theological Seminary, 1970), p. 73.

30. For an attempt to establish principles by which the delimitation of Q can proceed, see Petros Vassiliadis, "The Nature and Extent of the Q Document," *NT* 20 (1978): 49–73.

question of why this order is not more apparent in other places. Finally, the argument from doublets may have value for proving the existence of a common source or sources, but it does not demonstrate the existence of a written Q. Whether Q was a single written source, whether Q consisted of a collection of several different fragments, whether Q consisted of a combination of written and oral traditions, whether Q consisted of various oral traditions, or, less probably, was a single unified oral tradition are questions that are unlikely to be resolved in the immediate future.

In light of the extremely hypothetical nature of the Q source, it would appear that the wisdom of attempts to do redaction-critical work on the theology of the Q document or on the Q community is quite questionable.[31] The attempts to practice redaction criticism on Mark and arrive at his unique theological emphases is theoretical enough, for we have to posit his sources, which we do not have. However, we do have his Gospel.[32] On the other hand, the attempt to arrive at the theology of the Markan community is very questionable. Mark was written by an individual, not a community. Is the theology of Galatians the theology of the Galatian community? If it were, Paul would not have written Galatians. Paul wrote Galatians to change the theology of the Galatian community to that of his letter.[33] Furthermore, with regard to Q, we have neither the sources that Q used nor Q itself. Whether Q even existed as a single written (or even oral) source is most debatable. Whether it was a diverse collection of written and/or oral traditions available to Matthew and Luke but coming from different sources is unknown. How all this was related to the passion narrative is also unclear. And the possibility that Luke used Matthew and that there never was a Q, while not very likely, is still a theoretical possibility. In light of all this, it would appear that a redaction criticism seeking the Q theology and/or the Q community is work built on very "sandy soil."[34] J. W. Wenham has given a very helpful analogy with regard to the difficulty of succeeding in such a study. He raises the question of how successful any attempt to delimit the source of Matthew and Luke would be if we did not possess Mark but only possessed Matthew and

31. For a good survey of various theories of the theology and community of the Q material, see John S. Kloppenborg, "Tradition and Redaction in the Synoptic Sayings Source," CBQ 46 (1984): 34–62.

32. Some of the fanciful theologies of Mark that have been produced might raise questions concerning even this possibility, however.

33. Note that one does not speak of the "Josephus" community. And is Theophilus a "community"?

34. For an opposing view see Ronald D. Worden, "Redaction Criticism of Q: A Survey," JBL 94 (1975): 532–46.

Luke. Would the common omissions be detected? Would the "Markan" source be distinguished from other common material that Matthew and Luke obtained elsewhere? Would the "original" form of this material be ascertained? Would the correct order be discovered? Would we have discovered the many Markan theological emphases omitted or modified by one or both of the "later" Evangelists? Would the great Lukan omission (Mark 6:45–8:26) be omitted from Mark? And so on. No, there would be little hope of establishing a "Markan theology" and far less still for arriving at the theology of a Markan community in such a process. *A fortiori,* any reconstruction of a possible Q document is unlikely to be anywhere near the real thing, and establishing from this reconstruction what the community was like is even less likely.[35]

35. Wenham, "Synoptic Independence," p. 514 n.3.

4

The Matthew–Luke Agreements Against Mark

It is probably safe to say that the two-source theory, which posits the priority of Mark and the existence of Q, was more universally accepted fifty years ago than it is today. No doubt this is due to the various attacks upon the theory from several directions.[1] These attacks have focused on different aspects of the two-source hypothesis. At times the center of focus has been on the Q hypothesis; at other times it has been on the priority of Mark. Sometimes the order of the pericopes has been the focus of attention, and on other occasions the prominent issue has been the Matthew–Luke agreements against Mark in the triple tradition. Clearly the key question and major stumbling block for acceptance of the two-source hypothesis, however, involves the issue of the various Matthew–Luke agreements against

---

1. Some of the more significant works are J. Chapman, *Matthew, Mark, Luke* (London: Longmans, Green, 1937); B. C. Butler, *The Originality of Saint Matthew: A Critique of the Two-Document Hypothesis* (Cambridge: Cambridge University, 1951); Austin M. Farrer, "On Dispensing with Q," in *Studies in the Gospels: Essays in Memory of R. H. Lightfoot*, ed. D. E. Nineham (Oxford: Blackwell, 1955), pp. 55–88; William R. Farmer, *The Synoptic Problem: A Critical Analysis* (New York: Macmillan, 1964); E. P. Sanders, *The Tendencies of the Synoptic Tradition* (Cambridge: Cambridge University, 1969); B. Orchard, *Matthew, Luke and Mark: Griesbach Solution to the Synoptic Question* (Manchester: Koinonia, 1976); H.-H. Stoldt, *History and Criticism of the Marcan Hypothesis*, trans. D. L. Niewyk (Macon: Mercer University, 1980); M. D. Goulder, "On Putting Q to the Test," *NTS* 24 (1978): 218–34; etc.

Mark. If these agreements "require" that Luke knew (used) Matthew, then both the Q hypothesis and the priority of Mark become questionable. Q would then become unnecessary, for its existence is dependent on Matthew and Luke not knowing each other's work. Also, although one could still argue for a Markan priority if Luke used Matthew,[2] many of the arguments for a Markan priority would have been compromised and a Matthean priority would become more attractive. The Matthew–Luke agreements therefore must be dealt with and resolved in some way, if the two-source hypothesis is to be maintained.

The number of Matthew–Luke agreements against Mark that are found in the synoptic Gospels varies according to the definitions used to define what constitutes such an agreement. Frans Neirynck lists over 770 such agreements.[3] Stoldt, on the other hand, lists 272.[4] That these agreements are not a new "discovery" is evident from the fact that people like John Hawkins[5] and B. H. Streeter[6] saw the problem that such agreements make for the two-source hypothesis and sought to reconcile this with the priority of Mark and the existence of Q. Not all such agreements are of equal weight, and although classifying such agreements into groups is criticized by some,[7] such classification is both legitimate and necessary. While it is true that these agreements should not be discussed in isolation from their context, it is also true that one cannot treat them in their context without some prior understanding of the tendencies that these generalizations provide. That there is a "hermeneutical circle" involved in this is clear.[8]

But how are we to classify these agreements? Streeter used the following categories: Irrelevant Agreements; Deceptive Agreements; Influence of Q; and Textual Corruption. Such categories are clearly more "apologetic" than descriptive. Stoldt[9] uses more neutral categories: Mi-

---

2. So Farrer, "On Dispensing with Q"; Nigel Turner, "The Minor Verbal Agreements of Mt. and Lk. against Mark," *Studia Evangelica* I (Berlin, 1959): 223–34; A. W. Argyle, "Agreements Between Matthew and Luke," *ET* 73 (1961): 19–22 and "Evidence for the View that St. Luke Used St. Matthew's Gospel," *JBL* 83 (1964): 390–96; R. T. Simpson, "The Major Agreements of Matthew and Luke against Mark," *NTS* 12 (1966): 273–84; W. Wilkens, "Zur Frage der literarischen Beziehung zwischen Matthaeus und Lukas," *NT* 8 (1966): 48–57; etc.

3. Frans Neirynck, *The Minor Agreements of Matthew and Luke Against Mark* (Leuven: Leuven University, 1974), pp. 55–195.

4. Stoldt, *Marcan Hypothesis*, pp. 11–21.

5. John C. Hawkins, *Horae Synopticae* (Oxford: Clarendon, 1909), pp. 208–15.

6. B. H. Streeter, *The Four Gospels* (London: Macmillan, 1951), pp. 295–331.

7. So Farmer, *The Synoptic Problem*, pp. 118–19.

8. See Joseph A. Fitzmyer, *To Advance the Gospel* (New York: Crossroad, 1981), pp. 14–15.

9. Stoldt, *Markan Hypothesis*, pp. 11–21.

nor additional details in Mark that extend beyond the text of Matthew and Luke (i.e., common Matthew–Luke omissions of Mark); Minor additional details in both Matthew and Luke that extend beyond Mark (i.e., common Matthew–Luke additions to Mark); Concurrence of Matthew and Luke in expressions and wording, contrary to Mark; and Concurrence of Matthew and Luke in diverging from Mark's word form. The neutral quality of Stoldt's categories is both evident and to be commended, although this neutrality results in a certain awkwardness of expression. One should not, however, condemn Streeter's classification for being apologetic, since he sought to argue why such agreements did not refute the two- or four-source hypothesis. In other words Streeter's purpose was apologetic, and apologetic classifications are to be expected in such a work. The legitimacy of such classifications is determined by whether or not Streeter's explanations of the data are convincing. The classifications used below have sacrificed the objectivity of Stoldt for convenience and conciseness, as well as for "apologetic" reasons.

Matthew–Luke Agreements in Omission

Stoldt gives 180 examples of Matthew–Luke agreements of omission in the triple tradition against Mark. Stoldt concludes with a question: "How can it be explained that in 180 cases Matthew and Luke, independently and without knowledge of each other, joined in leaving out and ignoring the identical phrases and sentences of the Gospel of Mark—if this had been their source?"[10] Upon closer scrutiny and reflection, however, these agreements in omission are far less impressive than they appear at first glance.

If we compare Mark with Matthew and Luke, we find that Mark consists of 11,025 words. The parallel material in Matthew consists of 10,901 words and in Luke of 9,117 words.[11] Yet the number of words in Mark that are identical in Matthew is 4,432 (40%) and in Luke 2,873 (26%). This means that Matthew omits more than half of the Markan vocabulary and substitutes 6,469 (10,901 − 4,432) of his own words for the 6,593 (11,025 − 4,432) words of Mark that he omits. Luke similarly omits three-fourths of the Markan vocabulary and substitutes 6,244 (9,117 − 2,873) of his own words for the 8,038 (11,025 − 2,987) words

10. Ibid., p. 21. It should be pointed out, however, that some of these agreements of omission listed by Stoldt are rather ludicrous. Are the omissions of Mark 7:8, 13, 18–19 really agreements? Where is the Lukan parallel?

11. These statistics and those that follow come from Joseph B. Tyson and Thomas R. W. Longstaff, *Synoptic Abstract*, The Computer Bible, vol. 15 (Wooster, Ohio: College of Wooster, 1978), pp. 169–71. The data for the exact Matthew–Mark and Luke–Mark agreements come from columns J and K and columns P and Q on p. 170.

of Mark that he omits. Surely, if Matthew and Luke omit respectively 6,593 and 8,038 words of Mark's 11,025 words, there have to be numerous agreements in omission as a matter of course! The statistics given above may be misleading, since the replacement words of Matthew and Luke often replace the same sentences, phrases, and terms found in Mark, but the "rewriting" of so much of Mark must bring with it, simply on the basis of chance, numerous agreements in omission.

It should also be noted that when one looks specifically at some of these agreements, their omission is easily understandable on the basis of a Markan priority. Is Mark 1:1 ("The beginning of the gospel of Jesus Christ, the Son of God") really a significant omission? Would not each Evangelist want to begin his Gospel in his own distinctive manner? The fact is that no gospel writer is dependent on any other Evangelist for his introduction, although Matthew and Mark are somewhat alike. The omission of Mark 1:43 ("And he sternly charged him, and sent him away at once. . .") is likewise understandable, because both Luke and Matthew give abbreviated accounts of this incident and this verse does present a picture of Jesus that could be misunderstood. The deletion of Mark 2:2 ("And many were gathered together, so that there was no longer room for them, not even about the door; and he was preaching the word to them") is also quite understandable in that it is somewhat redundant in light of 2:4 and, since Matthew has radically abbreviated the story and omitted both references to the crowd, any omission by Luke of one of these redundant expressions would result in an agreement in omission. The common omission of Mark 2:26 (". . . when Abiathar was high priest. . .") can be explained by the historical difficulty created by the reference to Abiathar. In the Markan account of the raising of Jairus' daughter and the healing of the woman who was hemorrhaging (Mark 5:21–43) we find a number of common omissions of Matthew and Luke. These are Mark 5:26–27a, 29b, 30, 34d, 40c, 41b, and 42b. Again, at first glance these agreements look more impressive than they really are, for Matthew and Luke are clearly shorter versions of the account. Compared to Mark's 374 words, the Lukan account contains 280 words, and the Matthean account only 138. It would for all practical purposes be impossible for Matthew and Luke not to agree in their omissions against Mark.[12]

It is not possible to deal individually with all 180 instances of omission listed by Stoldt, but it is evident from what has been said above that many such agreements are not weighty when analyzed closely.

---

12. Compare Streeter: ". . . it would have been quite impossible for two persons to *abbreviate* practically every paragraph in the whole of Mark without concurring in a large number of their omissions" (*The Four Gospels*, p. 295).

The argument-for-common-omissions actually cuts two ways. If Mark is the "abridger" of Matthew and/or Luke, why does he have these 180 additions in his abridgement? Many scholars who raise this argument-from-common-omissions lose sight of the fact that the common omission of this material by Matthew and Luke makes far more sense than does Mark's addition of this material to his "abridged" Gospel and his consequent omission of such things as the Sermon on the Mount. If Matthew and Luke sought to abridge Mark in order to include their special material (Q, M, L), their omission of various Markan explanations (2:2, 18; 3:5, 9, 30; 5:26–27; 6:17, 21; 8:14; 9:26–27; etc.), explanatory comments (2:15; 6:31, 52, 7:3–4; 11:13b; etc.), Aramaic phrases (3:17; 5:41; 14:36), and so on, makes perfectly good sense, and statistically one would have to expect certain agreements in omission. Mark's hypothetical omission of the Q, M, and L material for the sake of brevity would argue diametrically against his having added such material to a Matthean and/or Lukan source.

In conclusion, the argument that Matthew and Luke knew each other, if based upon the agreements in omission, is not as strong as might first appear. Furthermore, lack of any convincing rationale for Mark's having abbreviated Matthew and/or Luke, and at the same time adding this other material, is more easily explained in favor of a Markan priority and the subsequent omission of this material coincidentally by Matthew and Luke.

Matthew–Luke Agreements in Grammar and Editing

There exists a large number of agreements between Matthew and Luke against Mark that involve such issues as verb tense, conjunctions, and individual terms. The significance of these agreements is much debated. For proponents of Luke's use of Matthew (whether via the Griesbach Hypothesis advocated by Farmer or Butler's theory that Luke used Mark and Matthew), these arguments are clear "proof" that Luke knew Matthew. For those holding the two-source hypothesis, these agreements are essentially "irrelevant."[13] One well-known example involves the use of the "historical present" (the use of the present tense in narration to describe past events). In Mark the historical present occurs 151 times, whereas in Matthew and Luke it occurs 78 and 6 times, respectively.[14] As can be imagined, there must therefore

13. So Streeter, *The Four Gospels*, pp. 295–98.
14. John C. Hawkins, *Horae synopticae* (Oxford: Clarendon, 1909), pp. 143–49. These figures include the twenty-one instances of the historical present in the parables of Matthew and the four instances in which they are found in the parables of Luke. There are no examples of the historical present in the parables of Mark.

be dozens of examples in which Matthew and Luke will agree on omitting Mark's historical present . A sampling of these are:

4.1

Matthew 9:2b	Mark 2:5	Luke 5:20
[author's italics]		[author's italics]
. . . and when Jesus saw	[5]And when Jesus saw	[20]And when he saw
their faith	their faith,	their faith
he *said* (*eipen*)	he said (*legei*)	he *said,* (*eipen*)
to the paralytic,	to the paralytic,	
"Take heart,		
my son;	"My son,	"Man,
your sins are forgiven."	your sins are forgiven."	your sins are forgiven you."

4.2

Matthew 9.4	Mark 2:8	Luke 5:22
[author's italics]		[author's italics]
[4]But	[8]And immediately	[22]When
Jesus,	Jesus,	Jesus
knowing	perceiving in his spirit	perceived
their thoughts,	that they thus questioned	their questionings,
	within themselves,	
said, (*eipen*)	said (*legei*) to them,	he *answered* (*eipen*) them,
"Why do you think evil	"Why do you question	"Why do you question
	thus	
in your hearts?	in your hearts?	in your hearts?

4.3

Matthew 21:1–2a	Mark 11:1–2a	Luke 19:28–30a
[author's italics]		[author's italics]
		[28]And when he had said this, he went on ahead, going up to Jerusalem.
[1]And when they drew near	[1]And when they drew near	[29]When he drew near
to Jerusalem	to Jerusalem,	
and came		
to Bethphage,	to Bethphage	to Bethphage
	and Bethany,	and Bethany,
to the Mount	at the Mount	at the mount
of Olives,	of Olives,	that is called Olivet,
then		
Jesus *sent* (*apesteilen*)	he sent (*apostellei*)	he *sent* (*apesteilen*)
two disciples,	two of his disciples,	two of the disciples,
[2]saying to them,	[2]and said to them,	[30]saying,
"Go into the village	"Go into the village	"Go into the village
opposite you,	opposite you,	opposite,
and immediately	and immediately	
	as you enter it	where on entering
you will find	you will find	you will find
an ass tied,	a colt tied,	a colt tied
	on which no one has ever sat;	on which no one has ever yet sat;
and a colt with her;		

4.4

Matthew 28:1 [author's italics]	Mark 16:1–2	Luke 23:56–24:1 [author's italics]
		[56]Then they returned, and
[1]Now after the sabbath,	[1]And when the sabbath was past, Mary Magdalene, Mary the mother of James, and Salome bought spices;	
		prepared spices and ointments.
	so that they might go and anoint him.	
		On the sabbath they rested according to the commandment.
toward the dawn of the first day of the week,	[2]And very early on the first day of the week	[1]But on the first day of the week, at early dawn,
Mary Magdalene and the other Mary	they	they
went (*elthen*) to see the sepulchre.	went (*erchontai*) to the tomb when the sun had risen.	*went* (*ēlthon*) to the tomb, taking the spices which they had prepared.

How can we explain these Matthew–Luke agreements? On the basis of the Griesbach Hypothesis, Mark simply added these historical presents to his sources (Matthew and Luke). On the basis of the two-document hypothesis, these agreements result from Matthew's greater preference of the aorist/past over Mark's historical present and Luke's strong aversion to the historical present. Farmer has argued that Luke did not have a strong aversion to the use of the historical present since he has six examples of this in his non-Mark material.[15] This argument is fallacious, however, because according to Farmer, Luke used Matthew. If Luke avoided at least seventy-two of the seventy-eight times in which the historical present is found in Matthew, certainly we cannot disallow his seeking to do the same if he used Mark! Actually the one clear example we possess of how the historical present is treated by a later gospel writer is found in the Gospel of Luke.[16] Luke's clear tendency, whether he used Matthew or Mark, is to eliminate the historical present. On the basis of the two-document hypothesis, all we need do to explain these agreements is to presume that Matthew had a similar, although not as thorough, tendency in this area as Luke. On the other

15. Farmer, *The Synoptic Problem*, p. 136.
16. This is not true, of course, if Luke were the first Gospel written, but few hold this position.

hand, according to the Griesbach Hypothesis, we must explain two equally strong but opposite tendencies: Luke sought to *avoid* the historical present in his Matthean source, and Mark sought to *add* the historical present to his Matthean source, even though his Lukan source avoided it. To explain the data, the Griesbach Hypothesis therefore requires two totally opposite tendencies on the part of Mark and Luke. The two-source hypothesis does not. The Griesbach Hypothesis also has difficulties in explaining why Mark, with his strong inclination toward using the historical present, did not follow Matthew in the following instances when he has the historical present in the triple tradition: Matthew 8:26; 9:28; 15:12; 17:20; 19:7 and 8. The theory that Matthew and Luke did not know each other does not encounter any real problem in this particular type of Matthew–Luke agreement against Mark.

A similar type of agreement consists of the over thirty instances in which Matthew and Luke have the conjunction *de* ("and") instead of the conjunction *kai* ("and") found in Mark.[17] Again, this statistic is more impressive at first glance than upon closer examination. *De* occurs 160 times in Mark, 491 times in Matthew, and 548 times in Luke. *Kai* occurs 1,078 times in Mark, 1,169 times in Matthew, and 1,455 times in Luke.[18] This means that *kai* occurs on the average of every 10.2 words in Mark, 15.6 words in Matthew, and 13.3 words in Luke, whereas *de* occurs once in every 68.9 words in Mark, 37.3 words in Matthew, and 35.4 words in Luke. It is evident from this that Matthew and Luke are inclined to use *de* significantly more than Mark (nearly twice) and are inclined to use *kai* significantly less. It is therefore not at all surprising that we would find Matthew–Luke agreements against Mark in this area. Finding thirty instances of their agreeing against Mark in using *de* rather than *kai* can be explained rather easily on the basis of a Markan priority. Sanders has furthermore pointed out that there was a tendency in the apocryphal Gospels when using Mark to decrease the use of *kai* and to use other conjunctions such as *de*.[19] On the theory of a Markan priority, we would only have to assume that Matthew and Luke had a similar tendency in their use of Mark. On the basis of a Matthean priority, on the other hand, we would have to assume the opposite tendency on the part of Mark in his use of Matthew.

17. M. De Solages, *La Composition des Evangiles de Luc et de Matthieu et Leurs Sources* (Leiden: E. J. Brill, 1973), p. 306, lists the following: Mark 2:24; 3:4, 6, 32, 33; 4:11, 16, 18, 20, 41; 5:13, 14; 6:35, 37, 38; 8:28, 36; 10:23; 11:4, 8, 31; 12:5, 33; 13:3, 12; 14:12, 13, 53, 54, 66; 15:15, 32; 16:1, 5.

18. These statistics come from Robert Morgenthaler, *Statistik des Neutestamentlichen Wortschatzes* (Frankfurt: Gotthelf-Verlag, 1958).

19. Sanders, *Synoptic Tradition*, pp. 228–30.

There are several other kinds of agreements that are not impossible to understand as coincidental. One of these is the use by Matthew and Luke of the more correct *agein* (to "lead") instead of *pherein* (to "bear/ carry") in Mark 11:2, 7; 15:1, 22 (cf. also Mark 12:15). Streeter long ago pointed out that *pherein* was more properly used of inanimate objects that one had to lift, whereas people or animals possessing legs are more accurately "led."[20] Farmer has sought to argue that *pherein* was encroaching on the meaning of *agein* in Hellenistic times and offers Luke 15:23 and Matthew 17:17/Mark 9:19 as examples.[21] However, in the former example the expression to "bring" the fatted calf is intimately connected with "kill it; and let us eat. . ."—so that the idea of *pherein* is not simply "lead it" but (as the RSV correctly translates it) "bring it," for the whole activity of killing, cooking, and feasting is in mind and the slaughtered-cooked calf must be "carried." As for Matthew 17:17/Mark 9:19, the impression of the account is that the child (Mark 9:24) may very well have been carried. Even if we grant, for the sake of argument, that the term *pherein* was encroaching on the meaning of *agein*, it is clear that *agein* is better Greek and that a common change of *pherein* to *agein* by Matthew and Luke would not be difficult to envision. On the other hand, if one holds to the Griesbach Hypothesis, one would have to explain why Mark would have wanted in these instances to change the perfectly acceptable *agein* (to "lead") in both his sources to the more difficult and less acceptable *pherein* (to "bear/ carry").

Other agreements that are not too difficult to understand are Matthew's and Luke's changing of "Elijah with Moses" (Mark 9:4) to the more natural and chronological "Moses and Elijah"; their placing of the two sets of brothers—Peter, Andrew, James, and John—side by side instead of separating them as in Mark's—Peter, James, John, and Andrew (Mark 3:16–18); changing Mark's less accurate description of Herod as "king" (Mark 6:14) to "tetrarch"; changing Mark's "after three days" (Mark 8:31; 10:34) to the less difficult and more traditional "on the third day"; changing Mark's "Master" (*rabbouni*) to "Lord" (Mark 10:51); and so on. Not all of the Matthew–Luke agreements against Mark are equally weighty and important. The great majority of them are not that difficult to explain on the basis of the two-document hypothesis. In fact De Solages argues that two-thirds to three-fourths of the Matthew-Luke agreements against Mark can be explained by their independent paraphrasing of Mark.[22] There is, however, a resid-

20. Streeter, *The Four Gospels*, p. 299.
21. Farmer, *The Synoptic Problem*, p. 129.
22. De Solages, *La Composition des Evangiles*, pp. 102–52.

uum of examples that pose much more of a problem for the two-document hypothesis, and it is to these that we must now turn.

The Most Significant Matthew–Luke Agreements

There are clearly a number of Matthew–Luke agreements against Mark that cannot be explained on the basis of coincidental editorial changes to the Markan text by Matthew and Luke. The number of these varies according to whose list one follows. Fitzmyer lists six: Matthew 26:68, 75; 17:3, 17; 9:7, 20, and their parallels;[23] Hawkins lists twenty[one];[24] and Stoldt apparently lists fifty-seven.[25] As one might surmise, the estimated number of "most significant" agreements is frequently dependent on whether or not one believes in the dependence of Luke on Matthew. Any reasonable list of such agreements, however, would include some or all of the following:

4.5

Matthew 3:11–12 [author's italics]	Mark 1:7–8	Luke 3:16–18 [author's italics]
	[7]And he preached, saying,	[16]John answered them all,
[11]"I baptize you with water for repentance,		"I baptize you with water;
but he who is coming after me	"After me comes he who	but he who
is mightier than I,	is mightier than I,	is mightier than I is coming,
	the thong	the thong
whose sandals I am not worthy to carry;	of whose sandals I am not worthy to stoop down and untie. [8]I have baptized you with water; but	of whose sandals I am not worthy to untie;
he will baptize you with the Holy Spirit *and with fire.* [12]*His winnowing fork is in his hand, and he will clear his threshing floor and gather his wheat into the granary, but the chaff he will burn with unquenchable fire.*"	he will baptize you with the Holy Spirit."	he will baptize you with the Holy Spirit *and with fire.* [17]*His winnowing fork is in his hand, to clear his threshing floor, and to gather the wheat into his granary, but the chaff he will burn with unquenchable fire.*" [18]So, with many other exhortations, he preached good news to the people.

23. Fitzmyer, To Advance the Gospel, p. 15.
24. Hawkins, Horae Synopticae, pp. 209–12.
25. Stoldt, Markan Hypothesis, pp. 19–21.

4.6

Matthew 9:7–8	Mark 2:12	Luke 5:25–26
[author's italics]		[author's italics]
⁷And he rose	¹²And he rose,	²⁵And immediately he rose before them,
	and immediately took up the pallet	and took up that on which he lay,
and went home,	and went out before them all;	*and went home,*
		glorifying God.
⁸When the crowds saw it, they were afraid,	so that they were all amazed	²⁶And amazement seized them all,
and they glorified God, who had given such authority to men.	and glorified God,	and they glorified God
		and were filled with awe,
	saying, "We never saw anything like this!"	saying, "We have seen strange things today."

4.7

Matthew 26:67–68	Mark 14:65	Luke 22:63–65
[author's italics]		[author's italics]
⁶⁷Then they	⁶⁵And some	⁶³Now the men who were holding Jesus
spat in his face,	began to spit on him,	mocked him and beat him; ⁶⁴they also blindfolded him
	and to cover his face,	
and struck him; and some slapped him, ⁶⁸saying, "Prophesy to us, you Christ! *Who is it that struck you?"*	and to strike him, saying to him, "Prophesy!"	and asked him, "Prophesy! *Who is it that struck you?"*
	And the guards received him with blows.	⁶⁵And they spoke many other words against him, reviling him.

To these can also be added the following Markan passages and their parallels: Mark 3:24, 26–29; 5:27; 6:33; 9:2, 19; 14:72.

Explanations for the Matthew–Luke Agreements

It has been argued in chapter 3 that Luke did not know Matthew.²⁶ Yet, if this is true, how can Matthew and Luke have these agreements

26. See above pp. 91–103.

against Mark? The traditional two-document hypothesis has a distinct difficulty here. Several suggestions have been made by Streeter to explain this.[27] There is little doubt, however, that Streeter's confidence in having "explained away" these agreements was much too optimistic, for Farmer has raised some serious questions against his argumentation.[28] On the other hand it would be equally wrong not to see that Streeter's explanations do at times have merit and are convincing. For the present writer, there does not exist one simple explanation of these agreements. Those who maintain that Luke's use of Matthew provides a simple explanation for these agreements must deal elsewhere with far more serious difficulties.[29] The explanation of these Matthew–Luke agreements, assuming that Matthew and Luke did not know each other, involves a whole complex of reasons, some of which are outlined below.

Coincidences Caused by Their Redactional Treatment of Mark

We have already discussed how Matthew and Luke, in eliminating 60 to 67 percent of the vocabulary of Mark, would at times naturally agree in common omissions of their source. To these can be added various agreements that resulted from their refraining from certain Markan grammatical tendencies, such as his use of the historical present, his use of *kai*, and so on. No doubt many of the less-significant Matthew–Luke agreements can be explained in this way.

The Overlapping of Q

Streeter suggested that certain agreements could be explained by the fact that Q contained an account or saying parallel to the one found in Mark and that the agreement of Matthew and Luke came about by their use of the Q parallel. We have already pointed out that one scholar has sarcastically referred to this explanation as the "blessed overlap!"[30] Yet certainly Streeter did not deserve such sarcasm, for he warned against appealing frivolously to Q as an explanation of these agreements. He in fact states: "Some scholars, however, have laid far too much stress on the bearing of the overlapping of Mark and Q on the problem of minor agreements. We have no right to call in the hypothesis of the influence of Q for this ulterior purpose except in places where the existence of obviously different versions, or of doublets very distinctly defined, provides us with objective evidence of the

27. See Streeter, *The Four Gospels*, pp. 293–331.
28. See Farmer, *The Synoptic Problem*, pp. 118–77.
29. See above pp. 91–103.
30. See above p. 110.

presence of Q."[31] Ironically enough, advocates of the Griesbach Hypothesis often make a similar appeal to overlapping sources as well.[32]

That written sources containing various gospel traditions existed before the writing of Matthew and Luke must almost certainly be true. Luke even makes mention of them (Luke 1:1). Is it likely that they did not overlap? It is inconceivable to think that along with Mark (or Matthew or Luke!) there were not also other collections of sayings or Gospel-like collections that existed.[33] Time and time again they must have overlapped.[34] Hypothetically there is therefore no reason why Matthew and Luke could not have been influenced by such accounts in the writing of their Gospels. If Farmer can appeal to overlapping traditions,[35] why cannot Streeter? If we modify this particular explanation to read "The Overlapping of Additional Sources" instead of "The Overlapping of Q," there is no reason to object to this explanation of certain Matthew–Luke agreements. Possibly the Matthew–Luke agreements against Mark in the baptismal accounts can be explained in this manner. Other agreements that may be due to such overlapping are the temptation; the Beelzebul controversy, the parable of the mustard seed, and the mission charge.

Textual Corruption

Streeter expended a great deal of effort in his attempt to explain that certain Matthew–Luke agreements were due to scribal corruptions.[36] Although one must beware here of sacrificing sound principles of textual criticism in order to support one's literary hypothesis, an early corruption of a Markan parallel in the triple tradition could, of course, result in a Matthew–Luke agreement against Mark. Furthermore, an attempt to "harmonize" a Lukan reading to that of Matthew, which was the church's favorite synoptic Gospel, could also result in such an agreement. Since "assimilation of parallel passages in the Gospels is the commonest form of textual corruption,"[37] it is not impossible that

31. Streeter, *The Four Gospels*, p. 306.

32. See C. M. Tuckett, *The Revival of the Griesbach Hypothesis: An Analysis and Appraisal* (Cambridge: Cambridge University, 1983), pp. 77–78.

33. At this point the discussion of pre-Markan collections—proto-Matthew, proto-Luke, and Ur-Markus—come in. See, for instance, H.-W. Kuhn, *Ältere Sammlungen im Markusevangelium* (Göttingen: Vanderhoeck & Ruprecht, 1970).

34. E. P. Sanders states: "While there are doubtless direct literary relationships among the synoptic Gospels, these relationships were probably complicated by the Evangelists' knowledge of overlapping traditions" ("The Overlaps of Mark and Q and the Synoptic Problem," *NTS* 19 [1973]: 464).

35. See Farmer, *The Synoptic Problem*, pp. 248, 272.

36. See Streeter, *The Four Gospels*, pp. 306–25.

37. Ibid., p. 307.

some of the Matthew–Luke agreements may indeed be due to such textual corruption. It is furthermore not unusual but rather common to find variants in the textual tradition of a synoptic Gospel that support the readings found in one of the other synoptic Gospels. Whether or not certain of the Matthew–Luke agreements can be explained as due to textual corruption is a matter for the specialist in textual criticism, but the very tendency of the scribes and copyists to harmonize the Gospel texts makes such a task most difficult.

Overlapping Oral Traditions

Another source for the Matthew–Luke agreements against Mark lies in their knowledge of oral traditions. It would be foolish to think that the only materials available to the Evangelists were one or two written sources. It would even be wrong to think that they possessed only a specified number of written sources. Since we know that the gospel traditions continued to be passed on in oral form for many years after our Gospels were written, we should not think that Matthew and Luke had only written sources before them. On the contrary, they had along with these written sources an even more extensive oral tradition, which possessed a fairly established form. No doubt there was a great deal of overlapping between these various sources, and at times the Evangelists may have preferred the form of the oral tradition over their written source or sources. This may be especially true when the written source deviated somewhat from the familiar oral tradition. It would therefore not be surprising if at times Matthew and Luke might agree in wording against Mark simply because they preferred the oral tradition to the Markan rendering. A possible example of this is:

4.8

Matthew 26:63b–64	Mark 14:61c–62	Luke 22:67–70
"I adjure you by the living God, tell us if you are the Christ, the Son of God."	"Are you the Christ, the Son of the Blessed?"	[67]"If you are the Christ, tell us."
[64]Jesus said to him, "You have said so. But I tell you,	[62]And Jesus said, "I am;	But he said to them, "If I tell you, you will not believe; [68]and if I ask you, you will not answer.
hereafter you will see the Son of man seated at the right hand of Power, and coming on the clouds of heaven."	and you will see the Son of man seated at the right hand of Power, and coming with the clouds of heaven."	[69]But from now on the Son of man shall be seated at the right hand of the power of God."

[70]And they all said, "Are you the Son of God, then?"
And he said to them, "You say that I am."

In Matthew and Luke there is an agreement that Jesus' reply to the high priest, while affirmative, was less straightforward than what we find in Mark. No doubt they are more "primitive" in this regard. A possible reason for this agreement is that Mark has eliminated the somewhat hesitant affirmation of Jesus ("You have said so, and I shall not deny it, but I would rather be referred to as the Son of man") and simply recorded that Jesus affirmed the title. Matthew and Luke may agree against Mark in this instance because they preferred the more traditional response, which they found in the oral tradition and with which they were familiar, to what they found in Mark.

Conclusion

In dealing with the problem of the Matthew–Luke agreements against Mark, it is easy to lose sight of the total range of phenomena involved in the Synoptic Problem. These involve all the arguments for Markan priority:

1. Mark is the shortest gospel.
2. Mark has the poorest writing style.
3. Mark has numerous harder readings.
4. Mark has many agreements in wording with Matthew against Luke and with Luke against Matthew; in comparison, there are few Matthew–Luke agreements against Mark.
5. Matthew and Luke never agree against Mark in the order of the material, and their deviation from Mark is more understandable than the reverse.
6. Certain literary agreements are best understood on the basis of the priority of Mark.
7. Markan redactional characteristics tend to appear more frequently in those sections of Matthew that contain the triple tradition, but Matthean redactional characteristics do not tend to appear in the triple tradition of Mark or Luke.

To these observations we must also add the various arguments in favor of the view that Matthew and Luke did not know and use each other's work:

1. M additions to the triple tradition "never" appear in Luke.
2. The Q material never appears in the same context in Luke as in Matthew.
3. The Q material appears in a more primitive context in Luke than in Matthew.
4. At times the Q material appears to be more primitive in Matthew, and even more often it appears to be more primitive in Luke.
5. Matthew and Luke never agree in order against Mark (this argument also argues for the priority of Mark).
6. The M material is lacking in Luke.

When we look at the Matthew–Luke agreements against Mark, they must be viewed in this total context, lest one gives to these agreements more significance than they deserve. Furthermore, one cannot help but raise the question of why, if Luke knew Matthew, there are only such "minor" agreements against Mark.[38] Fitzmyer seems to be quite correct when he states that these agreements "represent only a small fraction of the data to be considered in the Synoptic Problem. They constitute a problem which cannot be denied; they are one of the loopholes in the Two-Source Theory. Whatever explanation (or explanations) may account for this phenomenon, it scarcely weighs as evidence that completely counter-balances the other data pointing to a dependence of Luke (and of Matthew) on Mark."[39]

38. So F. Gerald Downing, "Redaction Criticism: Josephus' *Antiquities* and the Synoptic Problem," *JSNT* 9 (1980): 42–43.
39. Fitzmyer, *To Advance the Gospel*, p. 15.

5

The "Solution" of the Synoptic Problem

In chapter 1 a number of reasons were given as to why the similarities between Matthew, Mark, and Luke are best explained by the existence of some sort of literary relationship. These involved the close agreement at times in wording; the agreement in order; the presence of common parenthetical material; and the fact that Luke 1:1–4 explicitly mentions various written sources that Luke used in his writing. Throughout the history of the church, but especially in the last two hundred years, numerous suggestions have been made as to the nature of this literary relationship.

Early in the second century, Papias is quoted to have said that "Mark became Peter's interpreter and wrote accurately all that he remembered, not, indeed, in order, of the things said or done by the Lord" and that "Matthew collected the oracles [*ta logia*] in the Hebrew language and each interpreted them as best as he could."[1] Both the interpretation and the accuracy of Papias' words have been greatly debated. Did Papias claim that our Gospel of Matthew was originally written by the apostle Matthew and in Hebrew (or Aramaic, a dialect of Hebrew) rather than Greek? Since there is almost universal agreement that the present Gospel of Matthew is not a strict translation from Hebrew or Aramaic into Greek, the accuracy of Papias' statement with regard to the origin of Matthew is often questioned. Is it possible that

---

1. Eusebius, *Ecclesiastical History*, 3.39.15–16 (Loeb).

the *logia* does not refer to the present Gospel of Matthew but perhaps to a different work, such as an Aramaic Q; a "proto-Matthew"; a collection of Old Testament prophecies fulfilled in Christ, i.e., a "Testimony Book"; the Apocryphal Gospel of the Hebrews; and so on? It has also been suggested that the expression "Hebrew language" may refer not to the Hebrew language as such but rather to a Jewish manner of presenting the material.[2] On the other hand, others have suggested that Papias' statements deserve little credence and should be ignored.[3] It is true that Eusebius speaks rather negatively of Papias' intelligence,[4] but this may be due to his own bias against Papias because of the latter's millennial view, which Eusebius opposed.[5]

Whereas other early church fathers (Justin Martyr, Irenaeus, Clement of Alexandria, Origen, Tertullian, etc.) made comments about the authorship of the synoptic Gospels, Augustine was probably the first to seek to explain how they were related literarily.[6] According to Augustine, Matthew's Gospel was the first one written; Mark then used and abbreviated Matthew; and Luke used both Matthew and Mark. Although Augustine's *De Consensu Evangelistarum* contains many astute and valuable insights, it would appear that his "solution" of the Synoptic Problem is more dependent upon the present canonical order of the Gospels than upon a careful comparison of the synoptic Gospels and an explanation of the agreements/disagreements in wording, order, and so on, found within them. The careful analysis of the latter could only take place when a synopsis became available.

It was in the latter half of the eighteenth century that the attempt to resolve the Synoptic Problem gained full momentum. No doubt two events that gave great impetus to this were the publication of J. J. Griesbach's *Synopsis Evangeliorum* . . . in 1776 and the instigation of the "quest of the historical Jesus" by Lessing's publication of H. S. Reimarus' notes that same year. Soon a host of explanations appeared. These involved the following: an Ur-Gospel in Aramaic, which was used by each of the Evangelists (G. E. Lessing [1778]; J. G. Eichhorn [1794]); an early common oral tradition used by each (J. G. von Herder [1796]; J. C. L. Gieseler [1818]; B. F. Wescott [1888]); the use of common "fragments" or *memorabilia* (F. Schleiermacher [1821]); and various

2. So J. Kürzinger, "Die Aussage des Papias von Hierapolis zur literarischen Form des Markusevangeliums," *BZ* 21 (1977): 245–64.

3. Werner Georg Kümmel, *Introduction to the New Testament*, trans. by Howard C. Kee (Nashville: Abingdon, 1975), pp. 53–55.

4. *Ecclesiastical History*, 3.39.13.

5. So A. C. Perumalil, "Are not Papias and Irenaeus Competent to Report on the Gospels?" *ET* 91 (1980): 332–37.

6. See his *De Consensu Evangelistarum*, 1.2.

theories of mutual interdependence, such as the Griesbach Hypothesis ([1789]; W. R. Farmer [1964]), in which Matthew was first and was used by Luke, and Mark used both Matthew and Luke; the two-source hypothesis (K. Lachmann [1835]; C. H. Weisse and C. G. Wilke [1838]; H. J. Holtzmann [1863]; B. H. Streeter [1924]), in which Mark (or an Ur-Markus) was first and was used by Matthew and Luke, who also used another source, now lost, which scholars call Q; Mark was first, was used by Matthew, and Luke used both (A. M. Farrer [1957]); the theory that Luke was first (R. L. Lindsey [1969]); Augustine's view that Matthew was first and was used by Mark, and Luke used both Matthew and Mark. And so on. To these can be added theories of a "proto-Matthew" (L. Vaganay [1954]; P. Benoit [1961]) and a "proto-Luke" (P. Feine [1881]; B. H. Streeter [1924]).

Concerning the last two mentioned "solutions," it would seem that the theory of a proto-Matthew has in its favor primarily the testimony of Papias for a Hebrew Matthew. On the other hand, the arguments for a proto-Luke appear to have better textual support. For one, the sequence of the passion narrative in Luke 22:14–24:12 shows considerable variation from Mark, whereas elsewhere Luke tends to follow Mark rather closely. Second, the passion narrative in Luke also contains several non-Markan incidents that seem at times to be interwoven in the narrative rather than being simply L additions to the Markan narrative. Finally, it has been observed that the vocabulary of the Lukan passion narrative is less Markan than elsewhere. As a result of these and other arguments, the proto-Luke hypothesis appears to be gaining some adherents of late. Some have suggested that proto-Luke was essentially a "first draft" by Luke in which he combined Q and L before he used Mark. It should not be assumed, however, that proto-Luke does not have its critics as well.[7]

Of all the possibilities mentioned above, the two that seem to have the most support, or at least the most "press," are the Griesbach Hypothesis and the two-document hypothesis.

The Griesbach Hypothesis

Although the hypothesis that Matthew was the first Gospel written, that Luke used Matthew, and that Mark used both Matthew and Luke was first proposed in 1764 by Henry Owen,[8] it has been called the Griesbach Hypothesis because of its advocacy by J. J. Griesbach in 1783 and 1789. Its popularity and demise were partly associated with the

7. See Kümmel, pp. 132–38.
8. C. M. Tuckett, *The Revival of the Griesbach Hypothesis* (Cambridge: Cambridge University, 1983), p. 3.

rise and fall of the Tübingen Hypothesis. According to F. C. Baur, the "founder" of the Tübingen Hypothesis, the history of the early church was to be explained along the Hegelian lines of a thesis–antithesis struggle, which was later resolved in a new synthesis. This worked itself out as a struggle between Jewish Christianity, represented by Peter, James, and the apostles (thesis), and Hellenistic Christianity represented by Paul (antithesis), which was resolved in a "Catholic" Christianity represented by Luke–Acts, the Pastorals, and the Catholic Epistles (synthesis). In a similar way the Griesbach Hypothesis offered a thesis (Matthew—Jewish Christianity), antithesis (Luke—Hellenistic Christianity), and a synthesis (Mark—"Catholic"). Griesbach himself also maintained that if the author of the first Gospel was the apostle Matthew, it was impossible that he would have used the work of a non-apostle such as Mark.[9]

The revival of the Griesbach Hypothesis is in no small measure due to its vigorous espousal by W. R. Farmer. In his *The Synoptic Problem* Farmer has presented a useful, although biased, history of the Synoptic Problem and sought to argue that the rejection of the Griesbach Hypothesis in favor of the two-source hypothesis was due to reaction against the Tübingen Hypothesis and the support that the two-source hypothesis received from such notable scholars as H. J. Holtzmann, W. Sanday, B. H. Streeter, F. C. Burkitt, and others who accepted this view on "extra-scientific" or "nonscientific" grounds.[10] The more significant objections that Farmer and others after him have raised against the two-source hypothesis, however, involve the discussion of the phenomenon itself. It is now clear that the argument from order alone can be explained on the basis of not only the two-document hypothesis but the Griesbach Hypothesis as well.[11] Furthermore, the question of "primitiveness" or "redundancy" is not always as simple as once thought. But the greatest single argument for the advocacy of the Griesbach Hypothesis is clearly the agreements of Matthew and Luke against Mark in the triple tradition. This will always be the single greatest weakness of the two-source hypothesis. Farmer furthermore has raised a number of serious objections to the way that Streeter resolved this problem.[12]

Yet, whereas the attack of the advocates of the Griesbach Hypothesis upon the two-source hypothesis has revealed some serious weak-

9. Ibid., p. 7.

10. William R. Farmer, *The Synoptic Problem: A Critical Analysis* (New York: Macmillan, 1964), p. 190. Cf. also Bo Reicke, "From Strauss to Holtzmann and Meijboom," *NT* 29 (1987): pp. 1–21.

11. See above pp. 69–70.

12. Farmer, *The Synoptic Problem*, pp. 118–77.

nesses, the Griesbach Hypothesis is far from convincing as a theory. Time and time again the more primitive nature of Mark over Matthew and Luke is clear. Farmer's explanation concerning Matthew 19:17 ("Why do you ask me about what is good?") that "it is by no means certain that the text of Matthew is secondary"[13] to Mark 10:18 ("Why do you call me good?") is far less convincing than numerous arguments for the two-source hypothesis that he criticizes. It is impossible to conceive of Mark and Luke as having changed Matthew's account to "Why do you call me good?" as the Griesbach Hypothesis demands. On the other hand, the Matthean change of Mark, as the two-document hypothesis espouses, is perfectly understandable and natural. The use of Matthew's Gospel by Luke is likewise difficult to accept.[14] If one can believe that Luke used Matthew, with all the difficulties this entails, then the Matthew–Luke agreements against Mark should not be that difficult to accept.

The most basic problem that the Griesbach Hypothesis encounters, however, is that it simply cannot provide a credible explanation as to why Mark was ever written. Why Mark both "conflated" and "abbreviated" Matthew and Luke is most difficult to understand. Farmer has more recently argued that Mark was written to serve as an apologetic and to remove inconsistencies and contradictions in Matthew and Luke.[15] However, if Mark sought to do this, he was singularly inept, for—any attempts to deny this notwithstanding—the Gospel of Mark contains far more difficulties in the triple tradition than either Matthew or Luke. And yet Farmer claims that Mark sought to ameliorate the difficulties found in Matthew and Luke! In seeking to explain the various objections to the Griesbach Hypothesis, Farmer has furthermore had to propose some "incredulous expostulations."[16] To the objection of "why Mark would seek to omit the birth narratives" and so much other material, Farmer suggests that if Mark used Matthew and Luke, he probably also possessed the Book of Acts and, upon reading the speeches of Peter in the Book of Acts, observed that the ministry of Jesus began with the baptism. Thus he omitted the birth accounts.[17] Surely it is incredible to think that Mark, having Matthew and Luke in front of him and concentrating on those materials where these texts bore concurrent testimony to the same tradition, would base his Gospel's outline not on Matthew and Luke but upon Peter's speeches in

13. Ibid., p. 160.
14. See above pp. 91–103.
15. See his "Modern Developments of Griesbach's Hypothesis," NTS 23 (1977): 282.
16. Joseph A. Fitzmyer, To Advance the Gospel (New York: Crossroad, 1981), p. 30.
17. Farmer, "Modern Developments of Griesbach's Hypothesis," pp. 283–85.

Acts. To build an explanation upon Mark's use of Acts is to build upon a very sandy foundation indeed.

It must be conceded that the rightness or wrongness of the Griesbach Hypothesis is not dependent on its ability or inability to explain why Mark used his sources the way he did. We can never reconstruct with certainty the mental activity of the Evangelist when he wrote his Gospel, but one might expect that Mark would have used the Q, M, and L material in his sources in a manner and extent similar to his use of the triple tradition. But we do not find this at all. Furthermore, the plausibility of the Griesbach Hypothesis is greatly weakened by the difficulty of not being able to provide a credible explanation of the activity of Mark that is consistent and coherent.[18] On the other hand, Matthew's and Luke's use of Mark have never had such a difficulty, for their supplementation of their Markan source with other materials (Q, L, M, etc.) has always been most plausible. The fact that Farmer also has had to posit an early-second-century dating for the origin of the Gospel of Mark,[19] despite all the strong church tradition to the contrary, reveals an additional problem that the Griesbach Hypothesis faces.

As we have mentioned, the strongest argument in favor of the Griesbach Hypothesis lies in the area of the agreements of Matthew and Luke against Mark. It is therefore not surprising that proponents of this theory have emphasized this issue a great deal and that defenders of the two-source hypothesis have spent a great deal of effort "explaining" these agreements. There are times, however, that even the Griesbach Hypothesis cannot explain the phenomena very well. One of the strongest Matthew–Luke agreements against Mark is found in Mark 3:22–27 and the parallels. For example:

5.1

Matthew 12:24–30	Mark 3:22–27	Luke 11:15, 17–23
[24]But when the Pharisees heard it they	[22]And the scribes who came down from Jerusalem	[15]But some of them
said,	said,	said,
"It is only by Beelzebul,	"He is possessed by Beelzebul, and by	"He casts out demons by Beelzebul,
the prince of demons,	the prince of demons	the prince of demons;" . . .
that this man casts out demons."	he casts out the demons."	
	[23]And he	[17]But he,
[25]Knowing their thoughts,		knowing their thoughts,
	called them to him, and	

18. See here Tuckett, *Griesbach Hypothesis*, p. 13.
19. Farmer, *The Synoptic Problem*, pp. 226–27.

he said to them,	said to them in parables, "How can Satan cast out Satan?	said to them,
"Every kingdom divided against itself is laid waste,	[24]If a kingdom is divided against itself, that kingdom cannot stand. [25]And if	"Every kingdom divided against itself is laid waste,
and no city or house divided against itself	a house is divided against itself, that house	and a divided household
will stand; [26]and if Satan casts out Satan,	will not be able to stand. [26]And if Satan has risen up against himself	falls. [18]And if Satan
he is divided against himself; how then will his kingdom stand?	and is divided, he cannot stand, but is coming to an end.	also is divided against himself, how will his kingdom stand?
		For you say that I cast out demons by Beelzebul.

[27]And if
I cast out demons
by Beelzebul,
by whom do your sons
  cast
them out? Therefore they
shall be your judges. [28]But
if it is
by the Spirit of God
that I cast out demons,
then the kingdom of God
  has
come upon you.
		[19]And if
		I cast out demons
		by Beelzebul,
		by whom do your sons
		  cast
		them out? Therefore they
		shall be your judges. [20]But
		if it is
		by the finger of God
		that I cast out demons,
		then the kingdom of God
		  has
		come upon you.

[29]Or how can one enter a strong man's house	[27]But no one can enter a strong man's house	[21]When a strong man, fully armed, guards his own palace, his goods are in peace;
and plunder his goods, unless he first binds the strong man?	and plunder his goods, unless he first binds the strong man;	[22]but when one stronger than he assails him and overcomes him, he takes away his armor in which he trusted, and

Then indeed
he may plunder his house.
[30]He who is not with me is
against me, and he who
  does
not gather with me
  scatters.
	then indeed
	he may plunder his house.
		divides his spoil.
		[23]He who is not with me is
		against me, and he who
		  does
		not gather with me
		  scatters.

The Matthew–Luke agreements (see especially Matt. 12:26–28, 30, and their Lukan parallels) in this pericope have been frequently explained by the two-source hypothesis as due to an overlapping of Q with Mark. That the two-source hypothesis has a difficulty here need not be denied, *but* the Griesbach Hypothesis also has a serious problem in explaining this passage on the basis of the normal "griesbachian" behavior of Mark. According to the Griesbach Hypothesis, at least as proposed by Farmer,[20] the reason why there are few major Matthew–Luke agreements against Mark, in contrast to Matthew–Mark agreements against Luke and Mark–Luke agreements against Matthew, is that Mark did not wish to depart from any text to which Matthew and Luke bore "concurrent testimony." Yet if one carefully compares the parallel passages listed above, it is precisely where Matthew and Luke agree exactly and bear "concurrent testimony" (i.e., at Matthew 12:26b–28/Luke 11:19–20; Matthew 12:30/Luke 11:23; cf. also Matthew 12:32/Luke 12:10; Matthew 12:43–45/Luke 11:24–26) that Mark *does* depart from his sources![21] As a result, the Griesbach Hypothesis also has difficulty explaining this passage, which supposedly argues strongly in favor of this theory. Actually the more striking the Matthew–Luke agreements against Mark here and elsewhere, the more difficult it is to explain why Mark omitted their concurrent testimony; and if one seeks to explain this by stating that Mark was not bound by such concurrent testimony, one immediately raises the question of why there are not therefore many more Matthew–Luke agreements against Mark in the triple tradition.

It must be acknowledged that ultimately any solution of the Synoptic Problem can be explained by some mathematical-like suggestion of how the Evangelists used the sources available to them. One need but reflect on the fact that there exists today a "Flat-Earth Society," which maintains that the earth is in fact flat and supports this view with many ingenious theories and explanations. The revival of the Griesbach Hypothesis by Farmer and others, with the corresponding attack on the two-source hypothesis, has been of great value. It has clearly reminded us that the two-source hypothesis was, is, and will always be a "theory." It must never be accepted as a "fact" or "law." It must continually be questioned and challenged. On the other hand, although at times the Griesbach Hypothesis can "mathematically" ex-

---

20. Ibid., pp. 79, 83, 217.

21. Howard Biggs comes to a similar conclusion: "In fact, it looks as if, far from Mark following his sources where they bear concurrent testimony, he has painstakingly avoided the coincidences of Matthew and Luke" ("The Q Debate since 1955," *Themelios* 6, no. 2, [1981]: 23). Biggs is referring here to the parable of the mustard seed, but the same can be said of the Beelzebul controversy.

plain agreements in order and wording, it simply is not a convincing theory as to how Matthew, Mark, and Luke are related. It does far better in the abstract and in theory than in detail. Redaction-critical studies based on Matthew's and Luke's use of Mark are much more convincing than the far fewer attempts to do redaction criticism based upon the Griesbach Hypothesis. Matthew's and Luke's use of Mark ultimately "makes sense." It is understandable. The same cannot, at the present time at least, be said of the Griesbach Hypothesis' explanation of Mark's use of Matthew and Luke.

The Priority of Mark and Q

It seems reasonably clear from the various arguments presented above that the most basic literary relationship that exists between the synoptic Gospels is that Matthew and Luke both used the Gospel of Mark. The question of whether they used the same Mark that we have today or an Ur-Markus should be decided in favor of the former. While it would be unlikely that Matthew and Luke used the "original" Mark and also unlikely that they used exactly the same copy of Mark, there is no need to posit their use of an Ur-Markus or a recension of Mark. Such theories tend to raise more problems than they resolve. Generally an Ur-Markus begins to look so much like Mark that they are difficult to distinguish. Furthermore, a Markan recension is impossible to prove or disprove. Probably the Matthew–Luke agreements in the triple tradition can be explained as well by the redactional work of the individual Evangelists and some minor scribal errors in the Markan textual tradition as they can by the theory of either an Ur-Markus or a later recension of Mark.

Concerning the additional material common to Matthew and Luke but not found in Mark, it seems that despite the efforts of Taylor and others, the lack of a demonstrable common order of this material argues somewhat against the traditional Q hypothesis. It is probably better to refer to the "Q material" than to the "Q document." The exactness in wording of some of this material is not sufficient to require a specific written source for all the Q material, for this exactness can be equally explained by the use of either common oral material or common written sources. Also, the fact that at times the wording of the Q material is not very exact tends to weaken any argument that the exactness of some of the Q material requires a single written source that included both the exact and not-very-exact Q material in Matthew and Luke. It is probably best to say that besides Mark, Matthew and Luke also possessed and used various written and oral traditions in common, and these now appear in their Gospels as the Q material.

It also seems clear that along with Mark and the oral and written sources from which Matthew and Luke obtained their Q material, Matthew and Luke possessed other oral and written materials, which overlapped much of what they found in Mark and their Q sources and also included material not found in any of the synoptic Gospels. Although Luke 1:1–2 makes mention of such sources, it is impossible today to reconstruct them with any certainty.

Conclusion

The "solution" of the Synoptic Problem, which assumes the priority of Mark and the existence of Q, has involved a great deal of time and effort on the part of scholars over the centuries. Assuming that the Synoptic Problem has indeed been "solved," the question must be raised as to what practical value all this has for the study of these Gospels. Other than keeping scholars occupied and publishers busy publishing the myriad works on the subject, does the "solution" have any useful significance for the work of exegesis? Or is this all an esoteric rite of initiation into the gnostic fraternity of "Synoptikers"? It is to this question that we must now turn.

6

The Value of Literary Criticism

It has been said that probably more scholarly time and effort has been spent by New Testament scholars on the solution of the Synoptic Problem than on any other New Testament issue. Some scholars still question whether all this effort has produced a viable solution to the problem; some even question if a solution is possible. On the other hand, if we are optimistic and assume that scholarship has reached a solution such as indicated in the last chapter, the question still remains as to what practical benefits such a solution yields. How does the solution of the Synoptic Problem affect the study of these Gospels? Do we approach Matthew, Mark, and Luke any differently if we understand that Mark was written first and was used by Matthew and Luke in the composition of their Gospels? Does source criticism offer any practical benefits for the student of the Gospels? The following are some suggestions as to various ways in which the literary solution of the Synoptic Problem assists in the study of these Gospels.

Source Criticism and Historical Criticism

From the earliest New Testament scholarship, the quest for the solution of the Synoptic Problem was intimately associated with the quest for the historical Jesus. It is interesting to note that the publication of H. S. Reimarus' notes by G. E. Lessing (which inaugurated the quest for the historical Jesus) and the publication of J. J. Griesbach's *Synopsis Evangeliorum* both occurred in 1776. Many of the scholars who wrote about the quest for the historical Jesus also wrote about the Synoptic Problem. For them, the quest for the Jesus of history required that the most primitive and basic building block—the most "historical" source of the canonical Gospels—be found for the foundation of such a quest. For many scholars, especially in the nineteenth century, the solution of the Synoptic Problem was a prerequisite for a proper study of the life of Jesus of Nazareth. Only when the "Ur-source" of these Gospels was found could a truly objective historical investigation be made of the life of Jesus. It would be wrong to conclude, however, that a "solution" claiming that Mark was first was simply a reaction to D. F. Strauss's (and F. C. Baur's) negativism toward historical questions concerning the Jesus of history and their advocacy of Matthean priority.[1]

With the general acceptance of the two-source hypothesis, nineteenth-century research into the life of Jesus centered on the Gospel of Mark. Whereas in previous centuries Mark tended to be neglected and ignored in favor of Matthew, Mark now occupied the center stage in gospel studies. Scholars became convinced that if one eliminated certain miraculous features in Mark, one then possessed a basically reliable historical outline of the life of Jesus of Nazareth. The degree to which one followed the Markan outline depended, of course, upon one's theological position, but it was nevertheless agreed upon by almost all that, since Mark was the earliest Gospel, it was more historical and less "corrupted" by the theology of the early church.

Two events in the twentieth century changed all this. One was the publication of William Wrede's *Das Messiasgeheimnis In den Evangelien* in 1901.[2] Wrede, in this early redactional study of Mark, demonstrated that Mark was not an objective historical biography of Jesus at all. On the contrary, Mark was a theologian who wrote with a particular theological bias and emphasis. Wrede argued in fact that the "messianic secret" in Mark (Jesus' desire for secrecy) was a Markan theological emphasis rather than an actual pattern in the life of the historical Jesus. The impact of Wrede's work was great. The quest for the historical Jesus received a mortal wound, and if we were to pinpoint the death throes of this quest, it would probably be best dated with the publication of Wrede's work in 1901.[3] Since Mark, the basic Ur-gospel, was no

---

1. C. M. Tuckett has clearly refuted this view proposed by W. F. Farmer and H.-H. Stoldt (*The Revival of the Griesbach Hypothesis* [Cambridge: Cambridge University, 1983], pp. 3–7).

2. The English translation of this work appeared in 1971 under the title *The Messianic Secret*.

3. It should be noted that Albert Schweitzer's *The Quest of the Historical Jesus* (1910), which itself was one of the causes of the death of the old quest, first appeared in German in 1906 under the title *Von Reimarus zu Wrede*, i.e., *From Reimarus* [the one who started the quest] *to Wrede*.

longer to be seen as an objective historical biography of Jesus and since Matthew and Luke were less reliable still, a quest for the historical Jesus was now deemed impossible. With Wrede, confidence in the historical basis of the quest was destroyed, and the optimism surrounding such a quest came to an end.

Another "event" that affected the quest for the historical Jesus and the assessment of the historical value of the Ur-gospel (Mark) was the rise of form criticism after World War I. More will be said in detail concerning this later,[4] but suffice it to say here that the almost-simultaneous appearance of the works of K. L. Schmidt, Martin Dibelius, and Rudolf Bultmann, which inaugurated the form-critical investigation of the New Testament and of the synoptic Gospels in particular, demonstrated that Mark (and also the other Gospels) was not a simple objective biography of Jesus constructed along chronological lines. The skepticism raised by Wrede concerning both Mark and the possibility of a historical quest was now "confirmed" by the form critics. The quest for the historical Jesus seemed for the most part a dead issue. Wrede and the form critics had destroyed the confidence in the basic historical tool—the Ur-gospel, or Mark. Along with these two causes for fading interest in the quest, three more should be mentioned briefly. Albert Schweitzer helped bring about the death of the original quest by showing that the liberal Jesus of the questers was simply a Jesus created in their own image and that the real Jesus was in fact an enigma to the liberal. If the product of any quest was going to be a misguided apocalyptic preacher of judgment (so Schweitzer), why bother to search for such a Jesus! As a result, liberal scholarship became disinterested in the quest. Two other contributing factors involved the work of Martin Kähler and Wilhelm Dilthey. Kähler clearly demonstrated that the Jesus who was important for faith in the church was never the liberal Jesus of the critical-historical method but the Christ of faith (i.e., the supernatural Christ of our Gospels); Dilthey demonstrated that the whole idea of objective historical research was both impossible and even undesirable. As a result, the former, like Schweitzer, helped destroy the motivation for the quest; the latter, like Wrede and the form critics, helped destroy confidence in its very possibility.

That the earlier questers built their research upon a naive view of the Evangelists is now clear. None of the Evangelists, not even the "earliest" (Mark), was interested in producing an objective historical biography of the life of Jesus. How could one expect committed Christians

4. See below pp. 161–228.

like Matthew, Mark, and Luke to be "objective"? In fact who is ever totally objective about Jesus? Jesus himself said, "He who is not with me is against me" (Matt. 12:30). Furthermore, the different order and arrangement of some of the gospel materials in the synoptic Gospels should have been sufficient warning against interpreting the order of Mark in a strict chronological fashion. Yet the resulting skepticism toward the historical veracity of the Gospels that reigned in Germany after World War I was unjustified. In his famous address to the "Marburgers" on October 20, 1953, Ernst Käsemann said, "We should also be overlooking the fact that there are still pieces of the Synoptic tradition which the historian has to acknowledge as authentic if he wishes to remain an historian at all."[5]

We still must ask how our knowledge of the relationship between the synoptic Gospels assists us in historical criticism. One way is by means of the "Criterion of Multiple Attestation." Essentially this criterion works as follows: Assuming that the Markan, the Q, and the unique Matthean (M), Lukan (L), and Johannine material come from different sources, if a teaching or activity of Jesus is witnessed to in a number of these sources rather than just one (e.g., John or M), the probability of its historicity or authenticity is much greater. In other words, each source of the Gospels acts as a witness before the judgment seat of history, and the more independent witnesses (i.e., sources) that can give testimony, the stronger the case. An example of how this works is as follows. Did Jesus teach that the kingdom of God had actually come in some way in his ministry? (Or to word this differently—Did Jesus teach a "realized eschatology"?) We find support for this view in the Markan material (Mark 2:21–22), the Q material (Luke 11:20/Matt. 12:28), the M material (Matt. 5:17), the L material (Luke 17:20–21), and in John 12:31. With this kind of multiple support from a fivefold tradition, certainly any burden of proof should then lie with those scholars who would *deny* that Jesus taught that in his coming the kingdom of God had arrived in some unique way. Another example would be Jesus' use of the self-designation "Son of man", which likewise appears in all the gospel strata: Mark 2:10; Q (Luke 7:34/Matt. 11:19); M (Matt. 10:23); L (Luke 19:10); and John 5:26–27. It is, of course, true that this tool cannot provide historical certainty but only probability, but in historical matters this is all we can ever hope to achieve. Faith and belief may have unique access to historical certainty; but historical research can only deal with probabilities, and in this area

5. Ernst Käsemann, "The Problem of the Historical Jesus," in *Essays on New Testament Themes*, trans. W. J. Montague (Naperville: Allenson, 1964), p. 46.

the tool of multiple attestation that is based upon source criticism does prove useful.[6]

Another tool that source criticism has found useful is the "Criterion of Divergent Patterns from the Redaction."[7] By the use of source criticism we have become better able to ascertain the linguistic tendencies and theological emphases of the individual Evangelists. When we discover in a Gospel individual pieces of tradition that appear contrary to the normal style or emphases of that Evangelist, this witnesses to the fact that this tradition had such a solid place in the life of the church that the Evangelist was reluctant to omit it; he included it in his Gospel, despite his own theological emphasis, due to its being so well known. An example of this can be found in Matthew 11:13. It is evident from reading Matthew, especially when reading it alongside the other synoptic Gospels, that this Evangelist emphasized strongly the permanent validity of the Old Testament law (cf. Matt. 3:15; 5:17–20; 7:12; 12:5 [note the Markan and Lukan parallel]; 23:23; etc.). Yet in Matthew 11:13 we read, "For all the prophets and the law prophesied until John. . . ." Here, "despite the author," we find a tradition whose presence in Matthew can only be due to the fact that it was so clearly a part of the church's tradition that Matthew included it, even though it appears at first glance to conflict with his own emphasis on the permanence of the law.

This same criterion can also be used in a negative way. It would appear that materials in a Gospel that reflect an Evangelist's unique theological emphasis are probably less authentic or historical, especially if they appear only in his unique material (M in Matthew and L in Luke) or in his redactional work (summaries, explanatory clauses, seams, etc.). Literary criticism has enabled us to distinguish more clearly the tradition from the redaction of the Evangelists.

Source Criticism and Redaction Criticism

One of the clearest contributions of source criticism lies in the area of redactional studies. In fact it can probably be said that the single most important tool of the redaction critic is source criticism. This is especially true with regard to Matthew and Luke, although less so with Mark. With regard to the former two Gospels, source criticism enables

6. For a fuller discussion see Robert H. Stein, "The 'Criteria' for Authenticity," in *Gospel Perspectives*, ed. R. T. France and David Wenham (Sheffield: JSOT Press, 1980), 1:229–32.

7. Ibid., pp. 247–48.

us to see the work of each Evangelist more clearly than if we simply read their Gospels in isolation from Mark or each other, for by comparing them to Mark (or to one another with regard to the Q material), we can perceive their own theological emphases. By the careful comparison of Matthew and Luke with Mark (or with each other), we can observe where they chose to change their source, and this frequently gives us a clue as to their particular theological interpretation of the traditions. Of course one should be suspicious of extremely subtle interpretations that seem to conflict with the plain straightforward reading of the Gospels, for the Evangelists could hardly have assumed that their readers would have a synopsis before them! As a result, each understood that what he wished to say must be understandable by the simple reading of his Gospel. Yet source criticism does enable us to perceive the Evangelists' emphases more readily than if we could not compare the Gospels with the sources they used. Perhaps this can be shown best by some examples.

In the opening verses of the story of Jesus' healing of the paralytic we have the following:

6.1

Matthew 9:1	Mark 2:1–2	Luke 5:17
[1]And getting into a boat he crossed over and came to his own city.	[1]And when he returned to Capernaum after some days, it was reported that he was at home. [2]And many were gathered together, so that there was no longer room for them, not even about the door; and he was preaching the word to them.	[17]On one of those days, as he was teaching, there were Pharisees and teachers of the law sitting by, who had come from every village of Galilee and Judea and from Jerusalem; and the power of the Lord was with him to heal.

Even though the Lukan emphasis of Jesus' anointing by the Holy Spirit and his healing ministry is evident by the simple reading of Luke's Gospel, this emphasis becomes even clearer when we realize that the reference to "the power of the Lord was with him to heal" is a Lukan redactional comment, which he has inserted into the Markan narrative that he used. The close relationship between "power" and "Spirit" in Luke (cf. Luke 1:17, 35; 4:14, 36 [cf. with 4:18–19]; 24:49 [cf. with the following references: Acts 1:8; 2:1f.; 8:18–19; 10:38]) also indicates that this insertion must be read in the light of the birth narratives, which portray the coming one as conceived by the Holy Spirit (Luke 1:35), and in light of Jesus' anointing by the Spirit at his baptism (Luke 3:22).[8] Then Luke, unlike Matthew and Mark, tells how Jesus "full of the Holy Spirit" (Luke 4:1) is led by the Spirit into the wilderness to be tempted. Thereupon Jesus "in the power of the Spirit" (a Lukan addition to the Markan parallel—Luke 4:14) returns to Galilee and there in the synagogue—an account found only in Luke 4:18–21—Jesus turns to the following place in the Book of Isaiah and reads:

> "The Spirit of the Lord is upon me, because he has anointed me to preach good news to the poor. He has sent me to proclaim release to the captives and recovering of sight to the blind, to set at liberty those who are oppressed, to proclaim the acceptable year of the Lord." And he closed the book, and gave it back to the attendant, and sat down; and the eyes of all in the synagogue were fixed on him. And he began to say to them, "Today this scripture has been fulfilled in your hearing."

It is clear from all this that Luke wishes to tell his readers that Jesus' birth and ministry originated in the power of the Spirit, and in Acts Luke reveals that this same Spirit empowers the church as well. Our use of source criticism enables us to see this Lukan emphasis more clearly and much more easily.

Another example of this same emphasis is found in the Q material in Luke.

6.2

Matthew 7:11	Luke 11:13
[11]If you then, who are evil, know how to give good gifts to your children, how much more will your Father who is in heaven give good things to those who ask him!	[13]If you then, who are evil, know how to give good gifts to your children, how much more will the heavenly Father give the Holy Spirit to those who ask him!"

It is probable that the reference to "good things" in Matthew is more authentic, for it is easy to imagine that Luke would have changed Matthew's "good things," which no doubt *were* good things in a spirit-

---

8. Note how Luke emphasizes this by his use of the expression "in bodily form."

ual sense, to the best "thing" he could think of—the Holy Spirit. This Lukan redaction once again reveals to us the strong Lukan emphasis in this area.

We have pointed out in chapter 2 that one of Matthew's emphases lies in Jesus' being the promised "Son of David."[9] This is most clearly seen in those instances where Matthew has added this title to his source, as in the two examples below.

6.3

Matthew 15:21–22	Mark 7:24–25
[21]And Jesus went away from there and withdrew to the district of Tyre and Sidon.	[24]And from there he arose and went away to the region of Tyre and Sidon. And he entered a house, and would not have any one know it; yet he could not be hid.
[22]And behold, a Canaanite woman from that region came out and cried, "Have mercy on me, O Lord, Son of David; my daughter is severely possessed by a demon."	[25]But immediately a woman, whose little daughter was possessed by an unclean spirit, heard of him, and came and fell down at his feet.

6.4

Matthew 21:9	Mark 11:9–10	Luke 19:37b–38
[9]And the crowds	[9]And those	. . . the whole multitude of the
that went before him and that followed him	who went before and those who followed	disciples began to rejoice and praise God with a loud voice for all the mighty works that they had seen,
shouted, "Hosanna to the Son of David! Blessed is he who comes in the name of the Lord!	cried out, "Hosanna! Blessed is he who comes in the name of the Lord! [10]Blessed is the kingdom of our father David that is coming!	[38]saying, "Blessed is the King who comes in the name of the Lord! Peace in heaven and
Hosanna in the highest!"	Hosanna in the highest!"	glory in the highest!"

By the use of source criticism, we can see clearly this particular Matthean emphasis by the fact that he has added this expression to his Markan source. The ease by which such emphases are observed should

9. See above pp. 77–80.

also be noted. By the use of a synopsis we know that this particular emphasis in these instances comes from the hand of Matthew.[10]

Another Matthean redactional feature that is clearly seen in a synoptic comparison involves his emphasis on the fulfillment of the Scriptures in Jesus Christ.[11] Such an emphasis can be observed by the simple reading of the Gospel of Matthew, but the fact that time and time again Matthew added this to his source makes this all the more clear, as we see in the next two examples.

6.5

Matthew 8:16–17	Mark 1:32–34	Luke 4:40–41
[16]That evening	[32]That evening, at sundown,	[40]Now when the sun was setting, all those who had any that were sick with various diseases
they	they	
brought to him many who were possessed with demons;	brought to him all who were sick or possessed with demons. [33]And the whole city was gathered together about the door.	brought them to him;
		and he laid his hands on every one of them and healed them.
	[34]And he healed many who were sick with various diseases,	
and he cast out the spirits with a word, and healed all who were sick.	and cast out many demons;	[41]And demons also came out of many,
		crying, "You are the Son of God!" But he rebuked them, and would not allow them to speak, because they knew that he was the Christ.
	and he would not permit the demons to speak, because they knew him.	
[17]This was to fulfil what was spoken by the prophet Isaiah, "He took our infirmities and bore our diseases."		

6.6

Matthew 13:34–35	Mark 4:33–34
[34]All this Jesus said to the crowds in parables;	[33]With many such parables

10. Cf. also Matthew 12:23; 21:15 and parallels.
11. Cf. also Matthew 4:14; 12:17; 13:14; 21:4 and parallels.

indeed he said nothing to them
without a parable.

[35]This was to fulfil what was spoken by
the prophet. "I will open my mouth in
parables, I will utter what has been
hidden since the foundation of the
world."

he spoke the word to them, as they were
able to hear it;
[34]he did not speak to them
without a parable,
but privately to his own disciples he
explained everything.

Still another example of how we can observe a Matthean redactional emphasis by means of source criticism is found in the Sermon on the Mount. There we find a parallel in Luke's Sermon on the Plain:

6.7

Matthew 5:43–48

[43]"You have heard that it was said,
'You shall love your neighbor and hate
your enemy.'
[44]But I say to you,

Love your enemies

and pray for those who persecute you,
[45]so that you may be sons of your Father
who is in heaven; for he makes his sun
rise on the evil and on the good, and
sends rain on the just and the unjust.
[46]For if you love those who love you,
what reward have you?
Do not even the tax collectors
do the same?
[47]And if you salute only your brethren,
what more are you doing than others? Do
not even the Gentiles do the same?

[48]You, therefore, must be perfect,
as your heavenly Father is perfect.

Luke 6:27–28, 32–36

[27]"But I say to you
that hear,
Love your enemies,
do good to those who hate you, [28]bless
those who curse you,
pray for those who abuse you.

[32]"If you love those who love you,
what credit is that to you?
For even sinners
love those who love them.
[33]And if you do good to those who do
good to you, what credit is that to you?
For even sinners do the same. [34]And if
you lend to those from whom you hope
to
receive, what credit is that to you?
Even sinners lend to sinners, to receive
as much again. [35]But love your enemies,
and do good, and lend, expecting nothing
in return; and your reward will be
great, and you will be sons of the Most
High; for he is kind to the ungrateful
and the selfish.
[36]Be merciful,
even as your Father is merciful.

The reference to "being perfect" in Matthew 5:48 has frequently caused problems for readers. It would appear that Matthew has changed here the more authentic "merciful," which is found in Luke and has many parallels in Jewish literature, to "perfect."[12] This he has also done in Matthew 19:21 where we have these parallels:

6.8

Matthew 19:20–21	Mark 10:20–21	Luke 18:21–22
[20]The young man said to him,	[20]And he said to him, "Teacher,	[21]And he said,
"All these I have observed; what do I still lack?"	all these I have observed from my youth."	"All these I have observed from my youth."
[21]Jesus	[21]And Jesus looking upon him loved him,	[22]And when Jesus heard it,
said to him, "If you would be perfect, go, sell what you possess and give to the poor, and you will have treasure in heaven; and come, follow me."	and said to him, "You lack one thing; go, sell what you have, and give to the poor, and you will have treasure in heaven; and come, follow me."	he said to him, "One thing you still lack. Sell all that you have and distribute to the poor, and you will have treasure in heaven; and come, follow me."

This particular redaction of Matthew fits well his emphasis that "unless your righteousness exceeds that of the scribes and Pharisees, you will never enter the kingdom of heaven" (Matt. 5:20), and it serves as an excellent conclusion for Matthew 5:21–48, where the greater righteousness is taught by Jesus. The change of "merciful" to "perfect" indicates that, for the Evangelist, Matthew 5:48 serves as a conclusion not just for Matthew 5:43–48 (as Luke 6:36 does for Luke 6:27–36) but for all the references to "you have heard that it was said . . . but I say . . ." in Matthew 5:21–48. The latter verses, for the Evangelist, are therefore not to be interpreted as a repudiation of the Old Testament but rather as the "exceeding" righteousness, which Jesus demands (5:20) and which is required if one is to be "perfect."

One other example of a Matthean redaction is found in Jesus' teaching on "clean and unclean." If we compare the following parallel accounts, we find an interesting emphasis in Matthew.

6.9

Matthew 15:16–20	Mark 7:18–23
[16]And he said, "are you also still without understanding?	[18]And he said to them, "Then are you also without understanding?

---

12. See I. Howard Marshall, *The Gospel of Luke,* The New International Greek Testament Commentary (Grand Rapids: Eerdmans, 1978), p. 265.

[17]Do you not see that whatever goes into the mouth	Do you not see that whatever goes into a man from outside cannot defile him, [19]since it enters, not his heart but
passes into the stomach, and so passes on?	his stomach, and so passes on? (Thus he declared all foods clean.) [20]And he said,
[18]But what comes out of the mouth proceeds from the heart, and this defiles a man. [19]For out of the heart	"What comes out of a man is what defiles a man. [21]For from within, out of the heart of man,
come evil thoughts,	come evil thoughts, fornication, theft,
murder, adultery, fornication, theft,	murder, adultery, [22]coveting, wickedness,
false witness,	deceit, licentiousness, envy,
slander.	slander, pride, foolishness.
[20]These are	[23]All these evil things come from within, and they
what defile a man; but to eat with unwashed hands does not defile a man."	defile a man."

It is evident from the above that Matthew gives to the pericope a unique emphasis, which involves the fact that the words one speaks with one's *mouth* reveal one's heart. This emphasis is also found elsewhere in Matthew. Note his addition to the pericope concerning the unpardonable sin, which is found in neither the Markan or Lukan parallels: "I tell you, on the day of judgment men will render account for every careless word they utter; for by your words you will be justified, and by your words you will be condemned" (Matt. 12:36–37).[13]

From the above we can note that in Matthew there is present a strong emphasis concerning the care needed in speaking and a warning against the use of the mouth for evil. For the present writer, this Matthean emphasis first became clear through source criticism when noting Matthew's use of his Markan source in this passage.

When it comes to the Gospel of Mark, redactional-critical investigation is much more difficult because we do not have available the source Mark used in the writing of his Gospel. Attempts have been made to reconstruct certain pre-Markan complexes, but such reconstructions are quite hypothetical, and if Mark himself composed these complexes, their value for comparison with his Gospel in order to ascertain a

13. To these can also be added Matthew 5:33–37; 12:34–35; 21:16.

Markan redaction criticism is questionable. On the other hand, if most of the gospel materials available to Mark were in short, isolated traditions (except for possibly the passion narrative), we are able to arrive at his editorial work by the investigation of the Markan seams, insertions, summaries, organization, and so on.[14] Here, however, we are dealing more with form-critical insights and presuppositions (which will be discussed in the next section) than with source-critical ones.

Source Criticism and Hermeneutics in General

There are numerous instances where various hermeneutical insights are gained by the comparison of the synoptic Gospels. Some of these insights are furthermore independent of any particular solution of the Synoptic Problem. One of these lies in the area of the implications of the text.[15] If we can by source criticism arrive at the more primitive form of a text, then we can note how the various Evangelists understood and interpreted that text. In other words, if we can isolate the earliest form of the text or perhaps even the *ipsissima verba* or *vox* of Jesus, we can then note how each Evangelist interpreted that saying. In so doing we have a canonical and authoritative interpretation of that saying by the Evangelist that brings out certain implications or submeanings of Jesus' words. These interpretations furthermore possess a unique authority, since they come from the inspired authors of the Gospels. It must, of course, be noted that such a hermeneutical view assumes that the Scriptures are divinely inspired, a view the author accepts as true. For someone *not* believing in the inspired nature of the Gospels, such interpretations by the Evangelists may be viewed as "corruptions," "errors," "misunderstandings," "resource material for the study of the early church," and so on; but if one attributes divine (i.e., canonical) authority to these interpretations, source analysis provides rich insights into the meanings and implications of the texts.

Understanding the Meaning of the Text

An example of this principle involves Jesus' teaching on divorce. We find the following in the Gospels:

6.10

Matthew 19:9	Mark 10:11–12
[9]And I say to you; whoever divorces his wife,	[11]And he said to them, "Whoever divorces his wife

14. See below pp. 251–58.
15. At this point should be noted the author's indebtedness to E. D. Hirsch, Jr., *Validity in Interpretation* (New Haven: Yale University, 1967).

except for unchastity,
and marries another,
commits adultery."

and marries another,
commits adultery
against her; [12]and if she divorces her
husband and marries another, she
commits adultery."

6.11

Matthew 5:31–32	Luke 16:18
[31]"It was also said, 'Whoever divorces his wife, let him give her a certificate of divorce.' [32]But I say to you that every one who divorces his wife, except on the ground of unchastity,	[18]"Every one who divorces his wife
makes her an adultress; and whoever marries a divorced woman commits adultery.	and marries another commits adultery, and he who marries a woman divorced from her husband commits adultery.

To these can be added the following passage from Paul, who clearly was aware of Jesus' teaching on this subject.

> To the married I give charge, not I but the Lord, that the wife should not separate from her husband (but if she does, let her remain single or else be reconciled to her husband)—and that the husband should not divorce his wife.
> To the rest I say, not the Lord, that if any brother has a wife who is an unbeliever, and she consents to live with him, he should not divorce her. If any woman has a husband who is an unbeliever, and he consents to live with her, she should not divorce him. For the unbelieving husband is consecrated through his wife, and the unbelieving wife is consecrated through her husband. Otherwise, your children would be unclean, but as it is they are holy. But if the unbelieving partner desires to separate, let it be so; in such a case the brother or sister is not bound [1 Cor. 7:10–15a].

It seems reasonably clear in light of the threefold testimony of Mark, Q (Luke), and Paul, and by the difficulty of the saying when it lacks the exception for unchastity, that this form of the saying (i.e., without Matthew's "exception clause") is more authentic. It is also difficult to believe that Jesus spoke this saying on divorce in two separate forms on various occasions and that Mark, Q (Luke), and Paul remembered (or used) only the one form and Matthew only the other. Hypothetically, of course, this is possible, but it is far less likely than the view that the "exception clause" is an interpretative comment added by Matthew.

If we assume that the "exception clause" is a Matthean comment, of what value is this? The value lies in the fact that it reveals how Matthew understood Jesus' teaching on divorce, i.e., that it was an example of overstatement for effect. That Jesus frequently used overstatement and hyperbole is evident from such passages as Matthew 5:29–30; 6:2–4; 7:1, 3–5; 10:34; Mark 10:24–25; Luke 14:26; and so on.[16] Mark, Q (Luke), and Paul faithfully reproduce this overstatement, whereas Matthew provides us with an implication and submeaning of the statement, which he believed Jesus would accept and which is equally authoritative. Paul also reveals another, but different, submeaning of Jesus' statement in 1 Corinthians 7:15, which involves the situation in which an unbelieving partner deserts his or her believing mate. Through the source-critical analysis of this saying we have gained hermeneutical insight into the implications of the text in Mark 10:11–12 and Luke 16:18 and thus have also received help in how to apply this teaching to our present-day situation. The very fact that Jesus used overstatement in his teaching on divorce reveals how clearly he hated and opposed divorce. For him, no divorce is good, because every one witnesses to a failure of the pattern God ordained (Mark 10:6–9). That there may be "acceptable" causes for divorce other than the ones mentioned by Matthew and Paul is possible, but even speculating academically as to their nature appears to be out of tune with the will of God (cf. Mark 10:2)! Jesus' use of exaggeration clearly reveals this. There may be other instances in which divorce is a lesser of two evils, but any such instance witnesses to a failure of the divine pattern and purpose in marriage, and clearly the heavy burden of proof would be upon anyone seeking to justify such a divorce.

Another example of how one can gain insights as to the implications of a text by observing the redaction of the Evangelists is the parallel we find in Matthew 10:37 and Luke 14:26.

6.12

Matthew 10:37–38	Luke 14:26–27
[37]"He who	[26]"If any one comes to me and
loves father or mother more than me	does not hate his own father and mother
is not worthy of me;	
	and wife
and he who loves son or daughter	and children
	and brothers and sisters, yes, and
	even his own life,

16. For a fuller discussion of overstatement and hyperbole in the teachings of Jesus, see Robert H. Stein, *Difficult Sayings in the Gospels: Jesus' Use of Overstatement and Hyperbole* (Grand Rapids: Baker, 1985).

more than me	
is not worthy of me;	he cannot be my disciple.
[38]and he who	[27]Whoever
does not take his cross	does not bear his own cross
and follow me	and come after me,
is not worthy of me.	cannot be my disciple.

That we are dealing with the same saying is witnessed to by the fact that both Matthew and Luke have, after this saying concerning the family, the saying about taking up a cross and following Jesus. It is therefore probable that they are quoting the same saying of Jesus and are possibly using the same source. The authenticity of the saying in Luke 14:26 is almost guaranteed by its difficulty. Whereas Luke is essentially a "literal" translation of Jesus' words in Greek, Matthew has interpreted this saying with a thought-for-thought equivalent, for he knew that "to hate" was simply a Semitic way of saying "to love less."[17] This is clear in Genesis 29:30–31, where Leah's being hated (v. 30) simply meant that she was loved less than Rachel (v. 29). Here we find that Matthew's translation of his source gives us insight not so much into the implications of the text as to its actual meaning, i.e., the meaning intended by the original author, Jesus. Another example of this can be found in the Lord's Prayer, in Luke's translation of "debts" (Matt. 6:12) as "sins" (Luke 11:4). Still another that can be mentioned, but this time in Matthew, is the Matthean version of the Beatitudes, where we find: "poor in spirit" and "hunger and thirst for righteousness." These reveal that we should not read Luke's "poor" (Luke 6:20) and "hunger" (Luke 6:21) too simplistically as referring to merely a financial situation.

A final example of how we can find hermeneutical insight through the use of literary criticism is found in the parable of the lost sheep (Matt. 18:10–14/Luke 15:3–7). Matthew has arranged this parable differently than Luke. In so doing he has shown that, although the immediate context in Luke involved Jesus' rebuke of the Pharisees and scribes for their inability to accept God's love for the outcasts, one implication of the parable's meaning involves the issue of how the church should reach out in loving acceptance to the lost little ones within its own community. Matthew reveals this by inserting the parable into a chapter of instructions for the church. With the change of audience we now have a new application of this parable of Jesus to a different context.[18]

17. Ibid., pp. 77–78.
18. See below pp. 247–51.

Understanding the Limits of Exegesis

One final value of source criticism that should be mentioned is that it enables us to understand what not to expect from the Gospels and thus helps us avoid a wrong use of them. In our discussion of the priority of Mark (chapter 2), we noted that at times Matthew and Mark may agree against Luke in the ordering of the various pericopes and at other times Mark and Luke may agree in this regard against Matthew. From this it is clear that the ordering of the various gospel incidents and teachings is not always the same in the synoptic Gospels. As a result it would appear that the gospel writers were not primarily concerned with providing their readers with a strict chronological sequence of events.[19] Calvin long ago pointed out that "the Evangelists did not definitely set down a fixed and distinct time sequence in their records. They neglected the order of days, and were content to put together the chief events in Christ's career as they saw them. They certainly took note of the years. . . . But they freely confuse [i.e., intermix] the miracles which occurred at much the same period, and this we shall see clearly from a number of cases."[20] Even earlier, Papias commented that "Mark became Peter's interpreter and wrote accurately all that he remembered, not, indeed, in order, of the things said or done by the Lord . . . so that Mark did nothing wrong in thus writing down single points as he remembered them."[21]

One lesson that source criticism teaches us, then, is that the gospel writers were not interested in providing us with a strict chronological sequence of the events and teachings of Jesus' life. Therefore, to interpret them in this manner is to do violence to the intention of the authors of Scripture. It is "what" Jesus said and did, not "when," that was of primary importance for the Evangelists. To claim as "historical" the chronological sequence found in a synoptic Gospel, or to build an argument upon a certain sequence found in one or more of them, encounters the observation that frequently one gospel writer purposely places an account in a different order for topical or theological reasons.

19. A somewhat amusing example of what happens when this insight is lost was provided in the sixteenth century by Andreas Osiander. Noting that the order of Jesus' crossing of the Sea of Galilee and his raising of Jairus' daughter from the dead occur in a somewhat different progression in Matthew and Mark, he suggested the following solution: Jesus immediately upon crossing the Sea of Galilee (Mark 5:21) raised Jairus' daughter from the dead (Mark 5:21–43). After this he performed another healing (Matt. 9:1–8), called Levi (Matt. 9:9–13), and taught (Matt. 9:14–17). In the meantime Jairus' daughter died a second time and thus Jesus had to return and raise her a second time from the dead as recorded in Matthew 9:18–26.

20. John Calvin, *A Harmony of the Gospels Matthew, Mark, and Luke*, ed. David W. Torrance and Thomas F. Torrance (Grand Rapids: Eerdmans, 1972), on Matthew 4:18.

21. Eusebius, *Ecclesiastical History*, 3.39.15 (Loeb).

Source criticism teaches us this fact, and if we ignore its implications in this area, we shall fall into error.

Source criticism also provides us insight as to how one should treat the sayings of Jesus found in the synoptic Gospels. The pursuit of the actual sayings of Jesus, i.e., his *ipsissima verba*, has had many advocates in the last two centuries. Both the old quest for the historical Jesus inaugurated by H. S. Reimarus in 1776 and the new quest inspired by Ernst Käsemann in 1953 have had as their goal ascertaining the very words of Jesus. Perhaps no modern scholar has worked harder on this than Joachim Jeremias. This was the basic goal of a lifetime of study. In his view the quest for the *ipsissima verba* was an absolute necessity, for it is only when we arrive at them that we find the word of God in its pure, unadulterated form.[22] Without entering into the question of either the possibility of such a quest or its chance of success, we can learn a great deal from source criticism as to its "necessity." It is evident from source criticism that the individual Evangelists ". . . *do not intend to provide us with a record of the precise literal words of Jesus.*"[23] Quite the contrary, they felt free to paraphrase, modify certain terms, and add comments, in order to help their readers understand the "significance" of what Jesus taught. The Evangelists had no obsession with the *ipsissima verba*, for they believed that they had authority to interpret these words for their audience. Whether we see this approach as an inspired and authoritative interpretation of Jesus' words or as an unauthorized speculation or even as corruption depends, of course, upon one's theological presuppositions—but the freedom of the Evangelists in handling the words of Jesus and their relative disinterest in simply attempting to reproduce his actual words should raise the question of *why* we are pursuing the *ipsissima verba*.

Sometimes such a quest may be necessary for apologetical reasons, for if there is no correlation or correspondence between the Christ of the Gospels and the Jesus who actually lived, we are indeed guilty of Docetism.[24] Worse still, we have become idolators and worship a Christ of our own making! Therefore, such a quest is necessary on occasion for apologetical reasons, despite various existential objections to the contrary.

22. See Joachim Jeremias, *The Problem of the Historical Jesus*, trans. Norman Perrin (Philadelphia: Fortress, 1964), pp. 22–24.

23. George E. Ladd, *The New Testament and Criticism* (Grand Rapids: Eerdmans, 1967), p. 121.

24. So Käsemann, "Historical Jesus," p. 34. (Docetism was an early Christian gnostic heresy, which, due to its view that matter was evil, denied the incarnation, for the assuming of true humanity, i.e., flesh and blood, would have contaminated the pure Son of God. As a result Docetists argued that it only "seemed" (*dokeō*) as if the Son of God truly became a man.)

A final reason for this quest is hermeneutical in nature. If we can ascertain at times the *ipsissima verba* of Jesus, we are doubly blessed, for we then possess both the divine word of Jesus and the divine word of the Evangelists. If we are successful, we then possess both the original message and its divinely inspired interpretation, which is in turn a divine message as well. The comparison of the *ipsissima verba* of Jesus and the message of the Evangelists also helps us to understand the significance of that message for today. In the author's *An Introduction to the Parables of Jesus*[25] four basic rules are given for interpreting the parables: (1) Seek the main point of the parable; (2) Seek the point that Jesus sought to make in the first *Sitz im Leben*, i.e., seek out the *ipsissima verba* and seek to discover what Jesus meant by them; (3) Seek the point that the Evangelist sought to make in the third *Sitz im Leben*, i.e., seek to understand how the Evangelist interpreted Jesus' words for his own situation; and (4) Seek, in light of the first three principles, to discover the present significance of the text. In trying to discover the present-day significance of a text (which is, after all, the ultimate goal of interpretation), how much better off are we if we are able to arrive at both the meaning in the original *Sitz im Leben* as well as that of the Evangelists!

Conclusion

We have discussed a number of ways in which the work of source criticism is valuable in studying the synoptic Gospels. Others could be mentioned,[26] but it would appear that the greatest value of source criticism lies in the area of redaction criticism. The most reliable way of observing the work of Matthew and Luke is by noting how they used their sources. Once again, the success of understanding the theology of Matthew and Luke on the basis of a Markan priority must be mentioned. In the examples given above we see that Matthew's and Luke's use of Mark and Q makes good sense and is helpful in explaining what Matthew and Luke are seeking to teach in their Gospels.[27]

25. Robert H. Stein, *An Introduction to the Parables of Jesus* (Philadelphia: Westminster, 1981), pp. 53–71.

26. Bruce Manning Metzger sees the solution of the Synoptic Problem as a helpful tool for the textual criticism of those Gospels (*The Text of the New Testament* [New York: Oxford University, 1968], p. 210).

27. It is, of course, true that if one despairs of any solution of the Synoptic Problem, then the value of source criticism is greatly diminished. Cf., for instance, M. D. Hooker: ". . . any attempt at reconstructing what lies behind our gospels is highly speculative, and will in large measure reflect our own presuppositions about the material" ("On Using the Wrong Tool," *Theology* 75 [1972]: 580). If the conclusions reached in the previous chapters are correct, however, then Hooker's comments are unnecessarily negative.

PART II

The Preliterary History
of the Gospel Traditions

7

The Rise and Presuppositions of Form Criticism

The Development of Form Criticism

At the turn of the twentieth century there was a general consensus that the Synoptic Problem had been "solved." The dominating view was that the earliest Gospel, Mark, had been written around A.D. 65 to 70 and that Matthew and Luke, who used Mark, were written anywhere between A.D. 75 and 95. It was thought, however, that Q may have been written earlier, perhaps around A.D. 50 or a few years later. In Old Testament studies Herman Gunkel, Hugo Gressmann, and others began to study the preliterary history of the Old Testament traditions and sought to deal with the history of its various genres and literary forms. Gunkel was particularly influential in his investigation of the oral history of the literary sources of the Pentateuch (JEDP). It is therefore not surprising that after the hiatus in biblical studies created by World War I, similar attention was given in New Testament studies to the "forms" of the gospel materials that lay behind the written Gospels. This was particularly true in Germany, whereas in England source-critical work was still the dominant concern.[1]

1. For an excellent description of the milieu out of which form criticism arose, see Werner Georg Kümmel, *The New Testament: The History of the Investigation of Its Problems,* trans. S. MacLean Gilmour and Howard C. Kee (New York: Abingdon, 1972), p. 330.

Although some scholars, such as J. G. von Herder (1796) and B. F. Wescott (1888), had earlier referred to the role of oral tradition in the formation of the Gospels, it was a triumvirate of German scholars who truly initiated the form-critical investigation of the Gospels. In 1919 there appeared both K. L. Schmidt's *Der Rahmen der Geschichte Jesu* and Martin Dibelius' *Die Formgeschichte des Evangeliums* (the English translation is entitled *From Tradition to Gospel*). The former work sought to demonstrate that the Markan framework was due to the construction of the Evangelist himself, and that before he wrote his Gospel the units of tradition found in it circulated mostly as individual, isolated units. The latter work, which gave the name to the new discipline, was primarily concerned with the classification of the various forms of the gospel tradition. In 1921 the third cardinal work appeared. This was Rudolf Bultmann's *Die Geschichte der Synoptischen Tradition* (the English translation is entitled *History of the Synoptic Tradition*), which exerted a great and lasting influence on the new discipline.[2]

The aims and goals of this discipline have been debated from the beginning. For some scholars the goal of form criticism, as its name indicates, is simply to classify the gospel traditions according to their form. Most form critics, however, do not limit their study to the classification of form but go beyond this useful but elementary procedure and seek to use form-critical insights and techniques in order to establish the history of the gospel traditions, i.e., to practice *Traditionsgeschichte*. Some practice form criticism primarily to delimit what is traditional from that which is the unique contribution of an Evangelist.[3] Others use form criticism in order to study what the Gospels tell us about the "situation in life" of the early church (i.e., the second *Sitz im Leben*). And still others use form-critical investigation in order to make historical judgments concerning the subject matter of the materials, i.e., to make decisions concerning the life of Christ. As can be seen, the goals, aims, and claims of form criticism are much debated. It is therefore important that we investigate the various presuppositions upon which this discipline is built.

The Presuppositions of Form Criticism

Form criticism, like any discipline or tool of investigation, is based upon certain fundamental presuppositions. Since these form-critical

2. A fourth work, that of M. Albertz, *Die Synoptischen Streitgespräche*, which had been completed earlier and was ready for publication in 1918, also appeared in 1921 and indicates that form-critical thinking was clearly "in the air."

3. For a discussion of how form criticism and redaction criticism are related and how they differ, see Robert H. Stein, "What is *Redaktionsgeschichte?*" *JBL* 88 (1969): 45–56.

presuppositions have far-reaching effects with regard to both how this "tool" is used and what conclusions result, it is crucial that we look carefully at the various stated and unstated presuppositions. Eight of these presuppositions follow.

1. "Before the Gospels were written there was a period of oral tradition."[4]

It can hardly be denied that there existed a period before the Gospels were written in which the Jesus traditions were transmitted orally. This is essentially a truism. Unless the Gospels were composed and completed by the time of the ascension of Jesus (or earlier), there must have been an interval between his death and resurrection and the writing of the Gospels, a period when Christians "talked about" Jesus. In fact we know that this oral period of transmission continued even after the Gospels were written, for Papias (c. 130) states, "For I did not suppose that information from books would help me so much as the word of a living and surviving voice."[5] The basic question with this presupposition is not whether an oral period of transmission existed, for surely it did. Rather, it concerns two related issues. The first involves the length of the period between the writing of the Gospels and the events recorded in them, and the second, which is even more important, is whether this period was exclusively oral.

It was generally believed by the early form critics that our Gospels were written "late," i.e., from A.D. 70 to 100. This lateness of the Gospels was variously explained. The most common reason given involved the imminent expectation of the parousia, or second coming. Since the early church supposedly expected that the Lord would return very shortly, there seemed no need to preserve the gospel traditions in written form. The time was too short. Only as the reality of the parousia's delay became apparent did the concern arise for having the gospel

---

4. E. Basil Redlich, *Form Criticism* (London: Duckworth, 1939), p. 34.

5. Eusebius, *Ecclesiastical History*, 3.39.4 (Loeb). A. F. Walls ("Papias and Oral Tradition," in *Vigiliae Christianae* 21 [1967]: 137–40) has argued forcefully that we should probably not read into Papias' statement a preference for the apostolic oral tradition over the written Gospels, for the latter were also apostolic. What is important for Papias is "apostolic origin," and even in his day some of the apostolic oral tradition still existed. This, of course, raises the interesting issue of whether certain *agrapha* exist outside of the biblical materials. It is very likely that in fact there are such authentic sayings of Jesus outside of the canonical texts, but whether they are demonstrable is another question. For a discussion of this issue, see the classic work of Joachim Jeremias, *Unknown Sayings of Jesus*, trans. Reginald Fuller (London: SPCK, 1957). See also Jack Finegan, *Hidden Records of the Life of Jesus* (Philadelphia: Pilgrim, 1969); Marvin W. Meyer, *The Secret Teachings of Jesus* (New York: Random, 1984); and *Gospel Perspectives*, vol. 5, *The Jesus Tradition Outside the Gospels*, ed. David Wenham (Sheffield: JSOT, 1984).

traditions recorded in writing.[6] Yet, with the discovery of the Dead Sea Scrolls, this traditional argument has lost almost all its force. Although the Qumran community had a view of the end times as imminent (it was the "last generation" [1 QpHab 2:7; 7:2]), it was still involved in the production of a large amount of literary material. It is therefore clear that a view of the impending end of the world does not necessitate a halt or even a delay in writing. On the contrary, it should be noted that often those groups or sects who most energetically proclaim the end of the world have the busiest printing presses!

Another reason frequently given for the lateness of the Gospels is that as long as the eyewitnesses were alive, there was no real need for any written Gospels. It was when the disciples began to die off that the need for written records first became apparent. For example, the composition of the Gospel of Mark is frequently associated with the death of the apostle Peter.[7] And Eusebius states that Matthew wrote his Gospel to compensate for his going to be with the Lord.[8]

A third argument sometimes given for the lateness of the Gospels is that in the minds of some people, oral tradition was viewed as more sacred than written tradition. Both Papias' famous quotation and the rabbinic tradition are often mentioned in support of this view. A fourth and related argument is that there existed in Judaism an established pattern for the oral transmission of tradition and since Christianity arose out of a Jewish milieu, it was natural that this same pattern would be followed. It has also been suggested that as long as the church in Jerusalem existed, there was a central authority that could be appealed to in matters of dispute. With the destruction of Jerusalem and the loss in influence of the Jerusalem church, there resulted a leadership vacuum and a need for an authoritative control of the gospel traditions, and it was this that led to the writing of our Gospels.[9]

6. Martin Dibelius summarizes this view well when he states, "The company of unlettered people which expected the end of the world any day had neither the capacity nor the inclination for the production of books, and we must not predicate a true literary activity in the Christian Church of the first two or three decades" (*From Tradition to Gospel*, trans. Bertram Lee Woolf [New York: Scribner's, n.d.], p. 9). Dibelius adds: "The primitive Christian Churches were prepared for the disappearance of this world and not for life in it" (p. 240). See Erhardt Güttgemanns, *Candid Questions Concerning Gospel Form Criticism*, trans. William G. Doty (Pittsburgh: Pickwick, 1979), pp. 130–39, for a criticism of Dibelius on this point.

7. See the Anti-Marcionite Prologue of Mark; Justin Martyr, *Dialogue with Trypho*, 106; Irenaeus, *Against Heresies*, 3.1.2; etc.

8. Eusebius, *Ecclesiastical History*, 3.24.5f.

9. Stephen Neill states: "The original aim of Gospel-writing seems to have been not so much the edification of the Church . . . as the maintenance in its purity of the original missionary proclamation" (*The Interpretation of the New Testament 1861–1961* [London: Oxford University, 1964], p. 274).

All of the above reasons for the late dating of our written Gospels are at best hypothetical, and they are not without serious objections and rejoinders. Furthermore, even if they were able to explain why our present Gospels were so late in being written, they would not explain whether there existed other written notes, collections, and complexes that were used during the oral period. It is now clear that even during the rabbinic period the rabbinic teaching process was not exclusively oral.[10] It is also quite possible that before Mark was written there existed certain pre-Markan collections[11] as well as other notes and written material. If we take seriously the "many" of Luke 1:1 ("Inasmuch as *many* have undertaken to compile a narrative of the things which have been accomplished among us . . .", emphasis added), this would indicate that when Luke wrote his Gospel there existed more written material than just Mark and Q (or simply Matthew, according to the Griesbach Hypothesis).

The existence of an oral period before the Gospels were written is a fact. One existed even *after* they were written! It would be incorrect, however, to assume, as some form critics have in the past, that it was an exclusively oral period. Even whether it was a "primarily oral period" will be debated in the coming years, but it is probable that in the earliest years of the church the principal means for transmitting the gospel traditions was oral.

2. "During the oral period, the narratives and sayings, with the exception of the passion narrative, circulated mainly as single and self-contained detached units, each complete in itself."[12]

For the early form critics, the oral tradition circulated as individual pearls or units of tradition. The Evangelists (and here Mark is usually singled out on the basis that he wrote first) simply supplied the string that tied these pearls together. Another image used to describe the work of the Evangelists was that of *Sammlern*, "collectors" of material who used "scissors and paste" to bring these isolated traditions together and produce "pericope collections" (rather than Gospels). It was K. L. Schmidt, more than anyone else, who sought to demonstrate

10. See E. Earle Ellis, "New Directions in Form Criticism," in *Jesus Christus in Historie und Theologie*, ed. G. Strecker (Tübingen: J.C.B. Mohr, 1975), pp. 304–9; "Gospel Criticism," in *Das Evangelium und Die Evangelien*, ed. Peter Stuhlmacher (Tübingen: J.C.B. Mohr, 1983), pp. 40–41. Cf. also Birger Gerhardsson, *Memory and Manuscript* (Uppsala: C.W.K. Gleerup, 1961), p. 335, and *The Origins of the Gospel Traditions* (Philadelphia: Fortress, 1979), pp. 22–24; and most importantly, Rainer Riesner, *Jesus als Lehrer* (Tübingen: J.C.B. Mohr, 1981), pp. 491–98.

11. See Heinz-Wolfgang Kuhn, *ältere Sammlungen im Markusevangelium* (Göttingen: Vandenhoeck und Ruprecht, 1971).

12. Redlich, *Form Criticism*, p. 37.

this. He argued that when one looks carefully at the "seams" of Mark, i.e., the verses that connect the various pericopes together, they are often very general and rather vague. As for the individual accounts themselves, they tend to be independent, self-standing units whose meaning is not dependent on any necessary connection to what precedes or follows.

It would appear that there is a great deal to be said for Schmidt's thesis. When one looks at much of the material in the Gospel of Mark, it appears that the accounts were, for the most part, joined together on a non-chronological basis and that they indeed existed as independent units of tradition. The following introductions to the various pericopes in Mark do not seem to betray any intimate or necessary connection to what precedes. One can easily think of the pericopes as having begun with such introductions as "Once upon a time, Jesus . . . " or "Once Jesus . . . "

> Now John's disciples and the Pharisees were fasting; and people came and said to him . . . [2:18].

> Again he began to teach beside the sea [4:1].

> And he said to them . . . [4:21].

> And he said . . . [4:26, 30].[13]

> Now when the Pharisees gathered together to him, with some of the scribes, who had come from Jerusalem, they saw . . . [7:1].

> In those days, when again a great crowd had gathered, and they had nothing to eat . . . [8:1].

Note also in Matthew the following:

> "Then the kingdom of heaven shall be compared to ten maidens who took their lamps and went to meet the bridegroom" [25:1].

> "For it will be as when a man going on a journey called his servants and entrusted to them his property" [25:14].

Other examples could be listed, but the best way of observing this phenomenon is to read through the Gospel of Mark and observe the introductory verse of each new pericope to see if there is a necessary

13. Cf. Mark 4:30–33, which indicates that Mark 4:1–29 is a topical collection of parables and not a chronological account.

connection with what precedes, or if the sentence and the pericope that follow make good sense as a completely independent unit, with only the context of "Once Jesus . . ." being necessary. In Acts 20:35 and 1 Corinthians 7:10 we find two sayings of Jesus that are quoted without any hint of a context other than "Once Jesus said." It therefore seems reasonable to think that during the oral period various stories, parables, sayings, and so on, circulated apart from any specific context in Jesus' life. Furthermore, there is a natural limit to how many traditions one can group together in an oral tradition.[14]

Having acknowledged the essential truth of this presupposition, it must be pointed out that various form critics tend to make this an absolute principle and claim that all the gospel materials circulated as small independent units. For some, not even the passion narrative has been excluded.[15] Yet, from the very beginning, the earliest form critics maintained that the passion narrative was transmitted as a totality rather than as individual units.[16] There are several reasons for this view. For one, the passion narrative has within it both chronological and topographical details that tie the story together (Mark 14:3, 13, 26, 32, 53, 66; 15:1, 16, 22; etc.). At times the very day and hour are mentioned (Mark 14:1, 12, 17; 15:1, 33, 42; 16:1; etc.). It is also apparent that the passion narrative is a unity in which event follows event as a matter of course. One simply cannot end this account in the middle. After every aspect of the passion, one cannot help but ask, "Then what happened?" The passion narrative cannot be divided up into individual self-contained units, since the events both logically and of necessity follow one another. Finally, it should be noted that the celebration of the Lord's Supper in the Pauline version has a reference to ". . . the night when he was betrayed. . . . " It is therefore most unlikely that the participants who celebrated that meal together were unaware from the earliest times as to what happened on that day.

In addition to the passion narrative, there may also have existed various pre-Markan complexes. It would appear that some of the passages in Mark (1:21–39; 2:1–3:6; 4:1–34; 4:35–5:43; 7:1–23; 8:1–26; 12:13–37) may very well have existed together as complexes and collections before Mark wrote his Gospel.[17] If Q, proto-Matthew, and proto-Luke have any merit, they too, would provide us with additional

14. So Rudolf Bultmann, *The History of the Synoptic Tradition*, trans. John Marsh (New York: Harper, 1968), p. 322.

15. See Werner H. Kelber, ed., *The Passion in Mark* (Philadelphia: Fortress, 1976), especially pp. 153–59.

16. Karl Ludwig Schmidt, *Der Rahmen der Geschichte Jesu* (Berlin: Trowitzsch & Sohn, 1919), pp. 303f.

17. See Kuhn, *ältere Sammlungen*.

organized materials. Personal notes and memoranda would also have brought various materials together, if not on chronological grounds then on topical ones.[18] It may even be that there also existed a traditional summary outline much like the Gospel of Mark, which provided a chronological framework for the gospel materials. C. H. Dodd sought to establish this in a famous article entitled "The Framework of the Gospel Narrative."[19] He argued that a skeletal outline of Jesus' life and ministry was present in the oral tradition, that Acts 10:37–41 provides us with this outline, and that Mark built his Gospel on this traditional outline by inserting the various pericopes and topical collections available to him into the appropriate place in the outline. Whether such an outline existed and whether Dodd succeeded in demonstrating this are two separate questions. Both are debated. We should not assume, however, that the early church was as uninterested in history or was as anti-historical as some modern-day form critics. Although it may certainly be true that not all in the early church would have been as interested in history as Luke,[20] they must have had some idea of the course of Jesus' ministry. After all, the baptism could not have taken place after the crucifixion, nor the crucifixion after the resurrection! It is true that Mark is clearly responsible for the geographical framework of Jordan, Galilee, outside Galilee, and Jerusalem found in his Gospel, but this does not mean that this framework was his *de novo* creation. He could have based his outline on the basic historical framework that was associated with the life of Christ.

3. "The material in the Gospels can be classified according to their form."[21]

Within the Gospels we find different and often diverse kinds of material. Various attempts have been made to classify these materials, and the names given to them vary from author to author. The most popular classifications, however, are those of Dibelius, Bultmann, and Taylor. A "synopsis" of them appears in table 10.

Of the three classifications, it is evident that Taylor's is the most useful for several reasons. For one, his classifications are non-emotive in nature. Despite disclaimers to the contrary, the terms "legends" and

---

18. See Ellis, "New Directions," and Riesner, *Jesus als Lehrer.*

19. This article appeared in *ET* 43 (1932): 396–400. Cf. also his *The Apostolic Preaching and Its Developments* (London: Hodder and Stoughton, 1936). For criticism of Dodd's thesis, see D. E. Nineham, "The Order of Events in St Mark's Gospel: An Examination of Dr. Dodd's Hypothesis," in *Studies in the Gospels*, ed. D. E. Nineham (Oxford: Blackwell, 1955), pp. 223–39, and Güttgemanns, pp. 311–18.

20. Cf. Luke 2:1–2 and 3:1–2.

21. Redlich, *Form Criticism*, p. 50.

Table 10

Dibelius	Bultmann	Taylor
Paradigms	Apophthegms Conflict Didactic Biographical	Pronouncement Stories
Novellen	Miracle Stories	Miracle Stories
Paränesis	Sayings Logia Prophetic Legal "I" Parables	Sayings and Parables
Legends	Historical Stories	Stories about Jesus
Myths	Legends	

"myths" imply a negative judgment concerning the historicity of the material included under these categories. Even though this may not be true concerning the "classical" usage of these terms, the fact remains that for the vast majority of people the terms "legends" and "myths" give a negative historical evaluation to the material so classified and should therefore be avoided. Taylor's categories avoid any such negative connotations altogether and are therefore to be preferred. Furthermore, there are some serious questions as to whether, even by classical usage, the "stories about Jesus" can be classified as "myths." The stories about Jesus in the Gospels are better understood as possessing the form of historical narrative than the form of "myth." The classification of this material as "legends" and "myths" is primarily due to a negative historical judgment concerning its miraculous nature. It is not based on form at all.[22] A second benefit of Taylor's classification system is that he uses terminology that is understandable, especially for the English-speaking world. Finally, it must be noted that Taylor's categories are "speakable." Terms such as "paradigm," "paränesis," and especially the classical term "apophthegm" are almost impossible for English-speaking people to pronounce. As a result, we shall use the categories listed by Taylor, which seem to be most useful.

The first classification listed in table 10 is "pronouncement stories."

22. See Hans W. Frei, *The Eclipse of Biblical Narrative* (New Haven: Yale University, 1974), pp. 271–73.

Usually devoid of chronological or geographical details, a pronouncement story is an account in Jesus' life that serves as the basis for a significant concluding utterance. Two "pure" examples of this form are:

> And they were bringing children to him, that he might touch them; and the disciples rebuked them. But when Jesus saw it he was indignant, and said to them, "Let the children come to me, do not hinder them; for to such belongs the kingdom of God. Truly, I say to you, whoever does not receive the kingdom of God like a child shall not enter it." And he took them in his arms and blessed them, laying his hands upon them [Mark 10:13–16].

> And they sent to him some of the Pharisees and some of the Herodians, to entrap him in his talk. And they came and said to him, "Teacher, we know that you are true, and care for no man; for you do not regard the position of men, but truly teach the way of God. Is it lawful to pay taxes to Caesar, or not? Should we pay them or should we not?" But knowing their hypocrisy, he said to them, "Why put me to the test? Bring me a coin, and let me look at it." And they brought one. And he said to them, "Whose likeness and inscription is this?" They said to him, "Caesar's." Jesus said to them, "Render to Caesar the things that are Caesar's, and to God the things that are God's." And they were amazed at him [Mark 12:13–17].[23]

Bultmann has subdivided this category (his "apophthegms") into three further classifications: conflict ("Streitgespräche") as in Mark 12:13–17; didactic ("Schulgespräche") as in Mark 12:28–34; and biographical ("Biographische") as in Luke 9:57–62.

The second classification is listed as "miracle stories." One type of miracle story involves healing, and in each of these we find a recurring pattern. First we find a description of the problem (the diagnosis). Then we often, although not always, find a reference to the faith of those who came for healing. Next we find an account of the healing itself (the prescription or remedy). Finally we read of the result (the cure). Two examples of this, one with and one without a reference to the individual's faith are:

> And a leper came to him beseeching him, and kneeling said to him, "If you will, you can make me clean." Moved with pity, he stretched out his hand and touched him, and said to him, "I will; be clean." And immediately the leprosy left him, and he was made clean. And he sternly

---

23. Dibelius also lists as "pure" examples of this form, Mark 2:1–12, 18–22, 23–28; 3:1–5, 31–35; and 14:3–9.

charged him, and sent him away at once, and said to him, "See that you say nothing to any one; but go, show yourself to the priest, and offer for your cleansing what Moses commanded, for a proof to the people." But he went out and began to talk freely about it, and to spread the news, so that Jesus could no longer openly enter a town, but was out in the country; and people came to him from every quarter [Mark 1:40–45].

And immediately he left the synagogue, and entered the house of Simon and Andrew, with James and John. Now Simon's mother-in-law lay sick with a fever, and immediately they told him of her. And he came and took her by the hand and lifted her up, and the fever left her; and she served them (Mark 1:29–31).[24]

Taylor's third classification, "sayings and parables," is a general catchall that contains all the teachings of Jesus outside of those found in the pronouncement stories. Here it is clear that the classification does not depend upon form as much as upon content. Bultmann's subdivisions involve wisdom-like sayings of Jesus (logia); apocalyptic and prophetic sayings concerning the judgment or salvation to come (prophetic); rules and laws for the church community (legal); sayings in which Jesus speaks about himself or his activity ("I"); and parabolic sayings in which Jesus makes some sort of an analogy (parables).

The fourth and final category, "stories about Jesus," is divided into two separate classifications by both Dibelius and Bultmann. "Legends," for Dibelius, are religious stories about "holy people." These include not only accounts about Jesus but also those about John the Baptist and the disciples—such stories as the story of the boy Jesus in the temple (Luke 2:41–51); the account of Jesus' preaching in the synagogue at Nazareth (Luke 4:16–30); the call of the disciples (Mark 1:16–20); the anointing of Jesus (Luke 7:36–50); the story of Zacchaeus (Luke 19:1–10); the triumphal entry (Mark 11:1–10); the birth stories; and so on. Under "myth" Dibelius referred to those gospel stories that involved in some way or other the direct intervention of God in history. Dibelius listed three examples: the baptism of Jesus (Mark 1:9–11); the temptation (Matt. 4:1–11); and the transfiguration (Mark 9:2–8). Bultmann's subdivisions were "historical stories" and "legends." It should be noted with regard to this general classification, whether by Dibelius, Bultmann, or Taylor, that the category has nothing to do with form but is based solely on the content of the material.

The above classification systems are helpful in that they provide

---

24. See also Mark 1:23–28; 2:1–12; 5:1–20, 21–24, 35–43; 7:31–37; etc. To these healing miracles can also be added the accounts of nature miracles. See, for example, Mark 4:35–41; 6:35–44, 45–52; 8:1–9; etc.

convenient handles to refer to the various gospel traditions. Although classification is essential for the scientific study of any subject, it is an error to think that all the gospel materials fit neatly into specific categories or that all the classifications arise out of the form of the material. Actually only two of the categories possess a distinct form—the pronouncement stories and the miracle stories. The remaining types of material are essentially "formless."[25] Long ago, B. S. Easton pointed out that there is no *formal* difference between the logia—"whoever exalts himself will be humbled, and whoever humbles himself will be exalted" (Matt. 23:12); the prophetic word—"For whoever is ashamed of me and my words in this adulterous and sinful generation, of him will the Son of man also be ashamed, when he comes in the glory of his Father with the holy angels" (Mark 8:38); and the legal saying— "Whoever divorces his wife and marries another, commits adultery against her . . ." (Mark 10:11).[26] Along with the fact that only two of the four major classifications possess a specific form, we must also note that we frequently encounter in the material "mixed" or "impure" forms. Is the healing of the paralytic in Mark 2:1–12 primarily a miracle story or a pronouncement story? The same question can also be asked about the healing of the man with the withered hand in Mark 3:1–6. To claim that such stories are "impure forms," however, is less a judgment on the material than upon the system of classification being used. We must admit that at times the materials simply cannot be neatly pigeonholed. Rather than force these materials into some rather rigid categories or say that they are "impure," which appears to attribute a negative quality to them, it may be more appropriate to acknowledge that some materials simply do not fit the precise categories of form criticism.

Having acknowledged the value (and weaknesses) of such labels for discussing the gospel materials, the question must now be raised as to the value of the classifications for determining the setting out of which this material arose or for making historical judgments concerning the material itself. Dibelius argued that the pronouncement stories were shaped and transmitted in a particular setting of the early church— preaching.[27] On the other hand, the miracle stories were supposedly

25. The "I" sayings are an exception. It can also be questioned as to whether the "form" of a miracle story is due to literary considerations or matters of content. How else can one describe a healing miracle? One must discuss the problem, the remedy, and the cure.

26. Burton Scott Easton, *The Gospel before the Gospels* (London: Allen & Unwin, 1928), p. 74.

27. Dibelius (*From Tradition to Gospel,* p. 13) states, "Missionary purpose was the cause and preaching was the means of spreading abroad that which the disciples of Jesus possessed as recollections."

transmitted by a special class of storytellers and teachers, whose existence, however, we never read of in the New Testament. Bultmann disagreed with Dibelius and said that much of the material was shaped in Christian debates with the Jewish community. Schmidt and Albertz, on the other hand, saw the worship of the church as a more logical setting.[28] Gerhardsson has more recently argued that the primary *Sitz im Leben* for the material was not preaching or paränesis, for in paränesis one is not inclined to make quotations. A more logical *Sitz im Leben*, he suggests, is the conscious transmission of sacred tradition by the leaders of the church.[29]

It would almost certainly be an error to isolate certain forms of the tradition in specific settings. The fact that some of the material possesses a "mixed form" should warn us against this. It is absurd to think that a "miracle–pronouncement story" such as Mark 3:1–6 was the sole property of the preachers or the storytellers in the church. Or did they each recite only their own part of the story? The transmission of the gospel traditions almost certainly did not proceed exclusively along the lines of any one single *Sitz im Leben* in the early church. No doubt preaching, worship, and catechetical instruction all played a role in passing on the tradition. Yet, if we take Luke's explanation seriously, the primary means of transmission was the "ministers of the word" who were eyewitnesses from the beginning (Luke 1:2). In this regard the views of Gerhardsson and Riesenfeld have much to commend them.

Some form critics have also assumed that certain historical judgments can be made concerning the material on the basis of form alone. Sometimes the historicity of "formless" stories have been dismissed simply on the basis of their lack of form. "Mixed forms" have been divided up and made into two different stories. Certain accounts have been classified as "myths" and then assumed to be unhistorical because myths are unhistorical! Whether form criticism can legitimately make historical judgments concerning the transmission and content of the material will be discussed later,[30] but it needs to be pointed out at this point that no such judgments can be made simply on the basis that the material possesses a certain form. The form or formlessness of the gospel materials tells us nothing about their historicity. The rejection of the historicity of a clearly formed miracle story such as the resurrection

28. Humphrey Palmer has said rather sarcastically in this regard that whether or not the first Christians were adept at thinking up stories of Jesus to meet the needs of the Church," . . . form critics are [adept] at thinking up early-Church-situations to suit stories of Jesus" (*The Logic of Gospel Criticism* [New York: Macmillan, 1968], p. 185).

29. Gerhardsson, *The Origins*, pp. 38–39, 68.

30. See below pp. 180–216.

of Jairus' daughter (Mark 5:21–24, 35–43) and of a formless "myth" such as the transfiguration (Mark 9:2–8) is clearly independent of their form or lack of form. Such decisions are based primarily upon historical *a priori* considerations totally independent of form.

4. "The vital factors which gave rise to and preserved these forms are to be found in the practical interests of the Christian community."[31]

According to the form critics, the religious needs of the early church selected, preserved, molded, and even created the gospel traditions. That the practical or religious needs of the church played an important role in the preservation of the gospel materials goes without saying. John so much as tells us this when he states: "Now Jesus did many other signs in the presence of the disciples, which are not written in this book; but these are written that you may believe that Jesus is the Christ, the Son of God, and that believing you may have life in his name" (John 20:30–31).[32] Not everything Jesus said or did, in other words not every tradition about Jesus, was preserved (cf. John 21:25), for sayings and events with little significance or religious value for the church tended to be forgotten. Even a quick reading of the Gospels indicates that some material would have been especially meaningful for Jewish Christians in discussions with their fellow Jews,[33] and that other material was used apologetically to demonstrate that Jesus and his followers were no threat to the civil authorities[34] or to explain to believers why Christ died by crucifixion.[35] Other material was useful for church polity and ethics,[36] for missionary work among the Gentiles,[37] and so on. It would be wrong, however, to think that such material could only serve one purpose and was transmitted in only one context. The use of the pre-Pauline Christological hymn in Philippians 2:6–11 as an example of humility (2:5) indicates that the same material could serve different purposes in different contexts (as a Christological hymn or as an example of humility). One need only reflect on how one

31. Redlich, *Form Criticism*, p. 55.

32. Morton S. Enslin states, "When they [the Gospels] were written, their function was to make saints, not historians" (*The Prophet from Nazareth* [New York: McGraw-Hill, 1961], p. 1).

33. See Mark 2:1–12, 13–15, 18–22, 23–28; 3:1–6, 22–30; 7:1–13, 14–23; 8:14–21; 11:27–33; Luke 13:10–17; 14:1–6; etc.

34. See Matthew 27:62–66; 28:11–15; Mark 12:13–17; 14:55–65; 15:6–15, 33–39; etc.

35. See Mark 8:31; 9:31–32; 10:33, 45; 14:17–21; etc.

36. See Matthew 7:21–23; 18:1–35; 25:1–13; Mark 8:34–38; 10:2–12, 35–45; Luke 12:35–40; etc.

37. See Mark 1:16–20; 3:31–35; 7:1–23, 24–30; 12:1–12; Luke 7:1–10; etc.

Gospel text can be used legitimately in preaching to make different points to realize this.[38]

For many form critics, however, there often takes place a *non sequitur*, which assumes that the *Sitz im Leben* that preserved and molded the gospel traditions also gave them their birth. As a result, at times the needs of the early church are seen as not only the preserver but also the creator of the traditions. The tradition was not only *to* the church and *for* the church but also *from* the church! A specific group that Bultmann saw serving in this creative capacity in the early church were the "Christian prophets."[39] Evidence for this view was seen in such verses as Revelation 3:20 and 16:15, where the risen Christ speaks to the prophet, as well as in the existence of prophets within the early church (cf. Acts 11:27–30; 13:1–3; 15:32; 21:10–14). When these prophets spoke the "sentences of Holy Law" (so Käsemann), supposedly no distinction was made between the sayings of the risen Christ and the sayings of the historical Jesus, for the early church saw no difference between them.[40] Unlike Dibelius' "storytellers" of which the New Testament says not a single word, it is clear that Christian prophets did exist in the early church. But does the New Testament suggest in any way that they created sayings or received revelation from the risen Christ and read them back upon the lips of the historical Jesus?

Upon closer examination, there seems to be little objective evidence to support such a view. For one, it should be noted that any reference to the role of the early Christian prophets in Acts actually argues against this thesis, because the proclamation of these prophets gives no evidence that they claimed that their message came from the risen Christ. On the contrary, the prophet Agabus introduces his oracle with "Thus says the Holy Spirit" (Acts 21:11) and is described as speaking "by the Spirit" (Acts 11:28).[41] It should also be noted that the words of

38. Graham Stanton states: "Almost every 'form' of oral tradition may be used in a wide variety of ways. Similarly, any given situation can utilize very different forms" ("Form Criticism Revisited" in *What about the New Testament?* ed. Morna Hooker and Colin Hickling [London: SCM, 1975], p. 23).

39. Bultmann, *Synoptic Tradition*, p. 127. This was suggested earlier by Colani, Gunkel, and von Soden and has frequently been suggested by other Bultmannians. The most recent advocate of this view is M. Eugene Boring. See his "How May We Identify Oracles of Christian Prophets in the Synoptic Tradition? Mark 3:28–29 as a Test Case," *JBL* 91 (1972): 501–21 and his *Sayings of the Risen Lord: Christian Prophecy in the Synoptic Tradition* (Cambridge: Cambridge University, 1982).

40. David Hill has pointed out that Käsemann's "sentences of Holy Law" may not have been eschatological *ius talionis* at all but may in fact have been wisdom sayings having nothing to do with legal norms (*New Testament Prophecy* [Atlanta: John Knox, 1979], p. 171).

41. See David Hill, "On the Evidence for the Creative Role of Christian Prophets," *NTS* 20 (1974): 270.

the risen Christ in the rest of the New Testament do not appear to be confused with those of the earthly Jesus at all, but are kept quite distinct. This is evident when one compares Matthew 28:17–20; 2 Corinthians 12:9; and Revelation 3:20 and 16:15 with the sayings of the earthly Jesus in the Gospels. We find a similar phenomenon in the comparative literature as well, for the Old Testament prophetic literature was written in the name of the Lord but always through his prophets. No Old Testament prophetic book names the Lord as its author; each always appears in the name of the prophet.[42]

An even stronger argument against the idea that Christian prophets frequently read back into the life of Jesus sayings of the risen Christ is provided by the apostle Paul. Paul, who also was a prophet (cf. 1 Cor. 14:1–19, where Paul prefers to prophesy rather than to speak in tongues), makes a clear distinction between the words of the historical Jesus in 1 Corinthians 7:10 ("To the married I give charge, not I but the Lord, that the wife should not separate from her husband . . .") and the words that the risen Christ says by the Spirit (cf. 1 Cor. 7:40) through his apostle in 1 Corinthians 7:12 ("To the rest I say, not the Lord, that if any brother has a wife who is an unbeliever, and she consents to live with him, he should not divorce her.") Gerhardsson correctly comments: "These passages are embarrassing evidence against the common opinion that in the early church no distinction was made between what was said 'by the Lord (himself)' and what was said by some one else 'in the Lord'; that words of Jesus were freely constructed, or that sayings of some early Christian prophet were freely placed in the mouth of Jesus."[43] Dunn has also pointed out that the need to test prophecy, which was present in the Old Testament, was present in the New Testament as well (cf. 1 Cor. 12:3; Gal. 1:8; 2 Thess. 2:15; 1 John 2:22; 4:1–3, 15; etc.) so that any new prophetic saying would have encountered a need to validate itself as an authentic saying of the historical Jesus. It should finally be pointed out that the early Christian prophets were by no means the only or the most important group within the early church. The leading figures within the early church were the apostles, who were "eyewitnesses and ministers of the word" (Luke 1:2). It is hardly likely that they would have tolerated the de novo creation of gospel materials by these early Christian proph-

---

42. See James D. G. Dunn, "Prophetic 'I'-Sayings and the Jesus Tradition: The Importance of Testing Prophetic Utterances within Early Christianity," NTS 24 (1978):179–81.

43. Gerhardsson, The Origins, p. 35. Cf. also David E. Aune: " . . . the historical evidence in support of the theory lies largely in the creative imagination of scholars" (Prophecy in Early Christianity and the Ancient Mediterranean World [Grand Rapids: Eerdmans, 1983], p. 245).

ets. The theory of the creation of large amounts of the gospel tradition by these early Christian prophets is not convincing. On the contrary, the theory is extremely circular and seems to be based and founded on the very proposition it seeks to prove.[44] It may well be that rather than seeing the prophetic utterances of early Christian prophets as giving rise to various sayings of Jesus, it is more likely that it was the remembered sayings of Jesus that gave rise to the inspired utterances of the early Christian prophets![45]

In light of the above it would appear that while most scholars agree concerning the important role that the needs of the church played in preserving and shaping the gospel traditions, one should be cautious in claiming that the needs of the church "gave rise" to such material or that a particular group, such as the Christian prophets, was responsible for its creation. A better way of looking at the correspondence between the practice of the community and the gospel traditions is that instead of assuming the church's creation and drastic reshaping of the gospel traditions in order to meet its needs, we should recognize that from the beginning the life of the community and its needs were determined by the Jesus traditions they held so dear.[46] In other words, even as the preservation of the gospel materials was influenced by the needs and interests of the community, so the reverse was also true. Perhaps even more so. The needs and interests of the community were determined primarily by the traditions it received. For example, it was not so much that the early church's attitude toward the sabbath preserved the gospel materials concerning the sabbath (such as Mark 2:23–28; 3:1–6; Luke 14:1–6; etc.) as that these gospel traditions shaped and molded the early church's attitude toward the sabbath. As a result, the practical interests that preserved and shaped the gospel traditions were determined by these very traditions. The materials created the needs! The fact that there are no accompanying gospel traditions for later needs—such as the question of whether Gentiles needed to be circumcised to enter the church—proves that the early church did not simply create gospel materials nor drastically reshape them to meet their needs.[47] As we shall note later, the existence of difficult passages in the Gospels also argues that at times loyalty to the sacred tradition of

44. For a more complete critique of this, see the articles referred to above by Dunn, "Prophetic 'I'-Sayings"; Hill, "Christian Prophets"; the definitive work of Aune, *Prophecy*; and especially Hill, *New Testament Prophecy*, pp. 160–85.

45. So G. B. Caird, "The Study of the Gospels: II. Form Criticism," *ET* 87 (1976):140.

46. T. W. Manson, *Studies in the Gospels and Epistles* (Philadelphia: Westminster, 1962), p. 6.

47. For further discussion of the significance of this fact with regard to the reliability of the gospel materials, see below pp. 189–91.

Jesus' words resulted in the preservation of certain materials, even when those materials did not meet any particular religious need of the community but instead caused problems.[48] The Counselor's role in the early church with regard to the gospel traditions apparently involved less a creative function in producing new gospel traditions than a didactic one. He would help the church both to remember the gospel traditions and to teach their post-Pentecost significance (John 14:26). It should also be borne in mind that, since the eyewitnesses were not only part of the early church but its leading element, the community's shaping of the tradition does not exclude, but rather presupposes, the superintendence of the apostolic eyewitnesses in this.[49]

5. "The material of the tradition has no biographical or chronological or geographical value."[50]

In this form-critical principle a helpful insight, namely that much of the material lacks temporal, geographical, or purely historical interests, has unfortunately been made into a universal axiom. Yet it is clear that (although at times various materials do not possess any such information) some pericopes do contain clear geographical ties. These may involve the Sea of Galilee (Mark 2:13; 3:7; 4:1, 35; 5:1; etc.); Capernaum (Mark 1:21, 29; 2:1; 3:20 [?]; 9:33); Gerasa (Mark 5:1); Nazareth (Mark 6:1); Gennesaret (Mark 6:53); Tyre (Mark 7:24); Dalmanutha (Mark 8:10); Bethsaida (Mark 8:22); Caesarea Philippi (Mark 8:27); the region across the Jordan (Mark 10:1); Jericho (Mark 10:46); and more. Within the passion narrative, Jerusalem and its environs are, of course, designated in the materials. Furthermore, before one too quickly eliminates all these geographical designations as later secondary additions that have no value, it should be noted that the very difficulty of some of them argue against their being later additions. Why would anyone "create" such difficult place names for the tradition as Gerasa or Dalmanutha? And why would one "add" that Peter's great confession took place in Caesarea Philippi, a location we never again find in the rest of the New Testament? Surely, if one were to create a place designation for Peter's great confession that Jesus was the Christ (Mark 8:29), "Jerusalem" would have been much more appropriate.[51]

---

48. See below pp. 188–89.

49. This does not seem to have been seriously considered by D. E. Nineham in his "Eyewitness Testimony and the Gospel Tradition—II," *JTS* 9 (1958):243. For him this shaping could only be understood as the product of the anonymous and impersonal church.

50. Redlich, *Form Criticism*, p. 62.

51. If one were to place Jesus' question and Peter's response after Mark 11:11a, this would certainly be far more dramatic.

Outside of the passion narrative, temporal designations tend to be few and far between. A possible exception is the chronological framework found in Mark 1:21–39, which sees these events as taking place in a single day in Capernaum. Is this a correct chronological portrayal or has Mark or the pre-Markan tradition arranged these events into "a day in the life of Jesus"?[52] In favor of the latter view is the fact that all the accounts within this passage are healing miracles, so that topical considerations appear to be a dominant factor in this arrangement. Furthermore, if outside the passion narrative all these pericopes *must* have circulated as independent units, then the question is a moot one. On the other hand, there is no conclusive reason why these events could not have taken place in Capernaum as described, especially if we permit Mark to recite the accounts in his own style (for instance, his use of "immediately"). It should also be noted that some stories by their very nature have a chronological designation associated with them. Examples of these are the controversy stories involving Jesus' behavior on the sabbath (Mark 2:23–28; 3:1–6; 6:1–6; Luke 13:10–17; 14:1–6; cf. also John 5:1–18; 7:22–24; 9:13f.). A much more significant example of a chronological tie between the gospel traditions is found in Mark 9:2. Here the transfiguration account begins with "And after six days. . . ." Taylor points out: "No other temporal statement in Mk outside the Passion Narrative is so precise."[53] As it stands in Mark, this temporal designation intimately ties together the confession of Peter at Caesarea Philippi and the transfiguration. The correct interpretation of the transfiguration, according to Mark at least, requires that this event be interpreted in the light of what happened six days before, for the voice from heaven refers back in a twofold way to the events that occurred at Caesarea Philippi. "This is my beloved Son" (Mark 9:7) is not only a rebuke of Peter's recommendation to build three booths (9:5) but a confirmation of his confession that Jesus was the Christ (8:29). And the words "listen to him" clearly refer back to Peter's unwillingness to listen to Jesus' teaching concerning his forthcoming passion (8:31–33), for in the transfiguration account itself Jesus has not said anything. There is no compelling reason to think that Mark was the one to bring these two events together. It seems rather that from the beginning the transfiguration was understood as an event occurring within the lifetime of Jesus that was associated with the confession of Peter at Caesarea Philippi. The uniqueness of this precise temporal tie in Mark (outside the passion narrative) also argues for its non-Markan

52. The interconnectedness of this section is most easily seen by reading the seams apart from the narrative material. Read Mark 1:21–22, 29, 32, 35.

53. Vincent Taylor, *The Gospel According to St. Mark* (London: Macmillan, 1959), p. 388.

character. Two other temporal designations that can be mentioned in passing are Mark 1:14 and 4:35.

Finally, it must be pointed out that whereas the primary factor for the preservation of the gospel traditions was the religious needs of the community, this does not mean that the early church lacked any historical interests. Luke certainly did not! This is evident from the way he ties the events of the gospel to the historical events of his day: "In the fifteenth year of the reign of Tiberius Caesar, Pontius Pilate being governor of Judea, and Herod being tetrarch of Galilee, and his brother Philip tetrarch of the region of Ituraea and Trachonitis, and Lysanias tetrarch of Abilene, in the high-priesthood of Annas and Caiaphas, the word of God came to John the son of Zechariah in the wilderness . . ." (Luke 3:1–2; cf. 2:1–2). Is there any reason to think that such historical and biographical interests would have been excluded from the concerns and interests of the transmitters of the gospel traditions? Was the early church more like Luke with regard to the historical events of the gospel or like twentieth-century form critics of an existential persuasion? Surely Luke's attitude is more typical of that of the early church, T. W. Manson's comment in this regard is worth quoting: "It is conceivable that he [Jesus] was at least as interesting, *for his own sake*, to people in the first century as he is to historians in the twentieth."[54] The fact is that we find a few incidents in the Gospels that appear to reveal what we would call an almost purely historical interest. One such incident is found in Mark 14:51–52: "And a young man followed him, with nothing but a linen cloth about his body; and they seized him, but he left the linen cloth and ran away naked." The common omission of this incident by Matthew and Luke is easily understandable and reveals how difficult it is to find "religious meaning" in the incident. "On the contrary, no good reason can be suggested for the recording of the incident unless it rests on a genuine reminiscence."[55] The naming of the disciples in Mark 3:16–19 also appears to serve historical rather than religious interests. The Markan comment in Mark 15:21 that Simon of Cyrene was the father of Alexander and Rufus is still another indication that Mark, like Luke, had historical interests as well.

It would appear that whereas much of the gospel tradition lacks any specific chronological or geographical designation, some of it indeed does. As we shall see, there is no absolute rule or tendency in oral

---

54. Manson, *Studies in the Gospels and Epistles,* p. 6.

55. Taylor, *St. Mark,* p. 561. Such attempts as R. Scroggs and K. I. Groff, "Baptism in Mark: Dying and Rising with Christ," *JBL* 92 (1973):531–48; and E. L. Schnellbächer, "Das Rätsel des *neaniskos* bei Markus," *ZNW* 73 (1982):127–35, to find religious meaning in this incident prove just the reverse. It is impossible to see the preservation of this account as being due to its religious value.

tradition that demands that such designations could not have been associated with the tradition from the very beginning. Although there is truth in the form-critical observation that much of the material lacks specific chronological, geographical, and biographical value, to make this principle into an absolute and universal law is to make the evidence fit the theory rather than the theory the evidence.

6. "The original form of the tradition may be recovered and its history traced, before being written down, by discovering the laws of the tradition."[56]

It was the opinion of the early form critics that since the gospel traditions fell into the category of "folk tradition," the observation of how that tradition functions and develops would reveal the rules or laws that the gospel traditions also followed in their development. Such laws were derived in part from German folklore, Greek literature, rabbinic literature, and the apocryphal gospels, but it was especially in the observation of how Matthew and Luke used Mark and Q that these laws were formulated. It was then assumed that, knowing how Matthew and Luke used Mark, one could then conclude that Mark used the oral traditions that were available to him in a similar manner. Some of the laws of the tradition "discovered" by the early form critics were that there is a tendency to add circumstantial details to stories; that indirect statements tend to become direct statements; that impure pronouncement stories are later than pure pronouncement stories; that there is a tendency to add geographical details to accounts; and so on. Form critics were confident that the scientific use of such laws would enable them to reconstruct the oral tradition by eliminating the extraneous encrustations that had been added to the tradition by the early church.

Recent criticism has sharply dampened the optimism that first surrounded the discovery of these laws. This criticism has come from two different areas. One involved a more careful analysis of the synoptic Gospels by E. P. Sanders, who carefully compared five possible tendencies of the tradition: increasing length; increasing detail; diminishing Semiticisms; direct discourse; and conflation. First he observed the post-canonical treatment of the materials found in the synoptic Gospels. Then he observed the evidence within the Synoptics themselves. His conclusions are for the most part negative for he states: "There are no hard and fast laws of the development of the Synoptic tradition. On all counts the tradition developed in opposite directions. It became both longer and shorter, both more and less detailed, and both more

56. Redlich, *Form Criticism*, p. 73.

and less Semitic. Even the tendency to use direct discourse for indirect, which was uniform in the post-canonical material . . . was not uniform in the Synoptics themselves. For this reason, *dogmatic statements that a certain characteristic proves a certain passage to be earlier than another are never justified.*"[57] Although a number of Sanders' conclusions can be debated, he has demonstrated that the basic laws of the developing oral tradition that the early form critics postulated are by no means "laws." Often they are not even tendencies! How can we make a tendency out of the fact that sometimes the tradition tends to become shorter and sometimes longer, that sometimes names tend to be added and sometimes dropped? Caird gives the examples of the epileptic boy of Mark 9:17 being an "only child" in Luke 9:38 and the withered hand of Mark 3:1 becoming a "right hand" in Luke 6:6. Then, however, he points out that the "green grass" of Mark 6:39 disappears in Luke 9:14 and comments: "But a law which tells us that tradition may either amplify or abbreviate, may either add details or omit them, is very little help in determining which of two accounts is the more original."[58] That there are certain tendencies in the passing on of traditions cannot be denied, but these are at best tendencies and not laws, and one can never be certain in any particular instance that this tendency was being followed.

An even more devastating attack on the "laws of the tradition" questions the whole study of such laws, when based upon *written* evidence such as the apocryphal gospels, rabbinic literature, and even the synoptic Gospels. The above-mentioned studies by the early form critics and Sanders are all based upon the assumption that the development of oral tradition proceeded in a similar manner as the development of the written tradition. Some recent studies have argued that they did not, but that on the contrary their development is mutually exclusive and may even be contradictory.[59] If this is in fact true, we then possess neither any clear "laws" as to how the gospel traditions developed during the oral period, nor even any tendencies about which we can be certain! Although much study remains to be done in this area, it is clear that the assumption that we already know the laws or tendencies during the oral period (which is so basic to form-critical research) is being seriously questioned today. The view of the early

---

57. E. P. Sanders, *The Tendencies of the Synoptic Tradition* (Cambridge: Cambridge University, 1969), p. 272.

58. Caird, "The Study of the Gospels," p. 140.

59. See A. B. Lord, *The Singer of Tales* (Cambridge: Harvard University, 1960), p. 128; M. D. Hooker, "On Using the Wrong Tool," *Theology*, 75 (1972): 572; Ellis, "New Directions," pp. 305–6; Güttgemanns, *Gospel Form Criticism*, pp. 196–211; Werner H. Kelber, *The Oral and the Written Gospel* (Philadelphia: Fortress, 1983), pp. 14–32.

form critics that the gospel materials passed through an "effortlessly evolutionary transition from the pre-gospel stream of tradition to the written gospel"[60] is being vigorously attacked head-on.

7. The eyewitnesses played no significant role in the process of oral transmission.

Although this presupposition is usually not stated so specifically, it is a common assumption of many form critics. Although lip service may at times be given to the eyewitnesses, their specific role in the transmission of the gospel materials is seldom acknowledged.[61] Taylor commented in response, "If the Form-Critics are right, the disciples must have been translated to heaven immediately after the Resurrection."[62] One of the greatest failures of the early form critics was that they did not see the central role that the eyewitnesses must have played in the oral transmission of the gospel traditions. It may be that the heavy sociological emphasis on the early Christian "community" was not hospitable to this. Yet, if Dibelius created a group of "story-tellers" and if "Christian prophets" were thrust into the center of the transmission process, why was so little attention paid to the eyewitnesses, who according to Luke were "ministers of the word" during the oral period (Luke 1:2)? No doubt theological rather than historical reasons played a dominating role in this regard. The New Testament, however, highly esteemed the testimony of the eyewitnesses.[63] As we shall see, it is the great merit of the Swedish school of form criticism represented by Riesenfeld and Gerhardsson that it has placed the eyewitnesses at the heart of the process by which the gospel materials were transmitted.[64] Regardless of why the early form critics neglected the role of the eyewitnesses in the transmission of the gospel materials, the fact remains that they did, and this neglect resulted in an unhistorical portrait of the entire process and a negative view as to the historical value of the tradition.

60. Kelber, The Oral and the Written Gospel, p. 6.

61. D. E. Nineham states, "According to the form-critics, eyewitnesses played little direct part in the development of the Gospel tradition, however much they may have had to do with its original formulation" and points out that this presupposition is "basic" to form criticism ("Eye-Witness Testimony and the Gospel Tradition—I," JTS 9 [1958]:13). Cf. here Riesner Jesus als Lehrer, pp. 19f. It should be noted that the term "eyewitness" does not even appear in the subject index of Bultmann's History of the Synoptic Tradition.

62. Vincent Taylor, The Formation of the Gospel Tradition (London: Macmillan, 1935), p. 41.

63. Cf. John 19:35; 21:24; Acts 1:21–22; 10:39, 41; 1 Corinthians 15:6; 1 Peter 5:1; 2 Peter 1:16; 1 John 1:1–3; cf. also the famous quotation of Papias which appears on p. 163.

64. See below pp. 197–203.

8. The evangelists played no significant role in their recording of the gospel traditions.

A last presupposition of the early form critics that must be mentioned was their negative assessment of the literary role of the Evangelists. For them, the Evangelists were merely editors and not authors. They functioned as *Sammlern*, "collectors" of the tradition who worked with "scissors and paste" and simply glued together the materials. Dibelius made a distinction between Luke as the "author" of Acts and the "collector and editor" of the Gospel of Luke![65] No doubt the sociological orientation of form criticism helped bring about this neglect, despite the fact that Wrede's *Das Messiasgeheimnis In Den Evangelien* (1901) was well received by the early form critics. In this work Wrede portrayed Mark as an author and a theologian rather than as a mere "collector." We shall have occasion shortly to look more fully into this issue,[66] but it should be noted here that even today among certain redaction critics it is more popular to talk as if the Markan "community" rather than the Evangelist produced this Gospel. Such terminology clearly reveals that even among redaction critics there is sometimes present an anti-individualistic and pro-sociological bias. Yet surely it is safer to talk of the Evangelist who produced the Gospel of Mark than the community that produced it, for whatever the relationship of the Evangelist to his community, we know that he, not the community, wrote this Gospel.[67] Furthermore, the Gospel of Mark may not at all reflect the theology of the community to which he was writing.[68] Mark may have sought to correct its theology. Surely it would be foolish to speak of the Galatian community that produced Galatians or the Corinthian community that produced 1 and 2 Corinthians. Paul did not write these letters because they reflected the theology and practices of those communities but because they did not. He wanted these churches to conform to his theology and practice as found in these letters. If the theology of the Galatian community conformed to the Book of Galatians, Paul would never have written this letter! Whether the community for which Mark wrote had the identical theology that is found in his Gospel is uncertain, although doubtful. What is certain is that the Evangelist held this theology, so that when we speak of the "theology of Mark" we mean primarily the theology of the Evangelist himself. It is furthermore questionable whether Luke even wrote for a community. The only sure audience of Luke–Acts is Theophilus. The socio-

65. Dibelius, *From Tradition to Gospel*, p. 3.
66. See below pp. 222–24.
67. William Manson's statement that "Communities do not create. . . ." should be noted here (*Jesus the Messiah* [Philadelphia: Westminster, 1946], p. 49).
68. Cf. H. Frankmölle, "Evangelist und Gemeinde" in *Bib* 60 (1979):182, 190.

logical emphasis present in form criticism and also at times in redaction criticism seems to confuse the meaning and origin of the text with what we can learn about the early church from the text. For form critics this was understandable but an error none the less. For redaction critics it is also an error but far less understandable.

Conclusion

In concluding this chapter on form criticism it may be useful to list the eight basic presuppositions that characterize this discipline:

1. Before the Gospels were written there was a period of oral tradition.
2. During the oral period, the narratives and sayings, with the exception of the passion narrative, circulated mainly as single and self-contained, detached units, each complete in itself.
3. The material in the Gospels can be classified according to their form.
4. The vital factors that gave rise to and preserved these forms are to be found in the practical interests of the Christian community.
5. The material of the tradition has no biographical or chronological or geographical value.
6. The original form of the tradition may be recovered and its history traced, before being written down, by discovering the laws of the tradition.
7. The eyewitnesses played no significant role in the process of oral transmission.
8. The Evangelists played no significant role in their recording of the gospel traditions.

The above list witnesses to both the helpful insights that form criticism has provided and why the results of some form critics have been so negative concerning the historical value of the gospel traditions. We shall deal more fully with the value of form criticism later,[69] but it must be pointed out again that each of these eight presuppositions has been challenged in varying degrees. Certain of them err by converting partial factors or truths into universal ones. The first five presuppositions fall into this category. The sixth presupposition is being seriously questioned today because it was based upon insufficient and misleading data. There may indeed be "tendencies" in the passing on of oral tradition, but these are in no way "laws," and how these tendencies

69. See below pp. 217–28.

are to be discovered is left unclear. The most serious objections must be raised against the last two unstated, but nevertheless assumed, presuppositions. Here certain form critics, especially the Bultmannian school, have made two errors that have had serious consequences. With regard to the seventh presupposition, it has led to a radical and negative view of the historicity of the gospel traditions. In many instances it would probably be more accurate to say that this presupposition supported an already existing radical and negative view of the historicity of the gospel materials, because this anti-historical view was prior to and helped formulate the presupposition. It may therefore be that an *a priori* antisupernaturalistic world view produced this basic form-critical presupposition, rather than that this presupposition produced a negative historical evaluation of the tradition.[70] The last presupposition, which we shall have opportunity to discuss again later,[71] had serious consequences hermeneutically, for it caused its followers to neglect what the Evangelists were saying in their Gospels.

70. Pierre Benoit labels this "The Anti-historical Aspect of Form-criticism" (*Jesus and the Gospel*, trans. Benet Weatherhead [London: Darton, Longman & Todd, 1973], 1:28).
    71. See chapters 10–12.

8

The General Reliability
of the Oral Transmission
of the Gospel Traditions

In the past, the discussion of how the gospel materials were transmitted during the oral period has tended to ignore certain data and considerations. Our understanding of the history of the Christian church in its earliest decades, our understanding of the early Christian environment, and even our understanding of the gospel materials themselves have all grown since the earliest form critics first wrote and founded the discipline of form criticism. As a result, it may well be that there are now "New Directions in Form Criticism,"[1] which require that we reassess the earliest portrayal of the process of oral transmission in the early church. It may be that many of the early conceptions of how the Jesus tradition was passed on in the decades following Jesus' death and resurrection must be seriously modified or even rejected. In chapter 7 it was evident that several of the presuppositions upon which early form criticism was constructed are questionable. We shall now look at certain factors that will demonstrate that the *Sitz im Leben* in which the gospel materials were transmitted was far less free and anonymous and far more controlled than first suggested. We shall also look at certain data in the Gospels that will argue in favor

1. Note the name of this article by E. Earle Ellis in *Jesus Christus in Historie und Theologie*, ed. G. Strecker (Tübingen: J.C.B. Mohr, 1975), pp. 305–9.

of the faithful transmission of these materials. Other considerations will also be presented to help us arrive at an overall attitude toward the historical reliability of these traditions.

Gospel Materials That Witness to the Traditions' Faithful Transmission

Within the Gospels there exist certain statements or activities of Jesus that are "unflattering" or theologically difficult. Some of these have caused biblical scholars unending trouble over the centuries. Numerous "harmonists" have sought to explain away the difficulties of these passages with varying degrees of success. If the church created, molded, and preserved only material that served its own religious needs, how do we explain the presence of such material in the Gospels as:

> And Jesus said to him, "Why do you call me good? No one is good but God alone" [Mark 10:18].

> These twelve Jesus sent out, charging them, "Go nowhere among the Gentiles, and enter no town of the Samaritans, but go rather to the lost sheep of the house of Israel" [Matt. 10:5–6].

> And he said to them, "Truly, I say to you, there are some standing here who will not taste death before they see that the kingdom of God has come with power" [Mark 9:1].[2]

Surely the presence of such "problem material" witnesses less to the creative activity of the early church than to its faithful transmission of sacred tradition. Even as the difficulty of such material witnesses to its essential authenticity,[3] it also witnesses to the faithfulness of the transmission process by which such traditions were passed on. William Manson comments: "If the tradition had unfolded itself smoothly out of the mind or theology of the Church, how do we explain the presence in it of enigmatic words such as the saying in Mt. XI.12 about the Kingdom of heaven suffering violence, which the Church probably did not understand, or of obscure parables . . . , or of utterances like Mk.

---

2. Cf. also Matthew 10:23, 34; 11:12; Mark 3:20–21; 7:27; 8:22–26, 33; 13:32; 14:51–52; 15:34; Luke 12:49–51. In his famous article "Gospels" P. W. Schmiedel lists several of these in his "Pillar Passages" for constructing any life of Christ (*Encyclopedia Biblica*, ed. T. K. Cheyne and J. Sutherland Black [London: Adam and Charles Black, 1914], cols. 1881–83).

3. See Robert H. Stein, "The 'Criteria' for Authenticity," in *Gospel Perspectives*, ed. R. T. France and David Wenham (Sheffield: JSOT, 1980), 1:247–48.

X.18, which by seeming to limit the perfect goodness of Jesus must have been offensive to its Christology, or of ethical principles like 'Resist not evil' and 'Love your enemies,' which certainly were not any mere overflow of the Church's moral life?"[4]

A second observation that should be made here involves a comparison of the known religious needs of the early church with the gospel materials. If, as the early form critics have argued, the early church created materials to meet its religious needs, then we would expect to find those needs reflected and dealt with in the Gospels. This is especially true with regard to the most important religious issues that the early church faced. For example, it is clear that the most crucial issue that the early church encountered involved the question of circumcision. Did Gentile converts need to submit to circumcision in order to become Christians? Or to word it differently, did a Gentile have to become a Jew in order to become a Christian? The church's decision was that they did not (Acts 15:1–35; Gal. 2:1–10). Yet where do we find any "circumcision materials" in the Gospels? Where do we find this issue reflected in the gospel traditions? Actually there is only one reference to circumcision in the Gospels and it, if anything, seems to justify the practice (John 7:22)! Surely, if the early church was creating gospel traditions to meet its religious needs, one would expect to find something on this subject in those traditions. Why did not some early Christian prophet utter a "holy law" to deal with this crucial issue? Other areas of controversy in the early church for which we do not find any reference in the gospel materials involve church polity, speaking in tongues, spiritual gifts, divorce between a believer and an unbeliever, and more. The lack of such material in the Gospels witnesses against the idea that the church created large amounts of the gospel materials and in favor of the view that the church tended to transmit the Jesus traditions faithfully.[5]

---

4. William Manson, *Jesus the Messiah* (Philadelphia: Westminster, 1946), p. 50. Compare the similar argument made by Origen: "If they [the Evangelists] were not honest, but, as Celsus thinks, were composing fictitious stories, they would not have recorded Peter's denial or that Jesus' disciples were offended" [at him] (*Contra Celsum*, trans. Henry Chadwick [Cambridge: Cambridge University, 1953], p. 81 [2.15]).

5. Cf. G. B. Caird's conclusion: "There is in fact not one shred of evidence that the early Church ever concocted sayings of Jesus in order to solve any of its problems" ("The Study of the Gospels: II. Form Criticism," *ET* 87 [1976]: 140). Thorlief Boman points out that there are twenty-four speeches in the Book of Acts and these take up approximately 300 of Acts' 1,000 verses. In these speeches, however, not a single saying or act of Jesus is recorded. (He does not count Acts 20:35.) He suggests that this demonstrates that the church did not create sayings of Jesus and read them back upon the lips of Jesus, for if they had, we would expect to find more of Jesus' sayings, miracles, stories, etc., in Acts (*Die Jesus-überlieferung im Lichte der Neueren Volkskunde* [Göttingen: Vandenhoeck & Ruprecht, 1967], p. 37).

Another argument in favor of the faithful transmission of the gospel materials involves a comparison of the favorite Christological title found in the Gospels with the preferred title for Jesus found in the rest of the New Testament. The favorite title of the early church, as witnessed to in Acts–Revelation, is the title "Christ," which is used of Jesus over 450 times. On the other hand, the favorite title for Jesus in the Gospels is clearly "Son of man," a designation found eighty-two times. In the rest of the New Testament, however, the title "Son of man" is found only four times (Acts 7:56; Heb. 2:6; Rev. 1:13 and 14:14), and only in Acts 7:56 is it used in the same sense as in the Gospels. As for the title "Christ," the term appears fifty-four times in the Gospels, but—if we eliminate the clearly editorial framework of the Evangelists,[6] the Johannine materials, and those passages in which no reference is being made to Jesus[7]—we have only twenty-four uses of this title for Jesus in the gospel traditions.[8] Furthermore, six of these are parallel expressions.[9] From the above it is clear that the favorite title for Jesus in the Gospels ("Son of man") is almost never used in Acts–Revelation, and the favorite title in Acts–Revelation ("Christ") is found far less frequently in the gospel traditions than in the rest of the New Testament. How can we explain this? How can one explain why the favorite title for Jesus in the early church occurs so infrequently in the Gospels and why the favorite title for Jesus in the Gospels appears in the same sense only once in all of Acts–Revelation? Certainly this is not what one would expect if the church freely created and modified the gospel traditions to fit and meet its religious needs. If the early church handled the traditions as freely and creatively as the early form critics claimed, one would not expect to find this. On the contrary, one would expect to find a relatively equal proportion of "Christ" and "Son of man" titles in the Gospels and in the rest of the New Testament.[10] The severely disproportionate usage of these titles argues strongly against the view that the early church created or radically modified the gospel traditions. Rather, it argues in favor of the view that the early

6. Cf. Matthew 1:1, 16, 17; 11:2; Mark 1:1; John 1:17; etc.

7. Cf. Matthew 22:42/Mark 12:35/Luke 20:41; Luke 3:15.

8. Matthew 2:4; 16:16, 20; 23:10; 24:5, 23; 26:63, 68; 27:17, 22; Mark 8:29; 9:41; 13:21; 14:61; 15:32; Luke 2:11, 26; 4:41; 9:20; 22:67; 23:2, 35, 39; 24:26.

9. *Matthew 16:16*/Mark 8:29/*Luke 9:20*; *Matthew 24:23*/ Mark 13:21; *Matthew 26:63*/Mark 14:61/*Luke 22:67*; Mark 15:32/*Luke 23:35*.

10. The fact that the Gospels were by no means the earliest New Testament writings should also be noted. By the time they were written there would have been ample time for the Christology of the early church to have affected the tradition.

church faithfully preserved the gospel traditions, which portrayed Jesus as having used for his favorite self-designation the title "Son of man" and having avoided the open usage of the title "Christ."[11]

The Early Church's High View of Tradition

Christians today who come out of a free-church background frequently have difficulty in understanding the role that "church tradition" plays and the high esteem in which it is held in other denominations, especially in denominations of long standing. Such terms as "early Church Fathers," "Lutheran," "Calvinism," "Nicean," "Wesleyan," and "Westminster Confession of Faith" inspire reverence and a sense of authority in some groups that many free-church people cannot always understand. In practice, of course, Baptists, Congregationalists, and "independents" often have their own set of important traditions in theology (e.g., the independence of the local church, freedom of conscience) and lifestyle (e.g., total abstinence, no smoking), which tend to be relatively unspoken and vary from region to region. It is therefore important that we note carefully how the New Testament viewed "tradition" and especially the gospel traditions.

While it is true that Jesus clearly condemned the rabbinic traditions that were circulating in his day because they violated the clear commandments of the law (cf. Mark 7:1–13), we find in the New Testament a high respect for the gospel traditions and other traditions of the early church. This attitude toward the early church traditions was not late in developing but is already witnessed to in 1 Corinthians 11:2, 23; 15:1, 3; Galatians 1:9; Philippians 4:9; and 1 Thessalonians 4:1. Such traditions were to be "held" on to (1 Cor. 15:1–2; 2 Thess. 2:15); life was to be lived "in accord" with the tradition (2 Thess. 3:6; cf. Phil. 4:9), for the result of this would be salvation (1 Cor. 15:1–2), whereas its rejection meant damnation (Gal. 1:9). The reason for this view was that this tradition had God himself as its ultimate source (1 Cor. 11:23).[12]

---

11. For a discussion of Jesus' use of these two titles, see Robert H. Stein, *The Method and Message of Jesus' Teachings* (Philadelphia: Westminster, 1978), pp. 121–27, 133–48.

12. Although Paul claimed that his gospel came from the Lord (cf. 1 Cor. 11:23; Gal. 1:9, 12), this does not exclude the fact that he received part of the content of the revelation through the "eyewitnesses and ministers of the word." See Oscar Cullmann, *The Early Church*, ed. A. J. B. Higgins (London: SCM Press, 1956), pp. 59–75; G. E. Ladd, "Revelation and Tradition in Paul," in *Apostolic History and the Gospel*, ed. W. Ward Gasque and Ralph P. Martin (Grand Rapids: Eerdmans, 1970), pp. 223–30; and Ronald Y. K. Fung, "Revelation and Tradition: The Origins of Paul's Gospel," *EQ* 57 (1985): 34–41.

This high view of the tradition is also witnessed to by Paul's own behavior. In his discussion of the marital questions about which the Corinthians had written (1 Cor. 7), Paul quotes a gospel tradition concerning divorce: "To the married I give charge, not I but the Lord, that the wife should not separate from her husband (but if she does, let her remain single or else be reconciled to her husband)—and that the husband should not divorce his wife" (vv. 10–11). Yet concerning another related issue he writes differently: "To the rest I say, not the Lord, that if any brother has a wife who is an unbeliever, and she consents to live with him, he should not divorce her" (v. 12). Here Paul makes a clear distinction between the gospel tradition and his own, but no less authoritative, teaching. Another clear example of Paul's respect for the gospel tradition is found in verse 25 of the same chapter: "Now concerning the unmarried, I have no command of the Lord, but I give my opinion as one who by the Lord's mercy is trustworthy." Concerning the situation of the unmarried in the church, Paul possessed no tradition from the historical Jesus that he could share with the Corinthians, but as an apostle he could by the "Spirit of God" (cf. v. 40b) give his recommendation. Again Paul's obvious distinction between the Jesus tradition and his own apostolic teaching should be noted. Clearly, for Paul, the gospel traditions were a given that one delivered and received, and the creation of new material to read back into the gospel tradition was not a prerogative for even an apostle. And if this were not a prerogative available for the apostle Paul, how much less would it be a prerogative of the anonymous church!

The high regard that Paul had for the tradition is also apparent in Romans 6:17, where the apostle says: "But thanks be to God, that you who were once slaves of sin have become obedient from the heart to the standard of teaching to which you were committed. . . ." Whereas today we tend to speak of how the early church delivered and transmitted the transmission and whether it did so with greater or lesser precision, the whole matter is reversed in Romans 6:17. It is not the tradition that is handed over to the believers, but the opposite. The believers are handed over to the tradition! Although the majority of other references in the New Testament refer to the delivery of the tradition to the church, here it is the church that is handed over to the tradition. It is the tradition that preserves the church! It is the "standard of teaching," i.e., the tradition, that ultimately serves as the final canon of authority. What is clear is that such a statement, along with the others already mentioned, reveals so high a view of the tradition that even apostles were not free to add new sayings of Jesus to it.

The Role of Eyewitnesses in Transmitting the Gospel Traditions

Within the New Testament we find numerous references that reveal the high regard in which eyewitness testimony was held. In the Johannine literature we have several appeals to eyewitness testimony in order to validate the apostolic message. In 1 John 1:1–3 John states, against the docetic teaching that denied the true humanity of the Son of God and argued that it only appeared (*dokeō*) that the Word became flesh (1 John 4:1–3), that he "heard . . . seen with [his] eyes . . . looked upon . . . touched with [his] hands . . . the word of life. . . ." It is his eyewitness experience with Jesus that enables John to refute the docetic heresy. He was there, and so he knows that Jesus was no phantom. In the Gospel of John the eyewitness testimony of the Evangelist is witnessed to by his words: "He who saw it has borne witness—his testimony is true, and he knows that he tells the truth—that you also may believe" (John 19:35). This same appeal is made in John 21:24: "This is the disciple who is bearing witness to these things, and who has written these things; and we know that his testimony is true." A similar appeal is made to the value of eyewitness testimony in 1 Corinthians 15:6, although here a specific event is being referred to: "Then he appeared to more than five hundred brethren at one time, most of whom are still alive, though some have fallen asleep." In the Petrine Epistles we find the same reference to the value of eyewitness testimony: "So I exhort the elders among you, as a fellow elder and a witness of the sufferings of Christ . . ." (1 Peter 5:1) and "For we did not follow cleverly devised myths when we made known to you the power and coming of our Lord Jesus Christ, but we were eyewitnesses of his majesty" (2 Peter 1:16).

It is in Luke, however, that we find the strongest emphasis on the role of the eyewitness in the transmission process of the gospel materials. For Luke, the role of the apostolic band in witnessing to the gospel message is of cardinal importance. The theme of Acts is found in the eighth verse of the first chapter. There the risen Christ says to his disciples, "But you shall receive power when the Holy Spirit has come upon you; and you shall be my witnesses in Jerusalem and in all Judea and Samaria and to the end of the earth." The coming of the Spirit at Pentecost did not change the content of that "witness" but primarily provided "power" and a divine enabling for the bearing of that witness throughout the world. The content of that witness is made crystal clear by Luke in this same chapter. When a successor for Judas is selected, for the symbol of "twelve" had to be maintained, the only requirement mentioned is that he had to have "accompanied us during all the time that the Lord Jesus went in and out among us, beginning from the baptism of John until the day when he was taken up from us" (vv. 21–22). Here it is clear that the main importance of the Twelve for Luke lies in their witness to Jesus' ministry and resurrection. For Luke, there is no distinction between *Historie* (the historical events of Jesus' life surrounding his ministry) and *Geschichte* (his resurrection and ascension). They are all part of the same tradition that the apostles were called to proclaim. As a result we find Peter saying to Cornelius, "And we are witnesses to all that he did in the country of the Jews and in Jerusalem" (Acts 10:39; cf. also Acts 5:32) and that he was one of those chosen by God to be a "witness" (10:41). Although the latter reference refers primarily to the resurrection itself, in light of verses 37–39 it must also be understood as including what Jesus "did in the country of the Jews and in Jerusalem."

This Lukan understanding of the role of the eyewitnesses in the transmission process is even more clearly stated in Luke 1:1–2. Here "those who from the beginning were eyewitnesses and ministers of the word" were the ones who "delivered" the "things which have been accomplished among us." To what extent the latter statement refers to the material in Acts is much debated, but it clearly refers to the traditions contained in the Gospel of Luke. It was, according to the Lukan prologue, the eyewitnesses who were the ministers of the "word." Here it is clear by the use of the one article for both "eyewitnesses" and "ministers of the word" that a single group is meant. It was through these eyewitnesses, Luke tells us, that the gospel traditions were delivered before being written down. Luke's teaching and intention here, and in the Acts passages already mentioned, are clear. During the period between the resurrection/ascension of Jesus and the writing down of the "narratives" (Luke 1:1), the gospel traditions were delivered by the eyewitnesses. To what extent "delivered" is a technical term in Luke 1:2 is uncertain.[13] Nevertheless, it must mean that the eyewitnesses were involved in the teaching of these traditions and also in passing them on. Whether this involved a memorization process such as we find in later Judaism is not clear. What is clear is that "in the second verse [of the Lukan prologue] a supreme and unique place is accorded to apostolic tradition."[14]

We have already mentioned that most of the early form critics

13. The double use of "delivered" and "received" by Paul in 1 Corinthians 11:23 and 15:3 does suggest that for Paul the use of these terms for the passing on and acquiring of tradition possessed at least a "quasi-technical" meaning.

14. Ned B. Stonehouse, *Origins of the Synoptic Gospels* (Grand Rapids: Eerdmans, 1963), p. 127.

tended to ignore the presence of eyewitnesses in the early church and to deny to them any significant role in the transmission of the oral traditions. The reason for this is not difficult to understand. How can one refer to the eyewitnesses of "miracle stories" if by definition miracles cannot happen? It was D. E. Nineham who has given the main defense of this form-critical presupposition.[15] Only a few of Nineham's arguments need be mentioned here, but some of the most important are:

1. The emphasis on eyewitness testimony in the New Testament is for the most part late and primarily serves an apologetic function;
2. The rounded pericope form of the tradition rules out the possibility that this is the result of eyewitness testimony;[16]
3. Form criticism is based upon an *a posteriori* observation of characteristics within the finished Gospels as opposed to the *a priori* presuppositions held by those who argue that the eyewitnesses must have played an important role in the transmission of these materials.

Nineham has done scholarship a great service by clearly and forcefully presenting the basic argumentation of the form critics for a negative assessment of the eyewitnesses' role in the transmission of the gospel materials. Upon closer examination, however, Nineham's argumentation possesses numerous weaknesses. Some of the New Testament references, to be sure, are late, but does the lateness of Luke's Gospel necessitate that Luke 1:1–4 be unreliable? Are the speeches of Acts purely a Lukan creation or does Acts 10:39, 41 (cf. 1 Peter 5:1) go back in some way to older tradition and perhaps to Peter himself?[17] Furthermore, even if Luke wrote with an apologetical purpose in mind, does this automatically falsify what he and the other New Testament writers said on this matter? Surely the term "apologetic" should not be so interpreted as to imply that untruth and/or deceit is connected with it. With regard to the present form of the accounts, Nineham apparently believes that eyewitness testimony requires a non-rounded

15. This appeared in a series of articles entitled "Eye-Witness Testimony and the Gospel Tradition," *JTS* 9 (1958): 13–25, 243–52; and 11 (1960): 253–64.

16. Concerning the Gospel of Mark, Nineham states that ". . . no plausible reason can be given why recollection derived directly from the living voice of St. Peter should have been cast in the stereotyped, impersonal form of community tradition" (Ibid., p. 243).

17. For a positive view of the historicity of the speeches in Acts, see W. Ward Gasque, *A History of the Criticism of the Acts of the Apostles* (Grand Rapids: Eerdmans, 1975).

form, but ironically enough it is the rounded form that some form
critics have argued is most historical and the non-rounded or mixed
form the least! Actually, why should we assume that an eyewitness
testimony must be non-rounded? If we assume for the moment that
Peter repeated a pericope every month up to the time that Mark wrote
his Gospel (c. 65), this would mean that he told the same account 420
times (35 years × 12). If he told it once every week, he would have
repeated it 1,820 times (35 × 52)! Surely Peter's eyewitness testimony
could become quite "stereotyped and generalized" in such a process.
Furthermore, would not the eyewitnesses have intentionally repeated
the gospel materials in a rounded form in order to help their hearers
remember this material? Jesus certainly used poetic forms and mnemonic devices to help his hearers retain his teachings. Why would it
seem strange for the eyewitnesses to do the same with their accounts
of the teachings and acts of the Lord of Glory?

As to the claim that form criticism is based upon *a posteriori* observations rather than *a priori* presuppositions, it should be noted that the *a
posteriori* observations of the form critics are clearly made in the framework of numerous *a priori* presuppositions.[18] The fact remains that the
clearest empirical evidence available as to how the gospel traditions
were transmitted is Luke 1:1–4. Here the eyewitnesses do not just play
an important part but assume the chief role in the process. Since we
should not presuppose that eyewitnesses could not have shaped the
materials in easily remembered forms or arranged them topically rather
than chronologically, and in light of the clear teaching of the Lukan
prologue, there is no reason to reject or minimize the role of the eyewitnesses in the transmission of the gospel materials. After all, Luke's
description of the process by which the gospel traditions were passed
on was nearly 1,900 years closer to the actual process of transmission
than modern-day form critics.

No doubt the view of the earliest church as an anonymous, charismatic, unorganized, and leaderless community has played a significant
role in the denigration of the role of the apostolic eyewitnesses in the
transmission of the gospel materials. Yet the New Testament portrays
the church as being far from anonymous. Unless the accounts in Acts
are grossly inaccurate, the early church had a center—Jerusalem, and a
leadership—the apostles. Of the period after the church had spread
out from Jerusalem to Samaria, we read: "Now when the apostles at
Jerusalem heard that Samaria had received the word of God, they sent
to them Peter and John . . ." (Acts 8:14). When it spread to Antioch,
"News of this came to the ears of the church in Jerusalem, and they

18. See pp. 183–85, 199–200, 212–13.

sent Barnabas to Antioch" (Acts 11:22). When the issue of circumcision as a requirement for church membership came to a head, the church in Antioch appointed Paul and Barnabas "to go up to Jerusalem to the apostles and the elders about this question" (Acts 15:2). It was at Jerusalem that the first church council passed a decree on this matter (Acts 15:23–29). Paul also knew and accepted the importance of the Jerusalem apostles: ". . . I laid before them . . . the gospel which I preach among the Gentiles, lest somehow I should be running or had run in vain" (Gal. 2:2). And it was at Jerusalem that he received "the right hand of fellowship" to go to the Gentiles and preach the gospel (Gal. 2:9). It should also be noted in this regard that Paul returned to Jerusalem after each of his missionary journeys! To claim that all of this is pure fabrication by Luke would be wholly unjustified. The early church was not without leadership. The discovery of the Dead Sea Scrolls, with their highly developed organizational structure, furthermore reveals that if the Qumran community possessed such careful organization, there is no reason why the early church was any less structured. The New Testament clearly presents a picture of the early church as centered in Jerusalem with the apostles as leaders or, to use the terms of the New Testament itself, the church is ". . . built upon the foundation of the apostles and prophets, Christ Jesus himself being the cornerstone . . ." (Eph. 2:20).

The church could also be described as "charismatic," if by that term we mean that it was uniquely aware of the Spirit's presence in its midst. Yet, being charismatic does not necessarily exclude a high view of tradition. On the contrary, many charismatic communities clearly regiment by their traditions the kinds of charismatic experiences, phrases, and behavior that are permissible. Paul in his letters clearly ". . . sees no antithesis between pneumatic piety and the high estimation of tradition."[19] The pneumatic character of the early church therefore does not in any way exclude the conscious and careful transmission of authoritative tradition. The view of the early church as a primitive, charismatic, free-spirited, and pure democracy, which later degenerated into an orthodox early Catholic Church, has a beautiful "Rousseau-like" simplicity. For many, such a romantic picture is irresistible. Such a description of the early church is nevertheless based upon fantasy and not upon what we can learn from the New Testament!

Probably no one has done more to popularize the view that the gospel traditions were transmitted according to the methods common in rabbinic Judaism than Birger Gerhardsson. Although others had

---

19. *TDNT*, 2:172; cf. Rainer Riesner, *Jesus als Lehrer* (Tübingen: J. C. B. Mohr, 1981), pp. 424–26.

suggested this earlier,[20] it was Gerhardsson's *Memory and Manuscript: Oral Tradition and Written Transmission in Rabbinic Judaism and Early Christianity* that described in fullest detail the rabbinic process for the transmission of oral tradition. Gerhardsson argues that this rabbinic process is the closest available analogy to what actually occurred in Jesus' own ministry and in the life of the early church. He begins his work with a detailed study of the rabbinic methodology for the passing on of holy tradition. In this comparative study of the rabbinic materials he describes how the *tannaim* carefully and deliberately passed on tradition to their disciples, who memorized these traditions word-for-word, using constant repetition and mnemonic devices. This pattern, Gerhardsson believes, existed among the rabbis of Jesus' day and provides the most immediate parallel for the way Jesus taught his own disciples. Jesus analogously, even if not in exactly the same way, taught his disciples carefully and deliberately to memorize his teachings and used mnemonic devices and repetition to aid them in this process. Jesus delivered his teachings to the disciples in fixed form and according to a rabbinic teacher-pupil analogy. The disciples in turn supervised the passing on of this fixed tradition in a similar manner to the church. The contexts in which this was primarily done were the church's celebration of the Lord's Supper, catechetical instruction of church members, and Bible study. This passing on of the tradition did not, however, exclude their making editorial changes in their handling of the texts, but these changes were due to the apostolic formation of the materials, not because of the anonymous church.

Gerhardsson's thesis (and that of his teacher, Riesenfeld) has received a number of serious criticisms. For one, the question has been raised as to whether the transmission process described in the rabbinic literature can legitimately be read back into the time of Jesus. Smith and Neusner have argued that whereas Gerhardsson's portrayal of the transmission process is valid during the tannaitic period, it is invalid before A.D. 70, i.e., in Jesus' *Sitz im Leben*.[21] They argue that the events of A.D. 70 produced a totally different situation and set of needs for Judaism, so that the rabbinic materials can only be used with great difficulty to describe pre-70 circumstances. The content and methodology of the Jewish tradition underwent a radical change after the fall of

---

20. Cf. William Manson, *Jesus the Messiah*, p. 48; Harald Riesenfeld, *The Gospel Tradition*, trans. E. Margaret Rowley and Robert A. Kraft (Philadelphia: Fortress, 1970).

21. Morton Smith, "A Comparison of Early Christian and Early Rabbinic Tradition," *JBL* 82 (1963): 169–72; Jacob Neusner, *The Rabbinic Traditions About the Pharisees Before 70* (Leiden: E. J. Brill, 1971), 3:146f.; and Philip S. Alexander, "Rabbinic Judaism and the New Testament," *ZNW* 74 (1983): 237–46. The latter is a most helpful and readable summary. See especially pp. 241–42 and 244–45.

Jerusalem. As a result, the process of transmission described by Gerhardsson, while true of second- and third-century Judaism, is simply not true of Jesus' day. Yet Neusner's and Smith's conclusions are not without their own critics.[22] Neusner's radical skepticism seems to be too extreme. Certainly we must reject the naive view that the rabbinic sources are objective historical sources unaffected by the transmission process. But it is unproven and unlikely that such a radical change in the transmission process would have resulted from the events of A.D. 70.[23] A second protest against the thesis of Gerhardsson lies in the fact that Jesus was no rabbi. Since he had no rabbinical training, the analogy of Jesus' teaching "like a rabbi" is invalid. That Jesus was not a trained rabbi goes without saying, although he was certainly a skilled teacher. Yet, despite his strong criticism of *what* the Pharisees and scribes taught, there is no reason why Jesus had to reject the method, or *how* they taught. Nowhere in the Gospels does Jesus criticize the Pharisees and scribes for requiring their disciples to memorize and for using mnemonic devices! Furthermore, it is dangerous to argue that Jesus could not have taught in this manner because he lacked rabbinic training. It would have been natural for Jesus to appropriate any useful and known didactic method to teach and preach his gospel. Another objection raised against Gerhardsson's thesis is that the gospel materials show too great a divergence to have been the product of such a transmission process. This is a serious problem, but it runs into the objection that the oral process of transmission is equated with the written process we find in our Gospels. The legitimacy of such an equation is being seriously questioned today.[24] We could also mention other objections, such as "belief in the living Lord presumably fostered more creativity than one finds in the Rabbinic material"[25] or that the "unhistorical" nature of the tradition does not permit such a process of transmission.[26] With regard to the former objection, however, we have

22. See, for instance, S. Zeitlin, "Spurious Interpretations of Rabbinic Sources in the Studies of the Pharisees and Pharisaism," *JQR* 65 (1974):122–35.

23. See Peter H. Davids, "The Gospels and Jewish Tradition: Twenty Years after Gerhardsson," in *Gospel Perspectives,* ed. R. T. France and David Wenham (Sheffield: JSOT, 1980), 1:76–82.

24. See above pp. 181–83.

25. E. P. Sanders, *The Tendencies of the Synoptic Tradition* (Cambridge: Cambridge University, 1969), pp. 27–28.

26. Smith clearly reveals the extent to which historical presuppositions and bias play a role in his position when he speaks of the material in the traditions, "which, by the standards of common sense, are incredible," as a tradition "which freely multiplied miracles," and as a "mess of contradictory scraps of evidence." When the birth stories and nature miracles are seen as "false accretions to the tradition," there simply cannot be a careful eyewitness transmission process by definition ("A Comparison of Early Christian and Early Rabbinic Tradition," pp. 173, 174, and 176).

clear evidence to the contrary. Paul, for example, did not feel free to create dominical material, as the contrast between 1 Corinthians 7:10 and 12 demonstrates. This objection errs positively in attributing too great a creativity to the apostles and negatively by attributing too little creativity to the tannaitic rabbis. Concerning the "unhistorical" nature of the gospel materials, if the Gospels are grossly unhistorical and the gospel materials simply incredible, then by definition no careful transmission process could have taken place. But such a conclusion is based upon a particular evaluation of the historicity of the events recorded in the Gospels, and this in turn is based upon an *a priori* presupposition that denies the supernatural in history.

In evaluating the thesis of Gerhardsson, it is clear that he has "struck a nerve" of the form critics. What he has said, however, is a helpful contribution to the discussion. It is now clearer than ever before that Jesus was a teacher. In fact the Gospels describe him as a teacher forty-five times and the term "rabbi" is used of him fourteen times. One of his prominent activities was teaching (Matt. 4:23). Like the rabbis, he proclaimed the divine law (Mark 12:28–34), gathered disciples (Mark 1:16–20; 3:13–19),[27] debated with the religious authorities (Mark 7:5f.; 11:27–33; 12:13–17, 18–27), was asked to settle legal disputes (Mark 12:13–17; Luke 12:13–15), and supported his teaching with Scripture (Matt. 12:40; 18:16; Mark 2:25–26; 4:12; 10:6–8, 19; 12:26, 29–31, 36).[28] He also used mnemonic devices, such as parables, exaggerations, puns, metaphors and similes, proverbs, riddles, and parabolic actions, to aid his disciples and audience in retaining his teachings. Above all he used poetry, *parallelismus membrorum*, for this purpose. Jeremias has listed 138 examples of antithetical parallelism in Jesus' teaching that are found in the synoptic Gospels alone,[29] and to these over fifty other examples of synonymous, synthetic, chiasmic, and step parallelism can be added.[30] In light of all this, it is evident that Jesus "carefully thought out and deliberately formulated [his] statements."[31]

There is also evidence in the gospel materials that Jesus "must have

27. The historicity of the "Twelve" has been challenged by a number of scholars, but the presence of Judas in the group (who in the early church would create such a group and then make one of them a traitor?) and the account in Acts 1:12–26 of the selection of Judas' replacement argue strongly for the historicity of this group. To this can be added the reference in the pre-Pauline tradition found in 1 Corinthians 15:5.

28. See Stein, *Jesus' Teachings*, pp. 1–2; Riesner, *Jesus als Lehrer*, pp. 246–76.

29. Joachim Jeremias, *New Testament Theology*, trans. John Bowden (New York: Scribner's, 1971), pp. 15–16.

30. See Stein, *Jesus' Teachings*, pp. 27–32.

31. Birger Gerhardsson, *The Origins of the Gospel Traditions* (Philadelphia: Fortress, 1979), p. 69.

required his disciples to memorize."[32] In Luke 11:1 Jesus is asked to teach his disciples a prayer that they could memorize and make their own and that would identify those praying this prayer as his disciples. In addition the disciples were to remember not only his teachings but his actions as well (Mark 8:17–21). It is true that in Matthew 10:18–20 the disciples are told not to worry about what they should say, for the Holy Spirit would give them the words to speak. Yet this was advice for martyrs in their hour of trial, not for their normal teaching mission! With regard to the mission of the disciples, we shall see in the next section that they must have received some training and that this mission provides a natural situation in the life of Jesus for his having delivered the gospel materials to the disciples.[33]

The high esteem in which Jesus was held by the disciples would also guarantee that the words of Jesus where cherished and carefully remembered by them.[34] Surely Jesus was revered more than even Hillel or Shammai—if such passages as Matthew 5:17; 7:21–23; 10:32–33; 11:6; Mark 8:34–38; Luke 14:26; etc., have any historical basis. It is furthermore difficult to believe that the disciples to whom Jesus said, "Blessed are the eyes which see what you see! For I tell you that many prophets and kings desired to see what you see, and did not see it, and to hear what you hear, and did not hear it" (Luke 10:23b–24) would not have exercised great care to memorize and preserve those words of Jesus which the prophets of old longed to hear. Gerhardsson is certainly correct when he says, "All historical probability is in favour of Jesus' disciples, and the whole of early Christianity, having accorded the sayings of the one whom they believed to be the Messiah at least the same degree of respect as the pupils of a Rabbi accorded the words of *their* master!"[35] This is especially evident when we realize that whereas the rabbinic disciples were primarily committed to their teachers' interpretation of the Torah, the disciples were primarily committed to the *person* of Jesus. They were followers not so much of Jesus' teachings

32. Birger Gerhardsson, *Memory and Manuscript*, trans. Eric J. Sharpe (Uppsala: C. W. K. Gleerup, 1961), p. 328.

33. See below pp. 203–5.

34. Jacob Neusner states: "No rabbi was so important to rabbinical Judaism as Jesus was to Christianity. None prophesied as an independent authority. None left a category of 'I' sayings, for none had the prestige to do so" (*Development of a Legend* [Leiden: E. J. Brill, 1970], p. 190).

35. Gerhardsson, *Memory and Manuscript*, p. 258. Gerhardsson also states, "Since Jesus was considered to be the Messiah, the *'only'* teacher (Matt. 23:10), his sayings must have been accorded even greater authority and sanctity than that accorded by the Rabbis' disciples to the words of their teachers" (p. 332). Cf. also W. D. Davies, *The Setting of the Sermon on the Mount* (Cambridge: Cambridge University, 1966), p. 466; and Riesner, *Jesus als Lehrer*, p. 37.

but of Jesus himself. As a result, Jesus' teachings in the Gospels and the early Christian literature stand out in glorious distinction and absolute separation from the teachings of all others, including the rabbis.

There are some weaknesses in Gerhardsson's thesis that must be noted. For one, although he acknowledges the probable existence of written notes or *private memoranda*,[36] he does not place any great emphasis upon them or discuss their real importance or use. No doubt greater emphasis will be given to such written materials in the future, but the existence of this kind of material is becoming more and more certain.[37] The degree of variation found among the common material in our Gospels will furthermore always be a problem for Gerhardsson. But does this variation argue in favor of the view that the gospel traditions were passed down with more freedom than Gerhardsson allows? Or is it possible that it was in the writing of the Gospels that this variation took place? Also, Gerhardsson's belief that the gospel materials were transmitted in an independent and isolated context raises some additional questions, even though it provides some helpful suggestions as to why we find so few sayings of Jesus in the New Testament epistles. His suggested *Sitz im Leben*(s) of worship, catechetical instruction, and Bible study are reasonable, but there remain difficulties in thinking that the gospel tradition stood in splendid isolation from all other traditional materials.

Having said this, Gerhardsson's main thesis—that the teachings of Jesus found in the gospel traditions owe their shape and origin to Jesus himself, and that the delivery of those traditions during the oral period was supervised by the "eyewitnesses and ministers of the word" (Luke 1:1–2)—is far more convincing than the view that this all took place in the "anonymous community" of the early form critics.[38] Gerhardsson furthermore has convincingly demonstrated that it is wrong to argue from the paucity of references to Jesus' words and deeds in the Epistles that their authors were unfamiliar with the gospel traditions. Are we to assume that the author of Acts was ignorant of the Jesus tradition

36. See *Memory and Manuscript*, p. 335, and *The Origins*, p. 23.

37. In this regard Riesner's *Jesus als Lehrer* is extremely valuable. It is interesting to note here that Martin Dibelius suggested that Paul had papyrus notes containing the teachings of Jesus available to him when he wrote 1 Corinthians (*From Tradition to Gospel*, trans. Bertram Lee Woolf [New York: Scribner's, 1935], p. 242).

38. In his critique of Gerhardsson's *Memory and Manuscript*, Davies has some serious criticisms of Gerhardsson's thesis, but his conclusion is quite positive: "This means, in our judgment, that they [Gerhardsson and Riesenfeld] have made it far more historically probable and reasonably credible, over against the skepticism of much form criticism, that in the Gospels we are within hearing of the authentic voice and within sight of the authentic activity of Jesus of Nazareth, however much muffled and obscured these may be by the process of transmission" (*The Setting of the Sermon on the Mount*, p. 480).

because of the relatively few references to it in Acts? Hardly, for he had just written the Gospel of Luke! Likewise to conclude from the paucity of gospel references in 1 John that this writer was also ignorant of the Jesus tradition is equally fallacious, for he either had written the Gospel of John or knew it well. By analogy, it is therefore dangerous to argue that Paul, or other writers of the New Testament Epistles, did not know the gospel traditions.[39]

A *Sitz im Leben* for the Gospel Traditions of Jesus' Ministry

In an important article, which unfortunately has never been translated into English, H. Schürmann has argued that there existed a clear pre-Easter situation in the life of Jesus in which the gospel materials were transmitted and shaped.[40] Schürmann argued convincingly that within the context of the disciple-teacher setting of Jesus' ministry, and above all in his sending out of the disciples to preach and to heal, we have a natural context for the passing on of the Jesus traditions to the disciples. There seems to be no good reason to deny the historicity of the disciples' mission to heal and preach repentance (Mark 6:12); the nearness of the kingdom of heaven (Matt. 10:7); the kingdom of God (Luke 9:2; cf. 10:9); the gospel (Luke 9:6). After all, they were chosen in part at least, according to Mark 3:14 (and its parallels), "to be sent out to preach." Luke records two such missions (Luke 9:1–6; 10:1–12), which makes it evident that this event (or events) was firmly anchored in the tradition.[41] Furthermore, some of the material associated with this mission is so difficult, that it is hard to imagine it as simply a creation of the early church. An example of this is in Jesus' words to the disciples, "Go nowhere among the Gentiles, and enter no town of

39. See Gerhardsson's "Der Weg der Evangelientradition" in *Das Evangelium und Die Evangelien*, ed. Peter Stuhlmacher (Tübingen: J. C. B. Mohr, 1983), p. 81. In this regard we should also note that if there had not been a problem in Corinth concerning the Lord's Supper (1 Cor. 11:17–22), concerning divorce (1 Cor. 7:1f.), or concerning Paul's apostleship (1 Cor. 9:1f.), we would never have known that Paul was acquainted with material from the Jesus tradition on these matters.

40. Heinz Schürmann, "Die vorösterlichen Anfänge der Logientradition," in *Der Historische Jesus und der Kerugmatische Christus: Beiträge zum Christusverständnis in Forschung und Verkündigung*, ed. H. Ristow and K. Matthiae (Berlin: Evangelische Verlangsanstalt, 1960), pp. 342–70.

41. Gerhardsson states: "This 'sending' has such a strong anchoring in the tradition that, all things being considered, it cannot be dismissed as a simple backdating of the early Christian missionary activity after Easter. . ." (*The Origins of the Gospel Traditions*, p. 73). Cf. also T. W. Manson, *The Sayings of Jesus* (London: SCM Press, 1949), p. 73; and Riesner, *Jesus als Lehrer*, pp. 453–54. Manson states: "The mission of the disciples is one of the best-attested facts in the life of Jesus."

the Samaritans, but go rather to the lost sheep of the house of Israel" (Matt. 10:5b–6).

If in the lifetime of Jesus we possess a mission of the disciples to heal and teach (Mark 6:30), we must then ask *what* they were to teach and preach. If the disciples saw Jesus as greater than John the Baptist (and some of them must have, since they left John the Baptist to follow him), if they believed his message possessed a divine authority and was a divine revelation (cf. Matt. 5:21–48; 7:24–27; 24:35; etc.), and if they knew that Jesus shaped his teachings in easily memorable forms and wanted them to keep his words (Luke 11:28—this verse should be understood in the light of Luke 1:2; 5:1) and share them with others (Matt. 10:27), they must have cherished and preserved the words of their Teacher and Lord and used them as the basis of their teaching.[42] Furthermore, Jesus had stressed the importance of his words. The keeping of them meant life or death (Matt. 7:24–27; Mark 8:38; Luke 6:47–49; 11:28); they would never pass away (Mark 13:31). Therefore, when they proclaimed the coming of the kingdom of God, they possessed their master's "the kingdom of God is like . . . ." They could not improve on this! Indeed, if the disciples went out on their mission in Jesus' name (Luke 10:16), it is simply inconceivable to think that they did not utter what he had told them and proclaim what he had whispered (Matt. 10:27). As a result of their faithful proclamation of Jesus' words, Jesus could say, "He who hears you hears me, and he who rejects you rejects me. . ." (Luke 10:16; cf. Matt. 10:40), for the message of the disciples was the message Jesus taught and gave them.

In this natural *Sitz im Leben* of the pre-Easter community, it would seem most probable that memorization played a considerable part in Jesus' instruction. The mnemonic forms that we find in the gospel traditions are not accidental. Parables do not spring out of anonymous communities.[43] Good parables and good poetic forms come from a creative genius, and Jesus was clearly such a genius. The presence of such forms also indicates that Jesus intended for his teachings to be memorized, so that they would be preserved in the hearts and lives of his listeners and be transmitted to others as well. "The only reasonable explanation is that Jesus sometimes cast his teaching in the forms of Semitic verse in order that it might be memorable."[44] To what extent methods found in the later rabbinic materials played a role in Jesus'

42. Schürmann ("Logientradition," pp. 356–57) points out that, if Jesus' proclamation came as the final and deciding last word of God in this age, it must have been significant for his followers!

43. Cf. Boman, *Die Jesus-Überlieferung*, pp. 11–13, 29. The fact that we do not find parables in the rest of the New Testament or in the early Christian tradition reveals this.

44. Caird, "Study of the Gospels," p. 139.

teaching will always be debated, but it is certainly wrong to assume that Jesus never repeated anything that he said and that he did not care if his listeners remembered what he taught. Since the disciples thoroughly believed that it was in Jesus' teachings that "the words of eternal life" (John 6:68) were to be found, one cannot help but assume that before the resurrection the teachings of Jesus and his acts would have already formed the sacred core around which the preaching of the disciples centered during their mission. The form of his teaching would therefore serve both as an aid for memory and as a convenient form to repeat to others.[45]

It is clear that Schürmann has demonstrated that if form criticism restricts the *Sitz im Leben* of the gospel materials to a post-resurrection setting, it has seriously erred. In Jesus' ministry itself we find a clear and extremely important (probably the most important) setting for the preservation, shaping, and transmission of the gospel materials. It is impossible to conceive of a mission of Jesus' disciples apart from their having been trained and taught and delivered the message that they were to proclaim. Schürmann's thesis also has the merit of fitting well Luke's description of the disciples as "eyewitnesses and ministers of the word" (Luke 1:2) whereas the earlier form-critical views do not. Schürmann has demonstrated that this eyewitness ministry of the word by the disciples had already begun before Easter, even if its most important period would take place afterwards. There is furthermore no need to think that this material was simply memorized by the disciples. Some of Jesus' teaching could well have been written down in brief notebook-like memoranda for use during their mission.

Other Considerations Favoring the Gospel Traditions' General Reliability

A number of other considerations must be mentioned before we seek to formulate an overall picture as to the method and reliability of the process by which the gospel materials were transmitted in the early church. One of these involves the memorization ability that existed in the first century. We must be careful not to equate the lack of notable memory skills among most members of present-day industrialized nations with the ability of those who lived in the first century.[46] Today we

45. Schürmann, "Logientradition," p. 363. John Bradshaw points out that because of the mind's ability to memorize poetic form," . . . it would be surprising if Jesus' hearers had less than perfect recall for poetic sayings" ("Oral Transmission and Human Memory," *ET* 92 [1981]:305).

46. For some examples of the great capacity for memorization on the part of some people, see Riesner, *Jesus als Lehrer*, pp. 450–53; Boman, *Die Jesus-Überlieferung*, pp. 11–13.

do not need to memorize. We possess paper and pens, typewriters, photocopy machines, tape recorders, computers, videocassettes, numerous written texts, and so on. As a result, the ability to memorize has atrophied, much like a muscle that lies unused over time. This can easily be demonstrated by a simple game. See who can memorize a verse of song or Scripture more quickly—a six-year-old child or a forty-year-old adult. It will almost always be the child who excels. Although the adult has learned to file and recall all sorts of information, the basic ability to memorize has deteriorated.[47] On the other hand, in societies with less access to writing materials and modern electronic means for preserving information, the degree to which the art of memorization has been developed and the capacity some people possess for retaining information is truly amazing.[48]

In this regard, we should note that the Jewish people were taught to remember faithfully the deeds and teachings of their God (Deut. 7:18; 8:2; 9:7; etc.) and to teach their children these things (Deut. 4:10; 6:7; 11:19; etc.). In a world where most families did not possess a written collection of Old Testament scrolls or even a single scroll, this could only be done by means of memorization. In the synagogue schools of the first century (the *Bet Sefer*) Scripture was often chanted in unison and read aloud, in order to help in memorization.[49]

A second factor to be reckoned with is that the early church would have had a natural interest in the historical Jesus. It should be noted in this regard that many of the early form critics were "kerygmatic" theologians and made a sharp disjunction between the historical Jesus and the Christ of faith. Although the basic reason for this was philosophical, exegetical support was sought in Paul's statement in 2 Corinthians 5:16, which reads in the New American Standard Bible: "Therefore from now on we recognize no man according to the flesh; even though we have known Christ according to the flesh, yet now we know Him

47. It is a moot point whether children develop their skills for memorization early and then let this skill deteriorate with time as they rely more fully on other means to record information or whether this ability is "innate" and then lost. What is important to note is that the ability to memorize is not as great in today's technical societies as in first-century Judaism.

48. It may also be that ancient and more primitive societies had less "interference" to cause loss in retention.

49. S. Safrai, "Education and the Study of the Torah," in *The Jewish People in the First Century*, ed. S. Safrai and M. Stern (Philadelphia: Fortress, 1974), 2:952–53. Boman points out in this regard that the only way oral tradition is passed on in other societies as well is by rote memory (*Die Jesus-Überlieferung*, p.32), and David Greenwood points out that literary historians have shown that in Greece and Iceland oral tradition was passed on by professional minstrels ("Rhetorical Criticism and Formgeschichte: Some Methodological Considerations," *JBL* 89 [1970]: 419).

thus no longer." It is now certain, however, that the expression "according to the flesh" (*kata sarka*) is not an adjectival prepositional phrase but an adverbial one. This means that it does not define the noun "Christ" but the verb "know." Paul rejects not the "Christ according to the flesh," i.e., the Jesus of history, but on the contrary he rejects an "according to the flesh" or "from a human point of view" (RSV) way of regarding Christ. The adverbial nature of this expression is witnessed by the fact that the same expression is used with regard to knowing other people, and Paul is certainly not saying that he is not interested in knowing historical people! What Paul is rejecting is a *kata sarka* way of looking at and regarding Christ and others. The disinterest and disdain toward the Jesus of history that numerous form critics exhibit should not be read back into the New Testament or the early church.

It is extremely difficult to accept the assumption of certain form critics that during the oral period the early church had no historical or biographical or chronological interests in the Jesus of history. It is true that they had no interest in a "non-miraculous" Jesus, as later postulated by eighteenth- and nineteenth-century "historical" researchers.[50] But the Jesus who walked through Galilee healing and teaching—who proceeded to Jerusalem and celebrated the Lord's Supper, who was betrayed, tried, crucified, and rose triumphantly from the dead—was of immense interest to the early church. They had committed themselves in allegiance to him even unto death. How could they have anything but an enormous interest in all he said and did? Of course, in the writing of the Gospels and the oral transmission of the gospel materials, the most important and meaningful stories tended to be preserved. And no doubt the most important and significant stories tended to be repeated most often and remembered best, but *any* information about Jesus was of interest and value at this time. It may even be that Jeremias' search for the "unknown sayings of Jesus"[51] may better reflect the attitude of the early church during the oral period than the lack of interest in the life of Jesus displayed by some later form critics. T. W. Manson has pointed out: "It is at least conceivable that one of the chief motives for preserving the stories at all, and for selecting those that were embodied in the Gospels, was just plain admiration and love for their hero. It is conceivable that he was at least as interesting, *for his own sake*, to people in the first century as he is to

---

50. Martin Kähler was surely correct in this (*The So-Called Historical Jesus and the Historic Biblical Christ*, trans. Carl E. Braaten [Philadelphia: Fortress, 1964]).

51. Joachim Jeremias, *Unknown Sayings of Jesus*, trans. Reginald Fuller (London: SPCK, 1957).

historians in the twentieth."[52] Such an interest would have helped preserve stories or sayings of Jesus even when their religious value was not great, although in a sense anything about Jesus would have had some "religious" value for those who loved him.

A third matter worthy of mention is the bilingual nature of the early church. Although not absolutely certain, it is highly probable that Jesus spoke both Aramaic and Greek.[53] It is also probable that the disciples spoke both languages and that for them, as for Jesus, their native tongue was Aramaic. Two of the disciples, Andrew and Philip, had Greek names, and we know that after the resurrection Peter undertook extensive missionary journeys to the Diaspora and would have had to speak Greek. It is also evident from Acts that almost immediately there existed within the early church in Jerusalem a group called "Hellenists" (Acts 6:1–6) and whatever the reason for this designation (perhaps because of being "hellenistically inclined"), it is clear that their mother tongue was Greek. Even among the "Hellenists," however, there were no doubt those who knew varying amounts of Aramaic. It is therefore quite certain that the translation of the gospel traditions from Aramaic into Greek[54] did not take place decades later in a far-distant land and by people quite isolated from the actual events. On the contrary, the translation into Greek probably took place after at most a few years, or more likely only months later. In fact, since Jesus had followers in the Decapolis and as far away as the cities of Tyre and Sidon (Mark 7:24–37), as well as Gentile followers in Galilee (Luke 7:1–10), the translation of the gospel materials from Aramaic into Greek may have already begun during the ministry of Jesus.[55] We can thus assume that this translation did not take place in far-off Greece or even Syria but in Jerusalem, for the Hellenist Christians who attended the Greek-speaking synagogue(s) (note Acts 6:9) would have required a version of the Jesus tradition in their native language.[56] The question remains then, as to who would have made such a translation. It is quite likely (in fact probable) that at least some of the "eyewitnesses and ministers of the word" were bilingual and would themselves have been responsible for the translation, for they were the leaders of the church in Jeru-

52. T. W. Manson, *Studies in the Gospels and Epistles* (Philadelphia: Westminster, 1962), p. 6.

53. See Stein, *Jesus' Teachings*, pp. 4–6; Joseph A. Fitzmyer, *A Wandering Aramaen* (Missoula: Scholars, 1979), pp. 1–56; and Riesner, *Jesus als Lehrer*, pp. 382–92.

54. The various attempts to demonstrate that Jesus taught primarily in Greek are clearly wrong. This is shown by the Aramaic fragments we still find embedded in the gospel traditions. See Stein, *Jesus' Teachings*, pp. 4–6.

55. Rainer Riesner, "Der Ursprung der Jesus-Überlieferung," *TZ* 38 (1982):512.

56. Whether some of the Hellenists were already followers of Jesus during his ministry cannot be proven, but it is not at all impossible.

salem, and the Hellenists acknowledged their leadership. It should also be noted in this regard that the Lukan prologue implies that the eye-witnesses and ministers of the word were the ones who "delivered" the gospel traditions from which the "narratives" were compiled. The narratives that Luke used were in Greek, so that Luke at least sees the transition from Aramaic into Greek as being overseen by the apostolic eyewitnesses. It thus seems reasonable to assume that the translation of the gospel traditions into Greek took place very early in Jerusalem itself and that the eyewitnesses were largely responsible for the proc-ess. As a result, there does not seem to be any reason why we should assume that a radical change would have taken place in the translation of the gospel traditions from Aramaic into Greek. There is also no reason to assume that the translation of traditions from one language to another requires major theological, philosophical, or cultural changes. This is especially so with regard to the change from Aramaic to Greek, for Judea had been "hellenized" long before the time of Jesus.[57]

The time element is still another factor that plays a role in evaluating the reliability of the transmission process during the oral period. Was there really sufficient time for the kind of development that some of the early form critics suggested? Is the transmission of folk traditions over a period of several *centuries* a legitimate analogy for comparison with the transmission of the "sacred" teachings of God's Anointed "within a closely knit religious movement with rather firm conceptions and exalted attitudes about such traditions"[58] over a period of just a few decades? It seems probable that Mark was written in the late sixties, and various pre-Markan collections, the Q material, and other material were no doubt written earlier. As a result, we are dealing in some instances with written traditions that came into being only a decade or two after the events themselves. In the context of numerous living eyewitnesses, this is hardly sufficient time for the kind of "cor-ruption" of the tradition suggested by some of the radical form critics.[59]

57. See Martin Hengel, *Judaism and Hellenism*, trans. John Bowden (Philadelphia: Fortress, 1974); and I. Howard Marshall, "Palestinian and Hellenistic Christianity: Some Critical Comments," *NTS* 19 (1973):271–87.

58. E. Earle Ellis, "New Directions in Form Criticism," in *Jesus Christus in Historie und Theologie*, ed. G. Strecker (Tübingen: J. C. B. Mohr, 1975), p. 306; cf. also "Gospel Criticism" in *Das Evangelium und Die Evangelien*, ed. Peter Stuhlmacher (Tübingen: J. C. B. Mohr, 1983), p. 42.

59. F. F. Bruce gives by way of example the following interesting analogy: "In a radio address broadcast in 1949, Professor Dodd said that in his younger days he felt the gap of some thirty-five years between the events recorded in the Gospel of Mark and the writing of the Gospel to be 'a very serious matter.' Later on he suddenly realized that thirty-five years did not seem at all such a long time: he and his contemporaries in 1949 had a vivid memory of the events of the summer of 1914, leading to the outbreak of

One final item that can be mentioned in passing involves the new insights gained with regard to the use of written materials and notes in the first century. There is no reason today to assume that Jesus' words and deeds were never written down until Mark and Q were composed, so that between the time of Jesus and these written works there existed a purely oral period. Jewish males learned to read and write, and each Palestinian community had a synagogue school where these skills were taught. The possible use of notes and written materials by the disciples has been alluded to in the past but will be emphasized to a greater degree in future discussions.[60] Absolute certainty about the extent to which such notes were used is, of course, impossible, but it is not at all improbable that in their preaching mission during the ministry of Jesus the disciples used notes and written materials as a basis for their preaching. The use of such notes would then have had a preservative effect upon the tradition process.

Conclusion

In this chapter we have looked at a number of reasons for arguing that during the oral period the gospel traditions were reliably transmitted and that the radical skepticism of some form critics as to their historicity and trustworthiness is unwarranted. These reasons were:

1. The very difficulty of some gospel materials reveals that at times such traditions were preserved not primarily for their value to the community but because they were the words of Jesus and therefore sacred.
2. The high regard toward the gospel traditions, i.e., that they were "sacred traditions," ensured that they were carefully preserved.
3. The existence and role of the eyewitnesses, and especially the disciples as "ministers of the word" (Luke 1:2), had a positive effect on the faithful transmission of the gospel materials.
4. There already existed a *Sitz im Leben* in the ministry of Jesus (the sending out of the disciples to preach) that would have caused

---

World War I (just as today many of us have a vivid memory of the events of the 1930s, leading to the outbreak of World War II). 'When Mark was writing,' he said, 'there must have been many people about who were in their prime under Pontius Pilate, and they must have remembered the stirring and tragic events of that time at least as vividly as we remember 1914. If any one had tried to put over an entirely imaginary or fictitious account of them, there would have been middle-aged or elderly people who would have said (as you or I might say), 'You are wasting your breath: I remember it as if it were yesterday!' " (*Tradition Old and New* [Grand Rapids: Zondervan, 1970], p. 41).

60. In this area Rainer Riesner's *Jesus als Lehrer* is a most thought-provoking work.

the disciples to record in their minds, and quite possibly also in notes, the teachings and deeds of Jesus.

5. Several other reasons were mentioned in passing—the ability to memorize, the natural interest in the life of Jesus, the bilingual nature of Jesus and the disciples, the early need to translate the gospel materials into Greek in Jerusalem, the small amount of time that existed between the writing of the Gospels and the events themselves, and finally the common use of written notes in that time—all of which indicate that the "oral period" was never purely an oral one.

All the above individually, but even more in conjunction with one another, argue in favor of both the faithful transmission of the gospel materials and their historical reliability.

We must still ask at this point, "How exactly were the gospel traditions transmitted from the first *Sitz im Leben* to the third?" Or to word this in another way, "How were the things Jesus actually said and did transmitted during the period when our Gospels did not exist and how was the writing of our Gospels related to this?" For the most part, both in their origin and in their form, the sayings of Jesus in our Gospels come from Jesus himself. Jesus "delivered" these sayings to the eyewitnesses and disciples. Although this group of eyewitnesses was larger than the Twelve (Luke 24:9, 13–35, 36–43; Acts 1:21–26; 10:41), the core members of the group were the twelve disciples. Jesus delivered his teachings to these eyewitnesses in forms easily retained, and it should not be assumed that in the process Jesus never repeated his teaching. While it is probable that Gerhardsson's portrayal of Jesus as teaching like a second-century rabbi is overstated, it is certain that he intended that his disciples should retain what he said. Jesus was an excellent teacher and used various forms for mnemonic reasons. Such devices as parables, poetry, and exaggeration were all used in order to aid retention. Through memory and quite possibly through the use of notes, Jesus' teachings were "received" and retained by the disciples. In their mission during the ministry of Jesus their proclamation of Jesus' words and deeds would have further helped them retain these "holy words," and any uncertainty or confusion would have been subsequently cleared up when they returned and shared the results of their mission with Jesus and the others. The fact that they were sent out in pairs would also have helped them to preserve the Jesus traditions, for what one might have forgotten the other could have remembered. After the resurrection of Jesus, these teachings became even more important in the minds of the disciples. Then, with even more zeal than before, they went about proclaiming the teachings of Jesus and "delivering" them to the converts. Then more than ever they devoted themselves to the "ministry of the word" (Acts 6:4). It is also probable that the form in which Jesus had cast many of his teachings became even more stereotyped by the disciples' constant retelling of the teachings of the Lord of Glory.

During the ministry of Jesus certain pronouncements and the circumstances that led to them (pronouncement stories), certain miracles (healing and nature miracle stories), and other stories about Jesus were also remembered. To some extent the pronouncement stories and healing miracles would by their very nature have shaped themselves, whereas other stories about Jesus would have been shapeless. No doubt some of these, too, were shared by the disciples during their mission and thus were even more indelibly engraved in their minds. Yet, whereas the sayings material was shaped and formed by Jesus himself, we might well wonder exactly how the pronouncement stories and above all the "stories about Jesus" received their shape. We must at this point realize that many form critics look at such a question as futile because of various presuppositions. If, as some maintain, the critical-historical method by definition excludes the supernatural, the discussion of the passing down of miracle stories from the first *Sitz im Leben* into the second is absurd, since no such events could have occurred in the first *Sitz im Leben!*[61] How can one refer to eyewitness tradition of "miracle stories" if by definition miracles cannot happen? There could not be any continuity here between the first and second *Sitz im Leben*, for the miraculous acts of Jesus by definition could not have happened! The silence of many form critics on this issue can therefore be readily understood. Since these accounts are classified as "myths" and "legends," one cannot speak of continuity. It is here that the "anonymous community" becomes especially helpful. Lacking any actual ground in history (except for some possibly misunderstood events), the appearance of such myths and legends can best be understood as arising from anonymous persons who in anonymous places at anonymous times composed such accounts in order to have Jesus fulfill

---

61. At this point it is clear that Nineham's claim that form criticism's neglect of the apostolic eyewitnesses is due to *a posteriori* observations and not *a priori* presuppositions is clearly false. Here it is obvious that the rejection of the supernatural by many form critics is an *a priori* presupposition that predetermines that the miracle stories and certain stories about Jesus could not have been passed on by the eyewitnesses. This is clearly not due to any *a posteriori* observation but an *a priori* presupposition about the nature of reality. If one precludes the supernatural from the life of Jesus then the disciples by definition could not have remembered accurately the miracle stories and "myths" about Jesus. As a result one must then posit a *Sitz im Leben* apart from the eyewitnesses in which these miracle stories and "myths" could have arisen. This is why the "anonymous community" is so attractive to some form critics.

various messianic and Old Testament expectations. On the other hand, even if we allow for the occurrence of actual miraculous events, we must still deal with the question of how these events were transmitted from the first into the second *Sitz im Leben.*

Did each eyewitness repeat these stories as he saw fit, with the result that there were numerous "forms" of these accounts circulating during the oral period? Did the early eyewitnesses as a "collegium" in committee-session produce a standardized form for each such account? It is highly unlikely that Jesus was personally responsible for formulating these traditions concerning himself.[62] At this point it must be mentioned that any reconstruction of what took place is extremely hypothetical. Nevertheless, the translation of the Jesus traditions into Greek provides us with a situation in which such traditions would have been given a kind of "official" form. It was essential for the hellenistic Christians that the words and deeds of Jesus be translated into Greek. This very process would have resulted in a somewhat standardized and apostolic Greek version of not only the sayings of Jesus but the story-like materials as well. In turn, the existence of a reasonably standardized Greek form of the narratives about Jesus might have even helped standardize the Aramaic forms of this material as well. It is not impossible that this apostolic translation of the gospel traditions from Aramaic into Greek functioned as an early recension of the materials, which would have served as an authoritative pattern from that time on. The use of written notes in such a process is also not beyond the realm of possibility.

Whereas all Christians, not just the disciples, "went about preaching the word" (Acts 8:4), it was the disciples who acted as the authoritative bearers of the Jesus tradition after the resurrection. The teachings that Jesus had delivered to them, the pronouncement and miracle stories which they had witnessed and which shaped themselves, and the other materials were then supplemented by the passion and resurrection narratives. All these were taught by them to the church. As the church grew, others were taught to be teachers of the tradition. Probably Gerhardsson and Riesenfeld have gone too far in limiting the *Sitz im Leben* in which these traditions were circulated. No doubt catechetical instruction of the new converts would have been a natural context for sharing these traditions, and the Bible-study setting Gerhardsson suggests appears quite possible, as does a worship situation. Yet to say that this material was thought of by the early church as too "sacred" for use as illustrations or isolated anecdotes is unconvincing. Such a limitation of possible settings would conflict with both Jesus' own example of teaching the multitudes and the mission of the disciples dur-

---

62. Gerhardsson, *Memory and Manuscript*, p. 188.

ing Jesus' ministry. Why the New Testament letters seem to avoid references to the gospel traditions is unclear. Nevertheless, they could have made reference to them if they desired (cf. 1 Cor. 7:10; 9:14; 11:23–25), and the Old Testament Scriptures were used in this way. It seems certain that Paul and the other writers of the New Testament Epistles assumed that their readers knew the gospel traditions. Although it is not completely clear why we find a paucity of gospel traditions in their writings, the limitation of the gospel traditions to a particular *Sitz im Leben* and no other does not seem convincing. There probably existed a primary milieu, such as catechetical instruction or Bible study, in which the eyewitnesses and ministers of the word taught the gospel traditions, but some people would have learned the traditions from the evangelistic preaching, the witnessing of others, and in worship settings.

In the process of translating the Aramaic gospel traditions into Greek, the eyewitnesses would no doubt have used the Septuagint for scriptural quotations and would have taken the opportunity to write down some of this material. As a result, from the very beginnings of the early church, possibly even during Jesus' ministry, there would have come into existence written notes and memoranda, some by the apostles for their personal use, some by other teachers to aid them in the ministry of the word. Memory, however, was probably the most common method by which the majority of the church preserved the Jesus traditions. With regard to the first written Gospel, we should note that since the John Mark of the tradition lived in Jerusalem and his home was a center of the early church (Acts 12:12), he was no doubt privy to much eyewitness testimony. To what extent he himself was an eyewitness of the gospel events (Mark 14:51–52?) is uncertain, but it is quite possible that the reason why Barnabas and Paul took him on their first missionary journey was not simply due to his relationship to Barnabas (Col. 4:10) but because he was well-versed in the Jesus traditions and would thus serve as a valuable catechetical instructor. The church tradition also associated John Mark with the apostle Peter, and this weighty tradition should not be dismissed lightly. Others around this time apparently also wrote down "narratives" and collections of materials that served a broader function than merely personal notes.

In writing his Gospel, Luke not only used Mark but other written and oral materials that he researched (Luke 1:3) and assembled during the time he spent in Judea. According to Acts 21:15–27:1, Luke spent several years in Judea.[63] With the interest Luke reveals in Luke–Acts

---

63. The authorial intention of the "we sections" in Acts is clearly that the reader should assume that the author is a companion of Paul during these sections. It is not that he should assume that this is a well-known fictional "we-travel literary form."

towards the gospel traditions and the history of the early church, he no doubt investigated all things closely during this time (Luke 1:3). With regard to the origin of Matthew, the issue is more confused. Tradition speaks of Matthew as having written the *logia* in Hebrew,[64] but our present Gospel of Matthew does not seem to be a translation from Hebrew into Greek and in fact is dependent upon a Greek Mark and Q!

Children and even adults sometimes play a game called "telephone." In this game the first person repeats a short story into the ear of another person, who then repeats it to another, who repeats it to another, and so on, until the last person then repeats the original story. The game is humorous and fun because of the great changes that take place in the story during the process. For some, "telephone" is analogous to the procedure by which the gospel traditions were transmitted in the early church—Jesus, the anonymous church, and/or Christian prophets created various stories or sayings, and after fifteen or twenty tellings in the chain Mark (and then Matthew and Luke) wrote them down. The written record would then be seen as being about as faithful a reproduction of what actually happened or was said as person number fifteen would be in his reporting of what person number one originally said in "telephone." Such an analogy is completely inappropriate and misleading, to say the least. We need only mention some of the dissimilarities that exist to reveal how irrelevant such an analogy really is. For one, we cannot compare our own inability to memorize with the ability present in the first century. Second, the lack of form of the "telephone" story contrasts with the specific memorable form of much of the gospel materials. Third, the method of memorizing in the game is quite unlike that which took place in the first century, for in the latter instance repetition was an important factor. Fourth, the reverence given to the Jesus traditions as sacred and holy is certainly different from the frivolity of the message in "telephone." Finally, the number of "telephone" intermediaries in our example is probably at least 1300 percent greater. Between the first and fifteenth member of the "telephone" chain there exist thirteen intermediaries. But how many intermediaries were there between Mark and the eyewitnesses? Tradition says none! Luke claims that for him there is at most only one, for the sources he used were based upon eyewitness accounts. He may also at times personally have heard eyewitness testimony. The analogy is therefore a poor one and should never be used.

A final comment must be made concerning the fact that the Jesus traditions in the canonical Gospels are not exact duplicates and often

---

64. So Eusebius, *Ecclesiastical History*, 3:24.5; 3.39.16; 6.25.4; Irenaeus, *Against Heresies*, 3.1.1; Augustine, *Agreement of the Evangelists*, 1.2.4.

reveal little concern for preserving the *ipsissima verba* of Jesus.[65] In the passing on or "delivering" of the tradition, the "eyewitnesses and ministers of the word" as well as the Evangelists not only remembered and repeated what Jesus said and did but also shared what the Spirit taught them concerning the meaning and significance of those words and deeds (John 14:26), for he guided them "into all the truth" (John 16:13). As a result they felt free to paraphrase and interpret the sayings and deeds of Jesus and did so not as separate footnotes but in the body of the tradition itself. Unlike the notes added at the bottom of the pages in modern study Bibles, however, their comments possessed in the providence of God canonical authority. It should be emphasized in this regard, however, that throughout this whole process ". . . the preaching of Jesus was interpreted, not invented."[66]

65. The lack of the Evangelists' concern for the *ipsissima verba* should make us question those attempts that seek to base one's theology upon such reconstructed authentic sayings and reject or see as inferior the canonical message of the Evangelists. See, for example, Joachim Jeremias, *The Problem of the Historical Jesus*, trans. Norman Perrin (Philadelphia: Fortress, 1964), pp. 12–15, 20–24.

66. Bruce D. Chilton, *God in Strength: Jesus' Announcement of the Kingdom* (Freistadt: F. Ploechl, 1979), p. 279. Cf. also T. W. Manson, *The Sayings of Jesus*, pp. 12–13, and Boman, *Die Jesus-Überlieferung*, p. 30. Manson and Boman point out that the major problem that the early church faced was not the need to create new materials but rather to select what was most important in the large Jesus tradition.

9

The Value of Form Criticism

In the preceding two chapters we have discussed the various presuppositions of form criticism and have argued in favor of the faithful transmission of the gospel materials during the oral period. Because of the negative use and resulting conclusions of this discipline by the more radical form critics, the discipline itself, including its name, is viewed with disapproval in certain circles.[1] Like any tool, however, form criticism tends to be neutral in itself and takes its direction from the particular presuppositions of the individual practicing it. And, like any implement, form criticism can be used positively or negatively.[2] In the hand of a concerned and skillful surgeon a knife can function as a scalpel that can remove a malignant tumor or infected appendix and give life to the patient. In the hands of a talented artist a knife can transform a dead piece of wood into an object of great beauty. In the hands of a criminal,

---

1. That such a view is not without some justification is seen in the following statement of Ernst Käsemann: ". . . the work of the Form Critics *was designed to show* that the message of Jesus as given to us by the Synoptists is, for the most part, not authentic but was minted by the faith of the primitive Christian community in its various stages" [author's italics] ("The Problem of the Historical Jesus," *Essays on New Testament Themes,* trans. W. J. Montague [London: SCM Press, 1964], p. 15).
2. Contrast Käsemann's statement above with Vincent Taylor, who states, "If in the hands of Professor Bultmann Form-Criticism has taken a sceptical direction, this is not the necessary trend of the method; on the contrary, when its limitations are recognized, Form-Criticism seems to me to furnish constructive suggestions which in many ways confirm the historical trustworthiness of the Gospel tradition" (*The Formation of the Gospel Tradition* [London: Macmillan, 1933], p. vi).

however, it can become a weapon delivering death. Radioactive cobalt can be used by a trained physician to destroy cancerous tissue and give life, but when carelessly handled can cause deadly radioactive contamination. In a similar way the investigative tools of form criticism function positively or negatively in biblical research according to the caution and presuppositions that guide their usage.[3] In this chapter we shall seek to define some of the positive insights of form criticism and how they are helpful in gospel research.

The Gospels: Not Chronological Biographies

In the minds of some people the very idea that the Gospels are not precise chronologies is regarded as a negative approach to gospel studies, rather than a positive contribution. Some would discount the work of form criticism as presenting a "lower" view of the Gospels than if they are seen as chronologically exact biographies of the life of Jesus. Yet this insight is indeed a positive one in that it corresponds to "reality" as determined by a reasonable assessment of the evidence. If this is kept in mind, it will guard us from falsely interpreting the Gospels as if they were journalistic records of Jesus' sayings and teachings written in the form of a present-day chronological biography. The lack of this insight has often caused well-meaning Christians to posit absurd theories to explain gospel phenomena that conflict with their view that the Gospels are chronologically arranged. As a result, Jesus is claimed to have raised Jairus' daughter twice from the dead, was twice crowned with thorns, was denied by Peter six or more times, and so on. When we understand that the gospel materials were frequently arranged for topical rather than chronological reasons, such errors can be avoided. This insight has not been gained solely through form critical investigation, for we have already noted in chapter 6 that source criticism demonstrates this as well.[4] We can avoid some of the difficulties created by the slightly different ordering of events from one Gospel to another by recognizing that chronology was not the only criterion for the arrangement of gospel materials. This brings us to the second insight.

Much Gospel Material: Originally
Independent Units

If we understand that various gospel traditions circulated as independent self-contained entities during the oral period, we are provided

3. It goes without saying that the evaluation of whether form-critical results are positive or negative is itself dependent upon the presuppositions of the person making the evaluation.

4. See above pp. 155–56.

with a helpful hermeneutical insight. Although at times it is extremely important to note the context in which a pericope, parable, or saying is found, for this reveals how the Evangelist interpreted this particular material, at other times a pericope may be placed with similar materials primarily for topical reasons. For example, should a parable such as Matthew 20:1–16 ("The Laborers in the Vineyard") be tied exegetically to the preceding teachings of Jesus (Matt. 19:23–30) or was its placement due primarily to the similarity of the sayings in 19:30 ("But many that are first will be last, and the last first") and 20:16 ("So the last will be first, and the first last")?[5] It seems clear that the parable was not originally connected to what precedes it in Matthew's text, for the parallels to Matthew 19:23–30 that are found in Mark and Luke do not have the following parable. It is most likely that in the oral period this parable circulated as a self-contained unit whose meaning was dependent only upon the general context of Jesus' life and teachings. Therefore, in preaching or teaching this parable, it is probably wiser not to seek as intimate a relationship with its immediate context as one would if dealing with such expository sections of Scripture as Romans 1:16–8:39 or Galatians 1:11–4:31. Likewise, in any collection of parables, pronouncement stories, sayings, and so on, there may not necessarily be any special hermeneutical connection between them other than the fact that Jesus was understood to have taught this material.

The healing miracle of the raising of Jairus' daughter (Mark 5:21–24a, 35–43) is another example of how this insight applies. How is the meaning of this miracle story dependent upon its context? Is its meaning dependent on a relationship to the healing story found in Mark 5:24b–34? Is it dependent on the fact that it occurs in Mark's text immediately after the healing of the Gerasene demoniac (cf. Mark 5:1–20)? Yet, in Matthew, it does *not* occur immediately after this incident! We can probably explain this difference in order by assuming that in the oral period the account of Jesus' raising of Jairus' daughter circulated as an independent unit whose meaning was complete in itself. Outside of the general framework of Jesus' life and teaching, nothing more was needed to understand this pericope. Although it is an exaggeration to say that each pericope contains the whole gospel within itself, individual pericopes can frequently stand by themselves and are often best interpreted as self-contained units whose connection with the surrounding materials should not be pressed.

The fact that the church frequently makes use of the Beatitudes, the

5. For the view that Matthew 20:16 is traditional and not a Matthean redactional comment and that Matthew added the parable at this point due to the similarity of Matthew 20:16 and 19:30, see Robert H. Stein, *An Introduction to the Parables of Jesus* (Philadelphia: Westminster, 1981), p. 128.

Lord's Prayer, various sayings of Jesus, or a parable such as the good Samaritan or the prodigal son in complete isolation from their literary context clearly reveals that such materials are able to stand by themselves as independent units. If the early church passed them on in this manner, it may be that the only context necessary for understanding them is the general context of Jesus' life and teachings. This is especially important to remember when such teachings appear in topical collections.

The Gospel Materials Were Preserved for Their Religious Value

One of the basic presuppositions of form criticism is that the gospel traditions were primarily preserved for their religious value.[6] This was a conclusion already revealed by literary criticism, but form criticism has reinforced our understanding of the important role played by religious concerns in preserving the gospel traditions. M. S. Enslin's comment about the Gospels is quite correct: "When they were written, their function was to make saints, not historians."[7] Without in any way denying that the traditions in our Gospels are valuable for historical research, it must be emphasized that the primary reason why these materials were preserved and written down was religious and that their meaning is found in their religious teachings. The Author (Jesus) and authors (the eyewitnesses and Evangelists) sought to use them to teach the truth of God—the gospel message. Therefore, attempts to use these materials for other purposes, even when legitimate, are tangential at best and may lose sight of their author(s)' meaning. Furthermore, if these materials were preserved because they met various religious needs in the first century, they can meet those same needs today. After all, despite changes in technology over the centuries, our basic human needs are still the same. We still die and need to prepare to meet our Creator; we still sin and need divine forgiveness; we still need divine direction as to what pleases God. One way in which the study of the Gospels can take on new significance is to ask of each pericope, "Why was this account preserved? What need did it meet in the life of the early church?" In asking these questions we are far more likely to discover both the original meaning of the passage and its significance for today.

Perhaps this can be best illustrated by an example. In Mark we read the following account of the raising of Jairus' daughter:

6. See above pp. 174–78.
7. M. S. Enslin, *The Prophet from Nazareth* (New York: McGraw-Hill, 1961), p. 1.

And when Jesus had crossed again in the boat to the other side, a great crowd gathered about him; and he was beside the sea. Then came one of the rulers of the synagogue, Jairus by name; and seeing him, he fell at his feet, and besought him, saying. "My little daughter is at the point of death. Come and lay your hands on her, so that she may be well, and live." And he went with him . . . While he was still speaking, there came from the ruler's house some who said, "Your daughter is dead. Why trouble the Teacher any further?" But ignoring what they said, Jesus said to the ruler of the synagogue, "Do not fear, only believe." And he allowed no one to follow him except Peter and James and John the brother of James. When they came to the house of the ruler of the synagogue, he saw a tumult, and people weeping and wailing loudly. And when he had entered, he said to them, "Why do you make a tumult and weep? The child is not dead but sleeping." And they laughed at him. But he put them all outside, and took the child's father and mother and those who were with him, and went in where the child was. Taking her by the hand he said to her, "Talitha cumi"; which means, "Little girl, I say to you, arise." And immediately the girl got up and walked (she was twelve years of age), and they were immediately overcome with amazement. And he strictly charged them that no one should know this, and told them to give her something to eat [Mark 5:21–24a, 35–43].

How does one teach or preach this account? Do we deal with the *geographical* material found in it? Do we describe such details as the dimensions of the Sea of Galilee (13.5 miles long by 7.5 miles wide; 696 feet below sea level; 700 feet deep); or the sailing boats of Jesus' day (Jesus sat in one that must have held over thirteen people); or the kinds of fish in the lake (twenty-four kinds, of which two were unclean)? Or does one seek to give a *chronological* account of this and the surrounding events and point out that this incident takes place after Jesus healed the Gerasene demoniac, immediately after he returned to the eastern side of the Sea of Galilee, and before he went to Nazareth? But what then of the fact that the order is somewhat different in Matthew? Or does one describe the *cultural* situation and the funeral customs of Jesus' day, perhaps comparing them to present-day funeral customs, which tend to minimize such mourning? Or perhaps the teaching/preaching of this pericope would afford the opportunity to show slides of the Dominican *archaeological* work in Capernaum and the beautiful white synagogue of Capernaum (which unfortunately dates from a later period, the third century A.D.) and talk of the latest finds (Peter's house?).

Surely, form criticism (and literary criticism as well) tells us that this account was not preserved and cherished in the early church because of its geographical, chronological, cultural, or potential archaeological value! Why was this story memorized and passed on while others were not? Why would "Alexander and Chloe" of Antioch treasure this account? And why would "Jacob and Mary" in Jericho love and cherish this story? Could it be that perhaps the latter had a daughter, "Miriam," who died at the age of twelve, and they knew that just as their Lord had raised Jairus' daughter from the dead so, too, he would one day raise their beloved Miriam? One day their Lord would reunite them, and so they would always be with the Lord (1 Thess. 4:17). For "Alexander and Chloe," this healing miracle was precious because it made them realize that Jesus was the master of life and death. They need not fear the rulers of this world. Even Caesar held no dread for them, for their Jesus was "King of kings" and "Lord of lords" (Rev. 19:16)! He who held "the keys of Death and Hades" (Rev. 1:18) would raise their loved ones and them as well, just as he raised the daughter of Jairus. That is why this story would be precious to them! It was primarily for its religious value that this story and other gospel traditions as well were preserved. The raising of Jairus' daughter taught the early church and still teaches us today a great Christological truth. The object of the Christian faith is the Master of Life and Death. If he is for us, whom need we fear? (Rom. 8:31). Second, this story taught them (and teaches us) that we who believe in Jesus have a living hope. Death has lost its sting; the grave has lost its victory (1 Cor. 15:55–57). That is the meaning of this miracle story. That is what the eyewitnesses meant to teach by the "delivery" of this pericope, and that is what the Evangelists meant to proclaim by their recording of this account. Form criticism has been most helpful in challenging the readers of the Gospels to focus on the basic reason why the individual accounts were preserved, and the religious meaning and significance of these accounts have become clearer as a result.

The Evangelists' Editorial Work

One of the most helpful results of form critical investigation is that it has enabled scholars to discern the editorial work of the individual Evangelists with far greater precision. Literary criticism is, of course, also helpful in this, for it enables us to compare the different Gospels and note their grammatical and theological tendencies as well as their unique vocabulary. Form criticism has supplemented the work of literary criticism by helping us to understand the shape of the tradition before it was written down. Thus it called attention to such things as how Mark joined the various pericopes and complexes together by means of his seams; how he arranged the material in his Gospel; how he was involved in the composition of the various summaries; how he inserted certain explanatory comments into the text; and so on. In its attempt to analyze the pre-Gospel form of the tradition, the redactional activity of the Evangelists has become clearer. Unfortunately, when the form critics did isolate this editorial work, they simply cast it aside and ignored its relevance. In their desire to investigate the situation of the church community during the second *Sitz im Leben,* they neglected the *Sitz im Leben* of the individual Evangelists. The church community, not the individual Evangelists, was the focus of attention for the form critics. It was the redaction critics who pointed out the importance of the Evangelists' contribution to the text and how this revealed a third *Sitz im Leben.* This newer discipline is nevertheless built on the isolation of the Evangelists' editorial work by the form critics. The essential difference between form criticism and redaction criticism is that the former viewed the editorial work of the Evangelists as "slag" that should be rejected in the mining of the Gospels in pursuit of the "gold" of the early church (and at times the historical Jesus). On the other hand, the latter recognized that the "slag" rejected by the form critics contained valuable "platinum," which was itself very profitable and worthy of analysis.

Jesus' *ipsissima verba*

From the very beginning, numerous form critics have been interested in the historical evaluation of the gospel traditions. In fact, for some scholars, the primary value of form criticism is that it enables us to go beyond the editorial work of the Evangelists and to remove the crustaceous additions of the church during the oral period and thus arrive at the actual words of Jesus.[8] The early attempt to make historical decisions as to the authenticity or non-authenticity of various sayings or pericopes in the Gospels on the basis of their "form" alone was clearly in error. We have seen in chapter 7 that one cannot simply proceed from the classification of the material to value judgments concerning the historicity of the material itself.[9] There nevertheless exist several tools or criteria that have proven helpful in the attempt to ascertain the actual words of Jesus—the *ipsissima verba.* These criteria involve a complex of source-, literary-, historical-, and form-critical insights, and the results, like all such investigative conclusions, cannot be claimed as "absolute certainties" but only as "possibilities" or at times "probabilities." Nevertheless, the conclusions reached serve at least an apologetical function both in demonstrating a continuity be-

---

8. The scholar who has done the most in this area is Joachim Jeremias. See *The Parables of Jesus,* trans. S. H. Hooke (New York: SCM Press, 1963), pp. 11–114, and *New Testament Theology,* trans. John Bowden (New York: Scribner's, 1971), pp. 1–37.

9. See above pp. 168–74.

tween the life and teachings of the historical Jesus and the Christ of the
Gospels as well as in establishing an overall attitude toward the historicity of the gospel materials. Where does the burden of proof lie?
Upon the affirmation or the denial of the historicity of the gospel traditions? If, by using these criteria, it can be demonstrated that the Gospels are faithful portrayals of Jesus' life and teachings (and this *can* be
demonstrated), then surely the burden of proof has clearly shifted to
those who would deny the trustworthiness of the gospel traditions.[10]

Interpretative Insights from Form Criticism

Form-critical research has provided numerous insights as to how
various forms found in the Gospels should be interpreted. One form
found frequently in the synoptic Gospels is poetic parallelism or *parallelismus membrorum*. In turn this can be subdivided into synonymous,
antithetical, step, synthetic, and chiasmic parallelism.[11] We will examine the first in some detail. In synonymous parallelism there is a correspondence between each of the lines or strophes. Each line essentially
repeats what precedes it. Knowing this enables the exegete to interpret
an unclear line of such a saying by means of another one (or others)
that *is* clear. An example of this is Luke 6:27–28: "But I say to you that
hear, Love your enemies, do good to those who hate you, bless those
who curse you, pray for those who abuse you." What does it mean to
"love your enemies?" In a day when love is seen primarily as "ro-
mance" or "feelings," it is helpful to recognize that Luke 6:27–28 is an
example of synonymous parallelism. This means that the three
strophes or lines that follow the command to love one's enemies are
essentially a threefold commentary on what Jesus and/or Luke meant
by this command. To "love your enemies" means to "do good to those
who hate you." It means to "bless those who curse you." It means to
"pray for those who abuse you." If we understand "love" as dealing
primarily with one's emotions or feelings, the saying of Jesus becomes
most difficult to understand. One cannot command feelings or emotions. Yet, if "love" is understood as "loving actions," i.e., of doing

10. For a more detailed discussion of these criteria, see Robert H. Stein, "The 'Criteria' for Authenticity," in *Gospel Perspectives* (Sheffield: JSOT, 1980), 1:225–63. Discussed in
this article are the criteria of (1) multiple attestation, (2) multiple forms, (3) Aramaic
linguistic phenomena, (4) Palestinian environmental phenomena, (5) the tendencies of
the developing tradition, (6) dissimilarity, (7) modification by Jewish Christianity, (8)
divergent patterns from the redaction, (9) environmental contradiction, (10) contradiction
of authentic sayings, and (11) coherence.
11. For a discussion of these types of parallelism, see Robert H. Stein, *The Method and
Message of Jesus' Teachings* (Philadelphia: Westminster, 1978), pp. 27–32.

such loving things as "doing good," "blessing," and "praying," then the command makes perfectly good sense. Knowing that this passage is an example of synonymous parallelism enables one to understand what Jesus meant by the command to love one's enemies.

The Lord's Prayer in Matthew 6:9–13 is another example of how form-critical insights help in the interpretation of difficult passages. After the invocation ("Our Father who art in heaven"), we have three "thou petitions," followed by three "we petitions." What did Jesus mean by the first "thou petition," "Hallowed be thy name"? The most common interpretation is that this petition refers to personal care in the verbal use of God's name and/or a heartfelt reverence for the name of God. The third "thou petition" is also usually interpreted as referring primarily to a personal request that one's life may be in tune with the commands and will of God. However, if we observe the form of these petitions, we note that the "thou petitions" are an example of synonymous parallelism. This means that each of the petitions is in essence repeating the same request. Now what does it mean for the kingdom of God to "come"? It is to experience the consummation of all things. It is for history to come to its end and for the Son of man to return in his glory. It is for the believer to sit at the messianic table with Jesus (Mark 14:25) and for the unrighteous to experience the great judgment (Matt. 13:24–30, 36–43). In light of this, the first and third "thou petitions" must be understood as looking far beyond anything God can do in the heart of any believer. Rather, they look forward to the day when God's name will be "hallowed" on earth just as it is in heaven and when God's will is going to be "done" on earth just as it is in heaven. The Lord's Prayer is therefore another way in which the early church prayed for the same reality for which it prayed in "*Marana tha*—Our Lord, come" (1 Cor. 16:22; cf. Rev. 22:20). Because of our understanding the "form" of these three petitions, we have great hermeneutical insight on how to interpret the unclear petitions with the help of a clearer one.[12] Similar insights can be gained by careful observation of chiasmic and antithetical parallelism.

Another literary form to be mentioned is the proverb. For some,

---

12. Other additional reasons can be given to support this interpretation. First, the fact that the imperatives are aorists and not present tenses indicates that the current form of these petitions is not thinking of a continual repeating of this "hallowing," "coming," and "being done." Second, the qualifying "on earth as it is in heaven" has the earth as the arena of activity, not the human heart, and the extent of this goes beyond anything that can occur in this age. Third, the prayer has a close parallel in the Kaddish, an early Jewish prayer, where these petitions are clearly eschatological in nature. For the latter see Joachim Jeremias, *The Lord's Prayer*, trans. John Reumann (Philadelphia: Fortress, 1964), pp. 21–23.

proverbs are difficult to interpret because of a lack of understanding of
how this form functions. A proverb is a general truth, usually stated in
poetic form as a universal axiom. As a result it should not be pressed
as a universal absolute. One need only look at some Old Testament
examples to realize that very often there are exceptions to the "general
truth" that the proverb teaches.

Honor the LORD with your substance
  and with the first fruits of all your produce;
then your barns will be filled with plenty,
  and your vats will be bursting with wine [Prov. 3:9–10].

Misfortune pursues sinners,
  but prosperity rewards the righteous [Prov. 13:21].

Train up a child in the way he should go,
  and when he is old he will not depart from it [Prov. 22:6].[13]

As a result of our understanding the general nature of proverbs, we are
better able to interpret various proverbs of Jesus, such as:

He who is faithful in a very little is faithful also in much; and he who is
dishonest in a very little is dishonest also in much [Luke 16:10].

. . . for all who take the sword will perish by the sword [Matt. 26:52b].[14]

Homiletical and Didactic Insights
from Form Criticism

The discovery of various mnemonic devices used by Jesus in his
teaching can also prove quite helpful for the proclamation of the gospel
today. If Jesus effectively taught the gospel by means of parables,
would this not perhaps still be an effective way to teach? Would not
many a Sunday sermon be more effective if it contained a modern-day
parable? C. S. Lewis' *The Lion, the Witch, and the Wardrobe* is a fascinat-
ing allegory that communicates the gospel message effectively. The
present writer remembers telling this story on three occasions in a
church setting. Two of them were Children's Day messages, and the
other was a special service for children. Thanks to C. S. Lewis (not to

---

13. Cf. Prov. 10:3–4; 15:1; 17:2; 22:16.
14. Klaus Koch points out that the "form" of the Beatitudes in the Sermon on the
Mount is that of the "apocalyptic blessing." As a result they are not to be interpreted as
exhortations to practice certain virtues but rather as eschatological blessings addressed to
those who are saved from the final judgment (*The Growth of the Biblical Tradition*, trans.
S. M. Cupitt [New York: Scribner's, 1969], pp. 6–8, 17–18).

the present writer's great storytelling ability), these three services were memorable ones, not just for the children but for the adults as well. On another occasion the author ended a sermon with a parable. It was not a very good parable, but the church thought about, reflected upon, and digested that parable, so that it proved to be a useful tool of communication. Would ending a sermon with a riddle be a helpful way of involving the congregation in the message? The use of such forms by Jesus made his listeners participate in his message. It might be wise for some present-day preaching to involve the listeners in a similar way. By using the various forms we find in the Gospels as a pattern for teaching or preaching, our communication would be greatly enriched.

Still another insight in this area involves the missionary teaching of the gospel traditions to non-literate societies. The use of various poetic forms—parables, similes, metaphors, for example—as well as the miracle-story and pronouncement-story form should by all means be preserved in order to help non-readers retain the Jesus traditions. Indeed, the training of authoritative "ministers of the word" who can pass on gospel traditions orally may be the most effective short-term means available for the rapid spread of the gospel in such special situations. Furthermore, in the process of translation every attempt should be made to retain the rhythm and form of the gospel materials found in the Greek text. This is not only for "purist" reasons but for functional ones as well. The existence of written texts should not serve as a hindrance to the memorization and transmission of the gospel materials today.

Light on the Early Church

A final contribution of form criticism that we shall mention is that it has demonstrated the value of the Gospels for studying the history of the early church. There is a sense in which we can say that the form critics have "discovered" four new texts for the investigation of the history of the early church—Matthew, Mark, Luke, and John. Even as a German work on seventeenth-century Germany printed in Berlin in 1940 can teach us much about seventeenth-century Germany, so it can also teach us much about Nazi Germany. One can read this work in order to discern the values and viewpoints of Germany in 1940. Likewise, as a fifteenth-century Italian painting of the crucifixion of Jesus can teach us much about the history of that event, so, too, it teaches us something about fifteenth-century Italy. (Have you ever noticed how first-century Roman soldiers and fortresses look exactly like fifteenth-century Italian soldiers and castles in such paintings?) In a similar way, although the analogy should not be pressed, the gospel traditions found in the canonical Gospels are valuable sources of information about the church during the oral period. The selection of the material preserved and transmitted during this period surely reflects the issues, concerns, and conflicts that the early church experienced. Various interpretative comments and explanations found in the tradition also give us insights as to the life of the church during this period. Whereas some form critics have overemphasized this aspect and have viewed much of the gospel materials as creations of the early church or as having experienced drastic modification, the fact remains that through form-critical investigation it is now evident that our Gospels can be used as sources for knowledge of the early church. Such an investigation of the Gospels must of course be done with care and reverence, for (1) what we are mining in the search for such information is the sacred Scriptures, and (2) we are no longer seeking the basic meaning of the text but are seeking rather to investigate it for the subject matter contained within it. In the latter instance we must be aware that we are no longer studying the Gospels for the same purpose for which they were originally written. Nevertheless, such an investigation is valid and can provide insight as to the nature of the church during the oral period.

PART III

The Inscripturation of the Gospel Traditions

10

The Rise of Redaction Criticism[1]

In Part II it was pointed out that the main concern of form criticism involved the investigation of the Gospels for the purpose of discovering what could be learned about the early church during the oral period. Form critics investigated each individual pericope and saying in order to learn about the church community at that time. Two analogies were given in chapter 9 to illustrate this form-critical approach. One involved a fifteenth-century Italian painting of the crucifixion and the other a 1940 book published in Nazi Germany on seventeenth-century Germany. We pointed out that the interests of form criticism would be like studying this painting to see what we could learn about fifteenth-century Italy or examining the book for what it could tell us about Nazi Germany. There would be no particular interest in what the painter or the writer themselves sought to reveal through their painting or book. In a similar way, most form critics were uninterested in the gospel writers. Such an interest would clearly have been irrelevant and contrary to the basic sociological interests of form criticism. As a result, it is not at all surprising that the Evangelists were neglected and ignored as individuals. They were not viewed as writers as much as editors or *Sammlern*. Dibelius expressed this view quite clearly when he wrote, "The composers [of the Gospels] are only to the smallest extent authors. They are principally collectors, vehicles of tradition, editors."[2] Elsewhere

---

1. For a more detailed discussion and bibliography, see Robert H. Stein, "What is *Redaktionsgeschichte?" JBL* 88 (1969):45–56.

2. Martin Dibelius, *From Tradition to Gospel*, trans. Bertram Lee Woolf (New York: Scribner's, n.d.), p. 3.

the Evangelists were portrayed as "scissors-and-paste men" who simply glued together various gospel traditions in order to produce "Jesus-
material collections" or "gospel excerpts."

Clearly such a view of the gospel writers could not endure for long,
for the biblical accounts of Matthew, Mark, Luke, and John are not
merely "Jesus-material collections" but Gospels, and the Evangelists
were not merely "scissors-and-paste men" but authors. Whereas the
form critics perceived that the individual pericopes were separate gospel "jewels," they lost sight of the fact that these jewels were arranged
and given a particular theological setting by each of the authors. Each
editorial setting, which the form critics ignored and cast aside, shed
light on different facets of the gospel jewels and created a somewhat
different portrait of Jesus. On the one hand, the Gospels are not contradictory, but neither are they identical. These portraits did not simply
evolve out of an "anonymous church community." Such highly creative works as Matthew, Mark, Luke, and John, or the Mona Lisa and
Macbeth, are not usually committee projects but arise out of individual
genius.[3] In contrast to the sociological and anti-individualistic view of
the form critics, today it is clear that the gospel writers must be viewed
as theologians, i.e., as "evangelists".[4]

Although Günther Bornkamm had written some earlier articles
involving the redaction-critical investigation of certain Matthean pericopes,[5] the first major work involving redaction criticism was Hans
Conzelmann's Die Mitte der Zeit, which appeared in 1953. (The English
translation appeared in 1960 and is entitled The Theology of St. Luke.[6]) In
this work Conzelmann investigated the way Luke used his sources in
order to discover the unique theological contribution made by this
Evangelist in his work. According to Conzelmann, Luke superimposed a

3. See George B. Caird, "The Study of the Gospels: III. Redaction Criticism," ET 87
(1976):168–69; cf. also H. Frankmölle, "Evangelist und Gemeinde," Bib 60 (1979):182,
190.
4. It must be pointed out that it is strange in light of the favorable reception which
William Wrede's Das Messiasgeheimnis in den Evangelien (1901) received from German form
critics that such a blindness towards the Evangelists could have developed.
5. These are now found in Günther Bornkamm, Gerhard Barth, and Heinz Joachim
Held, Tradition and Interpretation in Matthew, trans. Percy Scott (Philadelphia: Westminster, 1963).
6. This was translated by Geoffrey Buswell and published in New York by Harper &
Row in 1960. Claiming that Conzelmann was the first major work in redaction criticism
does not mean that there were no others before him who emphasized what later became
known as redaction criticism. Along with Wrede, who has already been mentioned, we
could list such people as E. Lohmeyer, R. H. Lightfoot, J. M. Robinson, etc. See Stein,
"What Is Redaktionsgeschichte?" p. 47. Furthermore a good introduction to the Gospels
has always included such things as the grammatical style, sources, and theology of the
Evangelists.

"salvation history" scheme over the gospel materials in writing his Gospel by dividing history into three distinct stages: the period of Israel; the period of Jesus, which was the "middle" of time (note the German title); and the period of the church. In so doing Luke sought to resolve the problem of the delay of the parousia by means of a greater emphasis on realized eschatology. Conzelmann's thesis, which was warmly received at first, has received some telling criticisms.[7] But he generated continuing interest in studying how the Evangelists used the traditions available to them and in discovering their theological emphases.

The second most influential contributor to the redactional study of the Gospels was Willi Marxsen, whose *Der Evangelist Markus* appeared in 1959. (The English translation appeared in 1969 under the title *Mark the Evangelist*.[8]) Marxsen's work consisted of two parts. The first and most valuable is a discussion of the relationship between form and redaction criticism. It is the general view of form criticism that the study of the Gospels involves two situations in life: the *Sitz im Leben* of Jesus and the *Sitz im Leben* of the early church during the oral period. Marxsen argued that there are actually three life situations found in the Gospels. In addition to the *Sitz im Leben* of Jesus and of the early church there is the situation of the Evangelists as well. Study of this third *Sitz im Leben*, in contrast to the sociological orientation of form criticism, is concerned with the unique points of view of the individual Evangelists. In the second part of his work Marxsen sought to demonstrate that Mark wrote his Gospel as a sermon to warn the church in Judea to flee to Galilee (the famous warning for the Jerusalem church to flee to Pella!) and there await the imminent parousia. Although this thesis of Marxsen is easily discredited,[9] and no one takes it seriously today, his discussion of the Gospels' three *Sitz im Leben*(s) has proven to be a most valuable and lasting contribution. There have been attempts to defend the form-critical view that there are only two *Sitz im Leben*(s) and that one must speak of the second as being twofold in nature, consisting of (1) the transmission of the gospel traditions by the early church, and (2) the editorial redaction of the individual Evangelists.[10] The inscripturation of the gospel materials into the Gospels, however, was a unique event and is best recognized as such by refer-

7. See I. Howard Marshall, *Luke: Historian and Theologian* (Grand Rapids: Zondervan, 1971), pp. 77–88.

8. Willi Marxsen, *Mark the Evangelist*, trans. James Boyce, et al. (New York: Abingdon, 1969).

9. Mark's explanation of Jewish customs (7:3–4; 14:12; 15:42) and of Aramaic terms (3:17, 22; 5:41; 7:11; 9:43; 10:46; 14:36; 15:22, 34) makes no sense if addressed to the Jewish Christians in Judea!

10. So Wolfgang Trilling, *Das Wahre Israel* (Munich: Kösel, 1964), p. 13.

ring to it as a separate (third) *Sitz im Leben*. This approach will also help us recognize that we are passing from a sociological situation (the "church") to a highly individualistic one (Matthew, Mark, Luke, or John). Furthermore, if (as recently suggested) the transmission of the oral traditions was significantly different from the process by which they were inscripturated,[11] this also argues in favor of keeping the second and third *Sitz im Leben*(s) distinct and separate.

If redaction criticism uniquely focuses its attention upon the situations in the lives of the Evangelists, we must still raise the question of exactly what the goal of this discipline is. For Conzelmann, this newer discipline seeks to ascertain that which "distinguishes him [the Evangelist]" from the sources he used.[12] For Marxsen, the investigation of the third *Sitz im Leben* of the Gospels involves the study of what the gospel writers did with the gospel traditions available to them.[13] Redaction criticism has generally followed the example of Conzelmann and Marxsen and concerned itself with "the unique theological purpose or purposes, views, and emphases that the evangelists have imposed upon the materials available to them."[14] As a result, it is a misnomer to equate the redaction-critical investigation of a Gospel such as Mark's with the investigation of the Markan theology. The goal of redaction criticism is much narrower than the description of the entire theology of an Evangelist, for it seeks to focus on what is unique in his theology when compared to his sources. Both goals are, of course, legitimate areas of research. However, the limited aims of redaction criticism must be kept in mind. Redaction criticism is not concerned, for instance, with all that Mark believed about "revelation." (Did Mark believe in the divine authority of the Old Testament? What was the extent of his Old Testament canon? What view of inspiration did he hold? Did he believe in natural revelation? And so on.) Nor is it interested in his total eschatology. (What was his view on millennialism? Did he believe in the annihilation of the wicked? And so on.) Redaction criticism is concerned rather with Mark's unique theological contribution to the gospel traditions he used.

As a result of this emphasis upon the unique elements in each Gospel, there has been a concentration of labor and energy upon the "diversity" of the Gospels and a corresponding loss of interest in their "unity." This is not unexpected when, by definition, what the Evangelists believed in common is ruled out of consideration. This becomes a real problem only when redaction-critical emphases of the Evangelists

---

11. See above pp. 182–83.
12. Conzelmann, *The Theology of St. Luke*, p. 13. Cf. also pp. 9, 12–14, 95.
13. Marxsen, *Mark the Evangelist*, p. 26.
14. Stein, "What Is *Redaktionsgeschichte?*" p. 53.

are mistakenly equated with the theology of the Evangelists. Seen in their totality, the theology of the Evangelists possesses a great unity. Certainly the early church in its incorporation of the Gospels into its canon must have seen them as presenting an essentially unified theology. The early existence of "harmonies" of the Gospels also witnesses to this view. An illustration might be helpful at this point. If the theology of three Lutheran theologians of the late sixteenth century were analyzed and only their unique differences emphasized, a warped picture would result, for they would have had far, far more in common than such a study might tend to demonstrate. When compared with an atheist, a Buddhist, a follower of Islam, and even a Roman Catholic, their unity would become immediately apparent. In a similar way the redaction-critical emphasis on the unique emphases of the Evangelists should not blind us to the great common faith in Jesus that they seek to proclaim.[15]

The goals of redaction criticism are limited. Scholarship in this discipline seeks to discover answers to these questions:

1. What unique theological emphases does the Evangelist place upon the materials he uses?
2. What theological purpose(s) did the Evangelist have in writing his Gospel?
3. What was the *Sitz im Leben* out of which the Evangelist wrote his Gospel?

These questions are, of course, not isolated and independent of one another but intimately interconnected. One discovers the purpose(s) of an Evangelist in part by discovering his unique theological emphases, which in turn help reveal the *Sitz im Leben* in which he wrote. As a result, redactional research must keep all these goals in mind as it proceeds in its investigation.

---

15. A similar error results when the only material concerning Jesus which is accepted as authentic is that which satisfies the criterion of dissimilarity. By definition such a Jesus will be non-Jewish and non-Christian—a strange Jesus indeed!

11

The Method and Practice of Redaction Criticism

In seeking to describe how one practices source, form, or redaction criticism we encounter a serious problem. The reason for this is that these disciplines are interrelated and must of necessity overlap. As a result, any sharp and distinct delineation between their methodologies and tools would be misleading. One cannot do form criticism without coming to some source-critical conclusions. Likewise, one cannot do redaction criticism without having reached some form-critical and source-critical conclusions. The difference between these three disciplines is primarily one of emphasis and interest. Even the question as to the "correct" order of procedure in these disciplines is difficult to answer. Does one first seek to practice source criticism on the Gospels, so as to discover the editorial work of the Evangelists, and then practice redaction criticism? Yet one of the tools used to resolve the Synoptic Problem (i.e., source criticism) is the knowledge of the redactional style and theological interests of the Evangelists.[1] In a similar way the question has been raised as to whether form-critical investigation should precede redaction-critical investigation.[2] Historically these disciplines did develop in the order of source, form, and redaction criticism, but in both source and form criticism the basic step of redaction criticism was necessarily being performed as well. That step was the

1. See above pp. 76–86.
2. See Robert H. Stein, "What is *Redaktionsgeschichte?*" *JBL* 88 (1969):55–56.

delineation of the editorial work of the Evangelists. Although all three disciplines have this step in common, it is at this point that each goes its own way. Source criticism seeks to ascertain which Evangelist's editorial redaction was used by the other gospel writers. (Does Matthew's and Luke's use of Mark seem more logical than Mark's use of Matthew and/or Luke?) Form criticism seeks to discover the redaction of the Evangelists and then sets it aside in order to investigate the oral traditions. Redaction criticism, on the other hand, treasures, examines, and reexamines the editorial work of the Evangelists in order to see what it can learn about their emphases and purposes in writing.

The practice of redaction criticism is most easily demonstrated in the triple tradition, where we can observe how an Evangelist (Matthew and/or Luke) made use of the literary source (Mark) that was available to him.

Luke 5:17–18

A good example of how Luke displays his redactional interests is found in the setting he gives to the story of the healing of the paralytic.

11.1

Matthew 9:1–2	Mark 2:1–3	Luke 5:17–18
[1]And getting into a boat he crossed over and came to his own city.	[1]And when he returned to Capernaum after some days, it was reported that he was at home. [2]And many were gathered together, so that there was no longer room for them, not even about the door; and he was preaching the word to them.	[17]On one of those days, as he was teaching, there were Pharisees and teachers of the law sitting by, who had come from every village of Galilee and Judea and from Jerusalem; and the power of the Lord was with him to heal.
[2]And behold, they brought to him a paralytic,	[3]And they came, bringing to him a paralytic	[18]And behold, men were bringing on a bed a man who was paralyzed,

lying on his bed;	carried by four men.	
		and they sought to bring him in and lay him before Jesus;

In his introduction to this incident Luke adds the following comment: " . . . and the power of the Lord was with him to heal." By this redactional insertion Luke reveals his interest in the healing ministry of Jesus. This is also evidenced by the fact that there are more healing accounts in Luke than in any other Gospel,[3] even though four Markan miracle stories are missing because of the "great Lukan omission" of Mark 6:45–8:26.[4] In addition to these Lukan healing miracles we need to take into account the miracles of Jesus' disciples in Acts.[5] We may also add to these other summaries and comments found in the Gospel of Luke concerning Jesus' healing ministry.[6] Of these there is one that is especially helpful in revealing Luke's emphasis on the healing ministry of Jesus. Again this is best seen by observing the triple tradition.

11.2

Matthew 26:51–54	Mark 14:47	Luke 22:50–51
[51]And behold, one of those who were with Jesus stretched out his hand and drew his sword,	[47]But one of those who stood by	[50]And one of them
	drew his sword,	
and struck the slave of the high priest,	and struck the slave of the high priest	struck the slave of the high priest
and cut off his ear.	and cut off his ear.	and cut off his right ear.
[52]Then Jesus said to him, "Put your sword back into its place; for all who take the sword will perish by the sword. [53]Do you think that I cannot appeal to my Father, and he will at once send me more than twelve legions of angels? [54]But how then should the scriptures be fulfilled, that it must be so?"		[51]But Jesus said, "No more of this!"
		And he touched his ear and healed him.

3. Luke 4:31–37, 38–39; 5:12–16, 17–26; 6:6–11; 7:1–10, 11–17; 8:26–39; 40–42, 43–48, 49–56; 9:37–43a; 13:10–17; 14:1–6; 17:11–19; 18:35–43.

4. Mark 6:53–56; 7:24–30, 31–37; 8:22–26.

5. Acts 3:1–10; 5:12–16; 8:4–8; 9:10–19, 32–35, 36–43; 14:8–18; 16:16–18; 19:11–20; 20:7–12.

6. Luke 4:23, 27, 40–41; 6:17–19; 7:18–23; 9:1–2; 10:17; 11:14; 22:51.

It should be observed here that Luke alone has a reference to Jesus' healing of the servant's ear. Other Lukan redactional insertions that emphasize the healing ministry of Jesus are Luke 5:15 ("and to be healed of their infirmities"); 6:17 ("and to be healed of their diseases"); 7:21 ("In that hour he cured many of diseases and plagues and evil spirits, and on many that were blind he bestowed sight"); 8:2 ("and also some women who had been healed of evil spirits and infirmities"); and 8:47 ("and how she had been immediately healed"). It is evident from the above that Luke seeks to emphasize the healing ministry of Jesus. That such an emphasis was already in the tradition and was not a *de novo* creation of Luke is, of course, obvious, but it is likewise obvious that the Lukan redaction in Luke 5:17 fits well the overall emphasis of Luke that Jesus, through the Spirit, possessed the power to heal and that this healing ministry continued on with the disciples who also, through the gift of the Spirit, possessed power to heal.

Closely associated with the healing theme in Luke 5:17 is another theme that Luke has carefully developed up to this point. This is the theme of Jesus having been empowered by the Holy Spirit—"the power of the Lord was with him to heal." For Luke, the new age is the age of the Spirit![7] Luke knew well that the title "Christ," or its Hebrew equivalent "Messiah," meant "the Anointed One," and following his sources he points out that Jesus at his baptism was "anointed" by the Spirit. Luke then adds that the Holy Spirit descended upon him "in bodily form, as a dove" (Luke 3:22). In so doing he heightens the significance of this event. After then giving his genealogy of Jesus (Luke 3:23–38), he picks up the tradition of Jesus' temptation but adds that Jesus "full of the Holy Spirit" (Luke 4:1) was led by the Spirit into the wilderness to be tempted. After this event Luke follows his source once again, but his redactional activity and emphasis are quite clear.

11.3

Matthew 4:12	Mark 1:14a	Luke 4:14a
[12]Now when he heard that John had been arrested, he withdrew	[14]Now after John was arrested, Jesus came	[14]And Jesus returned in the power of the Spirit
into Galilee;. . .	into Galilee,. . .	into Galilee,. . .

Unlike the other synoptic Gospels, Luke adds that when Jesus departed to Galilee he returned in "the power of the Spirit." The emphasis on the Spirit and the relationship of the Spirit with "power" is most

---

7. See I. Howard Marshall, *Luke: Historian and Theologian* (Grand Rapids: Zondervan, 1970), p. 91.

apparent here. This connection is found elsewhere in Luke, for we see this in Luke 1:17, 35; 24:49; Acts 4:31–33; 6:8–10, but it is in Acts 1:8 and 10:38 that this is seen most clearly:

> But you shall receive power when the Holy Spirit has come upon you; and you shall be my witnesses in Jerusalem and in all Judea and Samaria and to the end of the earth [1:8].

> You know the word which he sent to Israel . . . the word which was proclaimed throughout all Judea . . . how God anointed Jesus of Nazareth with the Holy Spirit and with power . . . [10:36–38a].

At the first possible chance after Jesus' baptism and temptation, which the tradition had intimately associated together, Luke inserts the account of Jesus' preaching at Nazareth. In this passage we find Jesus referring to his anointing by the Spirit:

> And he came to Nazareth, where he had been brought up; and he went to the synagogue, as his custom was, on the sabbath day. And he stood up to read; and there was given to him the book of the prophet Isaiah. He opened the book and found the place where it was written, "The Spirit of the Lord is upon me, because he has anointed me to preach good news to the poor. He has sent me to proclaim release to the captives and recovering of sight to the blind, to set at liberty those who are oppressed, to proclaim the acceptable year of the Lord." And he closed the book, and gave it back to the attendant, and sat down; and the eyes of all in the synagogue were fixed on him. And he began to say to them, "Today this scripture has been fulfilled in your hearing" [Luke 4:16–21].

The anointing of Jesus and his being endowed with power by the Holy Spirit is an important Lukan emphasis, and the extension of this gift (Luke 11:13—note here the Lukan redaction by comparing this verse with the parallel in Matthew 7:11) and empowering by the Spirit to the followers of Jesus is a strong emphasis as well (Luke 9:1; 10:19; 24:49; Acts 1:8ff.).

By comparing Luke with his sources we observe a Lukan redactional insertion in Luke 5:17 that, upon closer investigation, reveals a particular theological emphasis in Luke. To be sure, this was not created by Luke *ex nihilo*, but he heightened and systematized it in his own way. We are thus able to say that when Luke wrote his Gospel, one of the themes he sought to emphasize was that Jesus was anointed for his mission and role as "the Anointed One" by the Spirit, who empowered him to heal and to do many mighty works. This same Spirit was in turn promised to Jesus' disciples, who were anointed and empowered by the Spirit to heal and preach the gospel message.

Matthew 13:10–17, 18–19, 23

Within Matthew 13 we find another example in the triple tradition that demonstrates how redaction criticism functions. Here we observe the following parallels:

11.4

Matthew 13:10–19, 23	Mark 4:10–15, 20	Luke 8:9–12, 15
	[10]And when he was alone, those who were about him	
[10]Then the disciples came and	with the twelve	[9]And when his disciples
said to him,	asked him	asked him
"Why do you speak to them	concerning the parables.	what this parable meant,
in parables?"		
[11]And he answered them,	[11]And he said to them,	[10]he said,
"To you it has been given	"To you has been given	"To you it has been given
to know		to know
the secrets of the kingdom of heaven,	the secret of the kingdom of God,	the secrets of the kingdom of God;
but to them	but for those outside	but for others
it has not been given.	everything is in parables;	they are in parables,
[12]For to him who has will more be given; and he will have abundance; but from him who has not, even what he has will be taken away.		
[13]This is why I speak to them in parables, because	[12]so that	so that
seeing	they may indeed see	seeing
they do not see,	but not perceive,	they may not see,
and hearing	and may indeed hear	and hearing
they do not hear,		
nor do they understand.	but not understand; lest they should turn again, and be forgiven."	they may not understand.
[14]With them indeed is fulfilled the prophecy of Isaiah which says: 'You shall indeed hear but never understand, and you shall indeed see but never perceive. [15]For this people's heart has grown dull, and their ears are heavy of hearing, and their eyes they have closed, lest they should perceive with their eyes, and hear with their ears,		

and understand with their heart, and turn to me to heal them.' 16But blessed are your eyes, for they see, and your ears, for they hear. 17Truly, I say to you, many prophets and righteous men longed to see what you see, and did not see it, and to hear what you hear, and did not hear it.		
	13And he said to them, "Do you not understand this parable? How then will you understand all the parables?	
18"Hear then the parable		11Now the parable is this:
of the sower.	14The sower sows the word. 15And these are the ones along the path, where the word is sown;	The seed is the word of God. 12The ones along the path
19When any one hears the word of the kingdom and does not understand it,	when they hear,	are those who have heard;
		then
the evil one comes and snatches away what is sown in his heart;	Satan immediately comes and takes away the word which is sown in them.	the devil comes and takes away the word from their hearts, that they may not believe and be saved.
this is what was sown along the path.		
23As for what was sown on good soil, this is he who hears the word and understands it;	20But those that were sown upon the good soil are the ones who hear the word and accept it	15And as for that in the good soil, they are those who, hearing the word,
		hold it fast in an honest and good heart, and bring forth fruit
he indeed bears fruit, and yields, in one case a hundredfold, in another sixty, and in another thirty."	and bear fruit, thirtyfold and sixtyfold and a hundredfold."	
		with patience.

In the Matthean parallel we note that the term "understand [*syniemi*]" is used five times, in contrast to its being found only once in Mark and Luke: Matthew 13:13 ("nor do they understand"); 13:14 ("You shall indeed hear but never understand"); 13:15 ("and understand with their heart"); 13:19 ("When any one hears the word of the kingdom and does not understand it"); and 13:23 ("this is he who hears the word and understands it"). It is clear from the last four examples, all of which Matthew has added to his source, that "understanding" is an important Matthean emphasis. This becomes even clearer when we observe how Matthew concludes this chapter on the parables as follows: " 'Have you understood all this?' They said to him, 'Yes.' And he said to them, 'Therefore every scribe who has been trained for the kingdom of heaven is like a householder who brings out of his treasure what is new and what is old' " (13:51–52).

This Matthean emphasis also appears elsewhere in his Gospel. In Matthew 15:10 the Evangelist follows his source and writes, "Hear and understand." In 16:12, however, he adds to his source a reference to the disciples as having "understood" Jesus' teaching about their being alert concerning the "leaven" of the Pharisees and Sadducees. Then, in 17:12–13, he states that whereas the scribes "did not know" that John the Baptist was the fulfillment of the prophecy concerning Elijah's return, the disciples "understood that he was speaking . . . of John the Baptist," which is not found in the Markan parallel. Elsewhere Matthew adds comments about the Pharisees not knowing (". . . if you had known. . ." [12:7]) and includes in 16:3 the account of the Pharisees' and Sadducees' ability to know how to discern the face of heaven ("the sky") but their inability to discern the coming of the kingdom ("the signs of the times").

It is evident that we find a particular Matthean emphasis in these passages. For Matthew, what distinguishes the disciples of Jesus from the multitudes is that they not only hear but understand. Unlike the multitudes, whose "heart has grown dull," the true disciples "understand with their hearts" (13:15). Matthew emphasizes the need for "understanding," which of course involves an attitude of the heart. But it also involves a mental grasp and theological perception of the events surrounding the life of Jesus, his teachings, and how the Old Testament Scriptures find their fulfillment in him. This understanding involves the opening of their hearts and the resultant knowledge of the mysteries of the kingdom of God, which has now been given to them (13:11).[8]

---

8. See Gerhard Barth, "Matthew's Understanding of the Law," in *Tradition and Interpretation in Matthew*, trans. Percy Scott (Philadelphia: Westminster, 1963), p. 110.

The Matthean Fulfillment Quotations

A third example of how redaction criticism works involves the strong Matthean emphasis on the fulfillment of Scripture in the life and teachings of Jesus. It is of course evident that this is not a "discovery" of redaction criticism, for such an emphasis on the part of Matthew has been observed from the earliest studies of his Gospel. Yet this emphasis becomes especially clear when we seek to determine whether these references were present in the traditions that Matthew used. Concerning his famous "fulfillment" quotations, we find in the triple tradition the following:

11.5

Matthew 8:16–17	Mark 1:32–34	Luke 4:40–41
[16]That evening	[32]That evening, at sundown,	[40]Now when the sun was setting, all those who had any that were sick with various diseases
they	they	
brought to him many who were possessed with demons;	brought to him all who were sick or possessed with demons. [33]And the whole city was gathered together about the door.	brought them to him;
		and he laid his hands on every one of them and healed them.
	[34] And he healed many who were sick with various diseases,	
and he cast out the spirits with a word, and healed all who were sick.	and cast out many demons;	[41]And demons also came out of many,
		crying, "You are the Son of God!" But he rebuked them, and would not allow them to speak, because they knew that he was the Christ.
	and he would not permit the demons to speak, because they knew him.	
[17]This was to fulfil what was spoken by the prophet Isaiah, "He took our infirmities and bore our diseases."		

11.6

Matthew 12:15–21	Mark 3:7–12	Luke 6:17–19
[15]Jesus, aware of this, withdrew from there.	[7]Jesus withdrew with his disciples to the sea,	[17]And he came down with them and stood on a level place,

		with a great crowd of his disciples and a great multitude of people
And many	and a great multitude	
followed him,	from Galilee followed; also from Judea [8]and Jerusalem and Idumea and from beyond the Jordan and from about Tyre and Sidon a great multitude, came to him.	from all Judea and Jerusalem and the seacoast of Tyre and Sidon,
and he healed them all,		who came to hear him and to be healed of their diseases;
	[9]And he told his disciples to have a boat ready for him because of the crowd, lest they should crush him;	
		[18]and those who were troubled with unclean spirits were cured. [19]And all the crowd
	[10]for he had healed many, so that all who had diseases pressed upon him to touch him.	sought to touch him, for power came forth from him and healed them all.
	[11]And whenever the unclean spirits beheld him, they fell down before him and cried out, "You are the Son of God."	
[16]and ordered them	[12]And he strictly ordered them	
not to make him known. [17]This was to fulfil what was spoken by the prophet Isaiah: [18]"Behold, my servant whom I have chosen, my beloved with whom my soul is well pleased. I will put my Spirit upon him, and he shall proclaim justice to the Gentiles. [19]He will not wrangle or cry aloud, nor will any one hear his voice in the streets; [20]he will not break a bruised reed or quench a smoldering wick, till he brings justice to victory; [21]and in his name will the Gentiles hope."	not to make him known.	

It is clear from a comparison of these passages that Matthew has inserted these fulfillment quotations into his Markan source. Some additional examples that can be added to these are Matthew 13:14–15; 21:4–5; 26:54 and their parallels. In a passage found only in Matthew and Mark we find the following:

11.7

Matthew 13:34–35	Mark 4:33–34
[34]All this Jesus said to the crowds in parables;	
	[33]With many such parables he spoke the word to them, as they were able to hear it;
indeed he said nothing to them without a parable.	[34]he did not speak to them without a parable, but privately to his own disciples he explained everything.
[35]This was to fulfil what was spoken by the prophet: "I will open my mouth in parables, I will utter what has been hidden since the foundation of the world."	

It should also be noted that in Matthew's special material we find the following fulfillment quotations: Matthew 1:22–23; 2:15, 17–18, 23; 4:14–16; and 27:9–10. To these can be added various Old Testament quotations not found in his Markan or Q source, such as Matthew 9:13; 12:7, 40; 21:16; and 27:43. While it has always been known, because of the amount of material found in Matthew dealing with this theme, that the fulfillment of the Old Testament in the life of Jesus is a Matthean theme, redaction criticism has shown more clearly the Matthean nature of this emphasis.[9]

Matthew 18:12–14

With regard to the Q material, redaction-critical investigation must proceed more cautiously, for whereas in the triple tradition we possess the source of Matthew and Luke (i.e., Mark) in the Q material we do not possess the actual source used by Matthew and Luke. As a result, we must first reconstruct what their source was like, by a comparison of Matthew and Luke, before we can examine how the Evangelists used it. This is not impossible, but it does mean that we should proceed with care. The example we shall investigate is the parable of the lost sheep.

9. In a similar manner the appearance of the "messianic secret" material in primarily Markan redactional materials, such as his seams (Mark 5:43; 7:17, 24, 36–37; 8:26, 30; 9:9), insertions (Mark 1:44; 4:10–12), and summaries (Mark 1:34b; 3:12; 4:33–34; 9:30), reveals clearly that the secrecy motif is a Markan emphasis.

11.8

Matthew 18:12–14	Luke 15:3–7
	³So he told them this parable:
¹²What do you think? If a man has a hundred sheep,	⁴"What man of you, having a hundred sheep,
and one of them has gone astray, does he not leave the ninety-nine on the hills and go in search of the one that went astray?	if he has lost one of them, does not leave the ninety-nine in the wilderness, and go after the one which is lost, until he finds it?
¹³And if he finds it,	⁵And when he has found it, he lays it on his shoulders,
truly, I say to you, he rejoices over it more than over the ninety-nine that never went astray.	rejoicing.
	⁶And when he comes home, he calls together his friends and his neighbors, saying to them, 'Rejoice with me, for I have found my sheep which was lost.' ⁷Just so, I tell you, there will be more joy in heaven over one sinner who repents than over ninety-nine righteous persons who need no repentance.
¹⁴So it is not the will of my Father who is in heaven that one of these little ones should perish.	

In Luke the *Sitz im Leben* in which this parable and the following parables of the lost coin and the gracious father are placed is a controversy between Jesus and the Pharisees and scribes. Due to Jesus' association with tax collectors and sinners (15:1—"Now the tax collectors and sinners were all drawing near to hear him"), the "Pharisees and the scribes murmured, saying, 'This man receives sinners and eats with them' " (15:2). In this dispute Jesus used the following parables as "weapons of warfare"[10] to defend his behavior in associating with the tax collectors and sinners as well as to challenge the prejudicial attitude of the Pharisees and scribes.

It is almost universally accepted among scholars that the setting in life portrayed by Luke is correct. It fits extremely well into the life of Jesus, for we know that this was a charge frequently leveled against him:

10. See Robert H. Stein, *An Introduction to the Parables of Jesus* (Philadelphia: Westminster, 1981), p. 59.

. . ."Why does he eat with tax collectors and sinners?" [Mark 2:16].

. . ."If this man were a prophet, he would have known who and what sort of woman this is who is touching him, for she is a sinner" [Luke 7:39].

. . ."He has gone in to be the guest of a man who is a sinner" [Luke 19:7; cf. Matt. 11:19].

The gospel traditions clearly indicate that Jesus and the Pharisees were in constant conflict with each other and that one of the reasons for this was Jesus' fraternization with the outcasts of society. Yet Jesus' associations with these reprobates were not simply chance events, but on the contrary were by design. In Jesus' associating with publicans and sinners, God was now visiting his people. The kingdom of God had come in Jesus' ministry. God was visiting the rejected and lost of Israel (cf. Matt. 11:19 with Isa. 35:5–6; 61:1). The activity of Jesus in eating with publicans and sinners, the criticism of this behavior by the Pharisees and scribes, and Jesus' defense in seeking the lost (Mark 2:17) fit so well with what we know about Jesus' ministry that only unwarranted skepticism would reject the historicity of the parable's setting as found in Luke.

It would therefore appear almost certain that in the first *Sitz im Leben* and in subsequent tradition the parable was addressed to the Pharisees and scribes and had, at least in part, an apologetic function. However, in Matthew this parable is addressed to a different audience. The eighteenth chapter of Matthew is the fourth great block of dominical teachings found in the Gospel. Like the first two blocks (Matt. 5–7; and 10), these materials are addressed to the church (cf. Matt. 5:1–2; 10:1, 5; 18:1–4) whereas the third (Matt. 13) is addressed to the crowds (cf. Matt. 13:1–3). The same parable that has been directed to the Pharisees and scribes in Luke and the tradition is applied by Matthew to the disciples and thus to the church.[11] Such a change in audience is not unusual or unexpected, for sayings that Jesus originally addressed to a different audience could also be applicable to the disciples or church. As a result, we find that sayings spoken to the crowds (Luke 11:34–35 [cf. v. 29]; 12:57–59 [cf. v. 54]; 13:24 [cf. v. 22]; 14:26–27 [cf. v. 25]; 14:34 [cf. v. 25]) in one Gospel are addressed to the disciples in another (Matt. 6:22–23 [cf. 5:1]; 5:25–26 [cf. 5:1]; 7:13–14 [cf. 5:1]; 10:37–38 [cf. vv. 1, 5]; Mark 9:50a [cf. vv. 33, 38]).

11. Cf. John Calvin on Matthew 18:12, who observed and justified this change in audience by Matthew (*A Harmony of the Gospels Matthew, Mark and Luke,* ed. David W. Torrance and Thomas F. Torrance [Grand Rapids: Eerdmans, 1972]).

Besides having changed the audience of the parable in order to apply it to his particular situation, Matthew has also made an important terminological change. Instead of describing the sheep as "lost" (*apolōlos*), he describes it as "astray" (*planōmenon*), for this latter term fits better the audience Matthew is addressing and those to whom he is referring. He is not speaking to the "lost" outside the church but to the ones "straying" (18:12–13) within the church. This is also evident by the use of the term "little ones" (18:10) to describe those who are straying. This expression is found in both Matthew 18:6 and 18:10, where the former reference is to "these little ones who believe in me" and the latter is to the little ones whose "angels always behold the face of my Father who is in heaven." It is evident in Matthew's redaction that he applies the parable of Jesus to his own situation, in which members of the church are going, or are perhaps being led, astray. In similar fashion Matthew may have omitted the reference to "repentance" found in the Lukan parallel because he is thinking of brothers and sisters who need restoration rather than sinners who need repentance. Matthew realizes that not every wandering member of the church will be restored. This is evident from the next pericope, but even in the parable itself this is evidenced by the subjunctive clause in verse 13, "And if he finds it . . . ." Not all in the church who are wandering may be restored, but there are "little ones" within this group who possess true faith. The community must not despise or reject such wandering brethren but should, as the Good Shepherd did while on earth, seek them out and in gentleness and meekness restore them. That gentleness and meekness should not be confused with a sentimentality that avoids confrontation or discipline is demonstrated by the next pericope (Matt. 18:15–17). But the primary purpose and aim of such discipline is restoration, and the manner is characterized by love, not condemnation.

We see in this example how Matthew has taken a parable of Jesus—which in his source was originally addressed to Pharisees and scribes and served both as a proclamation of God's visiting the lost in the ministry of Jesus and an apologetic for his behavior—and applied it to his own specific situation. Is such a usage of Jesus' parable a "corruption" of his words? Any decision on this question will be based upon one's view of biblical authority. It is clear that Matthew *has* changed the audience of the parable.[12] But was the function of the Evangelists in

12. Of course, if we argue that Jesus originally spoke two similar parables, one to the Pharisees and scribes and the other to the disciples, such a conclusion is unnecessary. Here the issue of sources plays a dominant role. Does this Q material come from a similar source used by Matthew and Luke? If so, that source almost certainly did not contain two versions of this parable addressed to two different audiences.

writing their Gospels simply to repeat unchanged the *ipsissima verba* of Jesus? The Evangelists certainly did not think so! What Matthew has done here is to take the "meaning" of Jesus' parable, which is in part at least God's great love for the outcasts, and apply it to the outcasts within his own church—the wandering ones. The church through the centuries has believed that the Evangelists possessed divine authority to do this. As a result of Matthew's redaction, the church is doubly blessed, for now along with a more or less authentic parable of Jesus as found in Luke we also have a divinely inspired commentary on how this parable was applied in Matthew's day to a different situation. This certainly gives us greater insight on how we should proceed to apply it to our situation today. Another way of stating this would be to say that Matthew shows the "significance" for his own day of the original "meaning" of Jesus' parable. It needs only to be pointed out that Matthew's application of the parable flows naturally out of the meaning Jesus originally gave to it.[13]

Markan Redaction Criticism

Practicing redaction criticism in the triple tradition (Matthew–Mark–Luke; Matthew–Mark; Luke–Mark) and in the double tradition (Matthew–Luke) is relatively easy in comparison to practicing redaction criticism on the material in Mark, M or L. The reason for this is simple. In the triple or the double tradition we either possess the source used (Mark) or can, with the help of the accounts in Matthew and Luke, reconstruct that source (Q) with reasonable certainty. In redactional work in the triple and double tradition the primary means of investigation is source analysis, although within the double tradition form-critical analysis is also sometimes involved. With regard to the investigation of the Markan redactional emphasis, as well as the Matthean emphasis in the M material and the Lukan emphasis in the L material, we are primarily dependent upon form-critical analysis in order to understand the nature of the sources of Mark, Matthew, and Luke. It is especially important with regard to Markan redaction criticism that a clear methodology be followed, lest one builds his work on sand. Where can we most easily see the hand of Mark in his Gospel? Several years ago the present writer suggested that a correct

13. Using the terminology of E. D. Hirsch, Jr., we would say that Matthew's interpretation fits the "unconscious meaning" of Jesus (*Validity in Interpretation* [New Haven: Yale University, 1967]).

Markan redaction criticism could be ascertained by the investigation of the following materials:[14]

Markan Seams

One of the basic presuppositions of form criticism is that before the gospel traditions were written down, they circulated essentially as isolated pericopes, except for the passion narrative. Although this presupposition was seen to be correct in many ways, there was also a need to acknowledge that various complexes of material and possibly a summary outline of Jesus' ministry may have existed before Mark was written.[15] Nevertheless, when Mark composed his Gospel, he must have brought together various isolated gospel traditions. Although at times he sewed them to one another quite loosely and simply, some of his joinings, such as Mark 1:21–23a and 4:1–2, are more extensive and serve as "summary seams." In the formation of these seams Mark often reveals something of his own theological interests and concerns.[16]

Markan Insertions

Within the various pericopes, Mark on numerous occasions inserts explanatory and theological comments, and these are a rich source for investigating his redactional emphases. The most easily recognized of these insertions are the comments beginning with "for" (gar), which is a common Markan literary style.[17] Other Markan insertions can be detected by their interruption of the flow of a pericope, their heavy Markan vocabulary, and their strong Markan theological emphasis. Two examples of the latter would be Mark 14:27 and 16:7. Such insertions are invaluable for detecting Markan redactional emphases.

Markan Summaries

Within the Gospel of Mark, we also find a number of summary statements. Since these statements often recapitulate what has preceded or summarize new aspects of Jesus' ministry,[18] it is probable that

14. For a more detailed discussion of the following materials, see Robert H. Stein, "The Proper Methodology for Ascertaining a Markan Redaction History," NT 13 (1971):181–98. The criteria which are listed will also be helpful in the investigation of a Matthean redaction criticism in the M material and a Lukan redaction criticism in the L material.

15. See above pp. 167–68.

16. See Robert H. Stein, "The 'Redaktionsgeschichtlich' Investigation of a Markan Seam (Mark 1:21f), ZNW 61 (1970):70–94, for a more detailed discussion of the subject.

17. Cf. Mark 1:16, 22; 2:15; 3:10, 21; 5:8, 28, 42; 6:14, 17, 18, 20, 31, 48, 50, 52; 7:3; 9:6 (2), 31, 34; 10:22; 11:13, 18 (2), 32; 12:12; 14:2, 40, 56; 15:10; 16:4, 8 (2).

18. See Charles W. Hedrick, "The Role of 'Summary Statements' in the Composition of the Gospel of Mark: A Dialog with Karl Schmidt and Norman Perrin," NT 26 (1984):289–311.

they contain a great deal of the author's own redactional interests and emphases. Without denying that many of these summaries, especially the larger ones (such as Mark 1:14–15; 3:7–12; 6:53–56; 9:30–32; 10:32–34), contain traditional material, it is nevertheless true that there is found in these passages a great deal more editorial activity on the part of the Evangelist than when he simply records a traditional pericope. As a result, these summaries form a rich source for the investigation of Mark's redactional emphases.

Markan Modification of Pericopes and Sayings

Another useful area for investigating Mark's theological emphases is where the Evangelist modifies the individual units of traditions or complexes he used. *But* how does one know when or where Mark has modified the tradition? In repeating the traditional materials, Mark would often reproduce them in his own vocabulary and style, making it much more difficult to separate his editorial changes from the tradition. As a result, the mere presence of a Markan style or vocabulary does not necessarily reveal a Markan modification of the material, since it could be the result of Mark's retelling the tradition in his own words. Some suggestions have been made as to how one might detect a Markan modification:

1. Where Matthew and Luke agree against Mark, this may indicate that they were reluctant to follow Mark because he differed from the pre-Markan tradition with which they were familiar.
2. The presence of "impure" forms in Mark may be due to his having modified the purer forms of the tradition lying before him.
3. The presence of a historical inconsistency between the Markan account and what actually happened may reveal a Markan modification of the tradition.
4. The presence of an inordinate degree of Markan terminology and style at certain places in an account may suggest a Markan modification.

Of the suggestions listed above, the second and third have little, if any, value. The whole idea of using "pure–impure" forms as a basis for various historical or literary judgments has been seriously challenged,[19] and even if one could prove a historical inconsistency in Mark,[20] this

---

19. See above pp. 172–74.
20. It should be noted that the *hypothesis* that miracles do not happen is not a proof that the miracle stories in Mark are not historical.

would still not prove that Mark was the one who modified the account and made it non-historical. The first suggestion has some value, but serious Matthew–Luke agreements against Mark seldom occur in the synoptic Gospels. The fourth suggestion is helpful and even quite useful at times, but once again it must be pointed out that finding Markan stylistic features in an account is to be expected.[21] Actually, the presence of "non-Markan" vocabulary and stylistic features in a Markan account is more helpful in the sense that it shows the lack of a strong Markan redactional activity in these passages.

Markan Selection of Material

Although Mark may have included some traditions in his Gospel simply because they were contained in the complexes he used[22] or because they were well-known, the majority of the material found in his Gospel was chosen because it served his theological purpose. The simple, straightforward reading of Mark should therefore reveal a great deal about his "theology." It should also serve to warn us that subtle and tenuous conclusions concerning a Markan redactional theology are, to say the least, most questionable if they conflict with the selection of material found in his Gospel. An example of this was the view that Mark wrote his Gospel to combat or refute a *theios-aner* Christology, which magnified Jesus' role as a miracle worker. Such a view should never have received the support it did, because it is contradicted by the evidence that Mark's Gospel contains many miracle stories. Judging by his choice of material, it is clear that Mark delighted in and emphasized the miracles of Jesus. Furthermore, in his seams and summaries he also emphasized this aspect of Jesus' ministry.[23]

21. Martin Hengel points out in this regard that "The ancient historian took pride in so reshaping his sources that his model could no longer be recognized, and the mark of his own individual style emerged all the more clearly. This basic rule in the ancient use of sources is often too little noted by the sophisticated analysts who very neatly set tradition off against redaction" (*Between Jesus and Paul*, trans. John Bowden [Philadelphia: Fortress, 1983], p. 4).

22. An example of this may be Mark 2:19–20, which contains a reference to Jesus' death. This seems to be contrary to the general scheme found in Mark 8:31f., which reveals that it was only after the events of Caesarea Philippi that Jesus began to teach the disciples concerning his death. Is the reason Mark 2:19–20 appears "out of place" due to the fact that it was contained in a pre-Markan complex (Mark 2:1–3:5) ?

23. It is also now evident that there never was an established *theios-aner* concept in the world of the first century. See David Lenz Tiede, *The Charismatic Figure as Miracle Worker* (Missoula: Society of Biblical Literature, 1972) and Carl H. Holladay, *Theios Aner in Hellenistic-Judaism: A Critique of this Category in New Testament Christology* (Missoula: Society of Biblical Literature, 1977). For a clear refutation of the view that Mark was seeking to refute a *theios-aner* Christology, see Jack Dean Kingsbury, *The Christology of Mark's Gospel* (Philadelphia: Fortress, 1983).

Markan Omission of Material

If we were able to determine which gospel materials Mark had available, but which he chose to ignore and exclude from his Gospel, his omissions would be most helpful in arriving at those teachings and stories of Jesus that were not of major significance for him. The problem, of course, is the word *if*! How can we know which materials Mark had available to him? The obvious answer is that we cannot know that, and it follows that we cannot know what Mark chose to omit from his Gospel.[24]

Markan Arrangement of Material

The placement of a passage into a particular context often serves as a theological interpretation of that passage by an Evangelist. For instance, the placement of Matthew 10:34 ("Do not think that I have come to bring peace on earth; I have not come to bring peace, but a sword") before Matthew 10:35–39 ("For I have come to set a man against his father, and a daughter against her mother. . .") clearly reveals that Matthew interpreted verse 34 not as a political statement involving revolution, but as a religious one that spoke of the division Christ would occasionally bring into family situations. We must be aware, however, that not every arrangement of the material was due to theological reasons. Sometimes topical, geographical, or chronological considerations played a role. Furthermore, to the extent that a particular schema of Jesus' life was known, Mark would have felt constrained to follow that pattern. Nevertheless, there did exist a considerable degree of freedom by which he could legitimately arrange his material, and one particular kind of arrangement that seems particularly Markan is his "sandwiching" of one narrative into another.[25] Later in this chapter we shall look at an example of the theological significance of how Mark arranged his material.

24. Ernest Best states, "If we knew that Mark had a great amount of material about the teaching of Jesus, say a 'copy' of Q and only three exorcism accounts, and chose to omit most of the teaching and put in all three exorcisms, this would obviously lead us to conclude that for him exorcisms were most important. Equally had he at his disposal only the teaching of Jesus which he has inserted and a hundred exorcism stories from which he selected the present three then we would come to quite a different conclusion about the importance of the exorcisms for Mark. Unfortunately we are not in a position to draw either conclusion" (*The Temptation and the Passion: The Markan Soteriology* [London: Cambridge University, 1965], p. 103).

25. See Mark 3:22–30 into 3:20–21 and 3:31–35; 5:24–34 into 5:21–24 and 35–43; 6:14–29 into 6:6b–13 and 6:30f.; 11:15–19 into 11:12–14 and 11:20–25; and 14:3–9 into 14:1–2 and 14:10–11. Two other possibilities are Mark 14:55–65 into 14:53–54 and 14:66–72 and 15:16–20 into 15:6–15 and 15:21–32.

The Markan Introduction

It is evident from the ways Matthew, Luke, and John begin their Gospels that a great deal can be learned concerning the interests and purposes of these writers by observing their introductions. It is therefore not unreasonable to expect the same with regard to Mark. Even if some sort of schema, such as found in Acts 10:37–41, was traditional, there still existed a great deal of leeway as to how Mark would begin his Gospel. Certainly Mark 1:1 ("The beginning of the gospel of Jesus Christ, the Son of God") reveals something important about Mark's Christological emphasis. Mark's whole Gospel is about Jesus Christ, who is the Son of God.[26] As a result, we need to note that the opening Old Testament references (1:2–3) do not focus on John the Baptist but upon Jesus, i.e., not upon the messenger or voice but on the Lord whose coming John the Baptist announces. In a similar way the description of John the Baptist in Mark 1:4–8 does not focus upon John, but upon the one "mightier" than him (1:7) who will baptize with a greater baptism (1:8). Then comes the highlight of the opening introduction, when the voice from heaven affirms the opening superscription by saying, "Thou art my beloved Son . . ." (1:11).

The Markan Conclusion

The way a person concludes his work is certainly an indication of what that individual is seeking to say. One need only think of how often people try to ascertain what a book is about by turning to the concluding chapter or summary! Of all the sections of a work, the conclusion is usually the most significant for our understanding. "How does it end?" is an important question. In Matthew, Luke, and John we have at the end of their works important clues and even statements as to what the respective Evangelists are seeking to emphasize. John states:

> Now Jesus did many other signs in the presence of the disciples, which are not written in this book; but these are written that you may believe that Jesus is the Christ, the Son of God, and that believing you may have life in his name [20:30–31].

In Luke we read:

> Then he opened their minds to understand the scriptures, and said to them, "Thus it is written, that the Christ should suffer and on the third day rise from the dead, and that repentance and forgiveness of sins

26. There exists a textual problem with regard to the expression "Son of God."

should be preached in his name to all nations, beginning from Jerusalem. You are witnesses of these things. And behold, I send the promise of my Father upon you; but stay in the city, until you are clothed with power from on high" [24:45–49].

And Matthew records:

And Jesus came and said to them, "All authority in heaven and on earth has been given to me. Go therefore and make disciples of all nations, baptizing them in the name of the Father and of the Son and of the Holy Spirit, teaching them to observe all that I have commanded you; and lo, I am with you always, to the close of the age" [28:18–20].

It would be strange if Mark's conclusion did not in a similar way provide helpful material for investigating the purpose of the author. With Mark, however, we are confronted with a serious problem. The ending of Mark's Gospel is much debated. Although the best Greek manuscripts end at Mark 16:8, there are several reasons why it is not at all certain that the Gospel originally ended at this point. One of these reasons is that it would have indeed been strange for Mark to have ended his work with the conjunction "for" (*gar*). Although examples of Greek sentences that end with a *gar*, have been discovered, no book has been found ending in this manner.[27] Second, it has been pointed out that, of the five times "to be afraid" is found in Mark, it is never used absolutely except here, if verse 8 is indeed the ending of Mark. Third, the reference to the women as being afraid seems an inappropriate way to conclude the Gospel. Finally, we find Markan insertions in 14:28 and 16:7 that refer to a meeting of the disciples and Peter with the resurrected Jesus in Galilee. Yet, if the Gospel of Mark originally ended at 16:8, no such meeting, *which Mark has prepared us for*, is recorded.[28] As a result, whereas the conclusion of a work is usually most helpful in the investigation of the author's purpose, in the case of Mark it may not be, for the original ending of Mark may very well be missing.

Markan Vocabulary

In this particular instance we are not concerned with the examination of the Markan vocabulary in order to determine whether a specific passage primarily reflects the editorial work of Mark. We are concerned

27. Bruce Manning Metzger, *The Text of the New Testament: Its Transmission, Corruption, and Restoration* (New York: Oxford University, 1968), p. 228.

28. That these two insertions refer to a resurrection appearance and not the parousia is evident by the reference to Peter. See Robert H. Stein, "A Short Note on Mark xiv.28 and xvi.7," *NTS* 20 (1974):445–52.

rather with investigating the overall language of the Evangelist to see what we can learn of his theological emphases. It is evident that the vocabulary found in the writings of a staunch Calvinist will reveal his theological penchant, even as the vocabulary used in the writings of an existentialist will reveal his main theological and philosophical orientation. If we investigate the other Gospels, we gain a great deal of insight by observing their particular theological vocabulary. Significant in this regard is Matthew's frequent use of such terms as *to fulfill, disciple, Son of David, cause to sin* (skandalizō), *righteous-righteousness, what was spoken* (rhēthen); Luke's use of such terms as *Spirit, to heal* (iaomai), *repent-repentance, multitude, salvation-Savior-save, receive;* and the following Johannine vocabulary: *love, know, witness, Father* (as a title for God), *life, I am, world, light.* These terms provide clues as to the theological emphases of the respective Gospel writers. It is therefore not surprising that various Markan terms also witness to his theological emphases. Some of these are *teach-teacher-teaching, preach the gospel, authority, to be able* (dunamai)-*power* (dunamis), *amaze-marvel* (thambeomai-thaumazō-ekplēssomai), *follow, believe,* and so on.

Mark 8:31–10:45

One example of a clear Markan redactional emphasis is found in Mark 8:31–10:45. In this section we encounter the first of Jesus' passion predictions (8:31–32a). Thereupon follow Peter's error and reproach of Jesus (8:32b) and Jesus' rebuke of Peter (8:33). These verses are then followed by a section of teaching on discipleship (8:34–9:1). We discover the following pattern: (1) passion saying (8:31–32a), (2) error by disciple (8:32b–33), (3) teaching on discipleship (8:34–9:1).

After this we read the account of the transfiguration and the sayings concerning Elijah (9:2–13). At least before Mark and perhaps from the very beginning, the transfiguration was associated with Peter's confession at Caesarea Philippi and the following rebuke by means of a chronological tie ("And after six days" [9:2]). After this material we find the account of the healing of the epileptic boy (9:14–29). The reason for the appearance of this story here is not certain. Some have suggested that its location may be due to chronological considerations, i.e., because Jesus healed the paralytic boy immediately after his transfiguration. Others have suggested that the placement reflects the parallel of Jesus' descent from the Mount of Transfiguration and Moses' descent from Mount Sinai. Since this healing story, which reveals the disciples' general unfaithfulness (they are not able to heal—9:18b, 28–29), is similar to Moses' discovery of Israel's unfaithfulness (they made a golden calf–Exod. 32), it was placed next to the transfiguration account. According to this explanation, the placement of this account here was because of typological considerations. One other explanation that can be mentioned involves the general Markan theological emphasis found in 8:27–10:45, where the failure of the disciples is used to teach the meaning of true discipleship. In this pericope (9:14–29) there is clearly a shortcoming on the part of the disciples, for they are unable to heal. As a result, it may have been placed here by Mark because it also contains material involving the instruction of the disciples.[29] This last explanation has the merit of fitting well the Markan theological scheme found in 8:31–10:45.

In Mark 9:30–32 we encounter the second passion prediction in this Gospel. This is also followed by a blunder on the part of the disciples, who debate over who is greatest among them (9:33–34), and this leads again to a collection of teachings on discipleship (9:35–10:31).

In Mark 10:32–34 we encounter the third and final passion prediction. This again is followed by a failure on the part of the disciples, when James and John seek privileged positions in the kingdom of God for themselves (10:35–41), and additional teachings on discipleship (10:42–45).[30] As a result of Mark's arrangement of the material, we discover in Mark 8:31–10:45 the recurring pattern shown in table 11.

Along with this Markan arrangement we can also see the redactional work of the Evangelist in other ways in this section. Without in any way denying the historicity of Jesus' having predicted his passion, it appears that the Evangelist has played a significant part in the forma-

Table 11

Passion Saying	Error by Disciples	Teachings on Discipleship
(8:31–32a)	(8:32b–33) Peter	(8:34–9:1)
(9:30–32)	(9:33–34) Disciples	(9:35–10:31)
(10:32–34)	(10:35–41) James and John	(10:42–45)

29. Ernest Best, *Following Jesus: Discipleship in the Gospel of Mark* (Sheffield, England: JSOT, 1981), pp. 68–69.

30. It has been argued that the two healings of blind men (Mark 8:22–26 and 10:46–52) which precede and conclude this major section are meant to serve as an introduction and conclusion.

tion of the three passion predictions.[31] This is seen in the summary-like nature of all three predictions as well as the Markan vocabulary and style found in them. Some examples of this are:

1. (8:31) "And he began [ērxato] to." The use of "to begin" (arxomai) as an auxiliary verb followed by an infinitive is found twenty-six times in Mark and appears disproportionately in the Markan seams.[32]
2. (8:31) "many things" (polla). The adverbial use of polla is listed as one of the seven words and phrases characteristic of Mark by Hawkins.[33]
3. (8:31) "to teach." This verb is a favorite term in Mark and is used seventeen times to describe Jesus' activity. The emphasis it receives in Mark becomes clearer when we compare its occurrence in the Gospel of Matthew, in which Jesus' teachings are clearly emphasized. Yet Matthew omits the verb "to teach" from the parallel in Mark nine times (Mark 2:13; 4:1, 2; 6:34; 9:31; 10:1; 11:17; 12:14, 35), and one time he changes it (Mark 8:31).[34]
4. (8:32) "the word" (ton logon)—"plainly" in the RSV. In 1:45; 2:2; 4:14, 15(2), 16, 17, 18, 19, 20; and 8:32 Mark uses this term absolutely and in each instance seems to be referring to the gospel message.
5. (9:30) "would not have any one know it." We find a close parallel to this in Mark 7:24 ("would not have any one know it"), and the theme fits closely with the theme of the messianic secret in Mark.
6. (9:31) "for he was teaching." We have here once again another reference to the teaching ministry of Jesus.

31. G. Strecker has sought to prove that of the three predictions only one (8:31) is traditional. The others are Markan creations. As to 8:31 while this is traditional, it is not authentic but a *vaticinia ex eventu* ("The Passion—and Resurrection Predictions in Mark's Gospel [Mark 8:31; 9:31; 10:32–34]," *Interp* 22 [1968]:421–42). To see Mark's hand in the latter two predictions, however, does not require that they be *de novo* Markan creations. And the denial of the authenticity of Mark 8:31 by some scholars is based primarily upon the *a priori* presupposition that such prophecy cannot occur rather than upon exegetical considerations.

32. See Vincent Taylor, *The Gospel According to St. Mark* (London: Macmillan, 1959), p. 48; and Stein, "The 'Redaktionsgeschichtlich' Investigation of a Markan Seam," p. 74.

33. John C. Hawkins, *Horae Synopticae* (Oxford; Clarendon, 1909), pp. 10–11.

34. Other statistics also show Mark's emphasis in this area. In two places where Mark uses the title "teacher" for Jesus, Matthew changes it to "Lord" (Mark 4:38, 9:17). In three places where Mark uses "teacher," Matthew omits it (Mark 10:20, 35; 13:1). In all, Matthew, whose Gospel contains 65 percent more material than Mark's, uses the term "to teach" fourteen times to Mark's seventeen, "teacher" twelve times to Mark's twelve, and "teaching" three times to Mark's five. See Stein, " 'Redaktionsgeschichtlich' Investigation," pp. 84, 91–92.

7. (10:32) "And they were . . . going up . . ." (*ēsan anabainontes*). This is one of twenty-four instances in which the paraphrastic construction with the imperfect is used in Mark.[35]
8. (10:32) "and Jesus was walking ahead. . . ." This is another example of Mark's use of the paraphrastic construction with the imperfect of *eimi*.
9. (10:32) "and they were amazed. . . ." The term "amazed" (*thambeomai*) is found only three times in the New Testament; all are found in Mark and all three appear to be Markan constructions (cf. 1:27; 10:24). The intensive form of this root, "greatly amazed" (*ekthambeomai*), is found four times in the New Testament and all four examples are found in Mark (9:15; 14:33; 16:5, 6).
10. The general use of the imperfect—8:31 (*ērxato*); 8:32 (*elalei*); 9:30 (*pareporeuonto*), (*ēthelen*); 9:31 (*edidasken*), (*elegen*); 9:32 (*ēgnooun*), (*ephobounto*); 10:32 (*ēn*), (*ethambounto*), (*ephobounto*), (*ērxato*). The Markan summaries clearly have a proclivity toward the imperfect, so that their presence suggests the hand of Mark.[36]

With regard to certain teachings on discipleship in 8:31–10:45 we can also detect the hand of the Evangelist. A few of the more obvious examples are:

1. (8:34) "the multitude with his disciples." The awkwardness of this phrase reminds one of a similar awkwardness in Mark 4:10— "those who were about him with the twelve."
2. (8:35) "the gospel's." In the Gospels the noun "gospel" is found only in Matthew and Mark. In Matthew it occurs four times; in three of these instances the expression "the gospel of the kingdom" is used (Matt. 4:23; 9:35; 24:14), and once (Matt. 26:13) it is used absolutely, as in the Markan parallel (Mark 14:9). In Mark the term is used seven times, and of these seven occurrences five are absolute (Mark 1:15; 8:35; 10:29; 13:10; 14:9). It should also be noted that in Mark 8:35 the expression interrupts the rhythm of the antithetical parallelism found in the verse and is a probable Markan insertion into the saying.
3. (10:32) "followed." In this editorial seam the Evangelist may have used this term due to its appearance in Mark 8:34; 9:38; and 10:21 (cf. also 10:52).

35. See C. H. Turner, "Marcan Usage: Notes, Critical and Exegetical, on the Second Gospel, VIII," *JTS* 28 (1927): 349–51.
36. Hedrick, "The Role of 'Summary Statements,' " p. 292.

Having noted some of the redactional work of Mark, we now need to observe the theological consequences that result. The threefold pattern found in Mark 8:31–10:45 reveals that, for the Evangelist, Jesus' passion is neither accidental nor a tragedy but was clearly foreknown by Jesus. The cross was a divine necessity, as the "must" (*dei*) of Mark 8:31 reveals. Furthermore, the errors of the disciples are used as a foil by which Jesus' teachings on discipleship can be presented.[37] Discipleship, for Mark, means following Jesus and taking up a cross (8:34). It means a willingness even to lose one's life for Christ's sake or, to word it differently, to lose one's life for "the gospel's" sake (8:35). Discipleship, for Mark, means becoming servant of all (9:35), even as Jesus was servant of all (10:45). It involves the removal/repentance of any area of life that proves a hindrance in one's life (9:43–48). It requires a right perspective concerning possessions (10:17–31). It may even involve drinking Jesus' cup and experiencing his baptism (10:38–39; cf. 14:36). One cannot help but see in this section of Mark that "following" Jesus involves an *imitatio Christi* with respect to Jesus' example, and there is especially evident a strong emphasis with regard to following him "unto death."

Many suggestions have been made as to the *Sitz im Leben* to which or in which Mark wrote his Gospel. Was Mark writing to a community that was questioning why the Son of God died on the cross? Was he writing to a church that elevated the supernatural in Jesus' ministry and minimized his passion? Was he writing to a situation in which a "sufferingless" Christianity was being taught? Or was Mark writing to a church already beginning to experience persecution (perhaps under Nero) in order to prepare them for this period of trial? We are faced with the difficulty of tying together the *what* of the Markan redactional emphasis, i.e., his unique theological stress, with the *why* of his *Sitz im Leben*. It is clear that in Mark 8:31–10:45 the Evangelist emphasizes the theme of following Jesus and bearing one's cross. The reason why he stresses this is far less clear. We are faced here with the same situation that we find in the Markan "messianic secret." That Mark emphasized the theme of the messianic secret is undeniable. To this extent Wrede was correct. But why Mark stressed this is unclear. And, in his explanation of *why*, Wrede was incorrect. Nevertheless we must be thankful for what our redactional investigation of this passage has revealed, for we see more clearly than ever the importance Mark places upon following Jesus, even if such discipleship leads to sharing in his "cup" and

---

37. The view that Mark was seeking by this to discredit the disciples and especially Peter (see Theodore J. Weeden, *Mark: Traditions in Conflict* [Philadelphia: Fortress, 1971]) loses sight of Mark 14:28 and 16:7.

"baptism." This emphasis needs to be stressed continually, not only in times of persecution for the gospel's sake but also in times when Christianity is "popular," perhaps especially in the latter instance. The Jesus of Mark did not promise his followers wealth, health, and long life, but rather a "cross" (Mark 8:34). Those who suggest another kind of Christianity need to remember that Peter also made such a suggestion and was severely rebuked (Mark 8:32b–33)!

12

The Value of
Redaction Criticism

$\mathbf{H}$aving discussed the rise of redaction criticism and its
goals and having seen how one does redaction criticism, we must now
consider the value of this discipline for the study of the Gospels.[1] In
some circles redaction criticism, like form criticism, has received a bad
press because of the radical conclusions and theories of some practitioners of this discipline. It also cannot be denied that many of the
earliest redaction critics, like many of the early form critics, came from
the left of the theological spectrum and brought with them into their
investigation radical presuppositions as to the history of the traditions
and of the early church. Also, the subtlety of some redaction criticism
makes one think that Origen is alive once again and that his allegorical
method of interpretation has fallen fourfold upon the redaction critics
and been born again in their interpretations. We must remember, however, that the misuse of a tool does not cast shadows of suspicion upon
the tool itself but rather upon its users.

If the Evangelists used sources in the composition of their Gospels,
and Luke 1:1–4 affirms this, then the study of how the Evangelists
used these sources and the particular emphases they gave to them is a
perfectly legitimate and natural procedure. The proper response to the

1. The practice of redaction criticism need not be limited to the Gospels. Any work
which uses sources can be investigated with the purpose of observing how the author
used and edited those sources to make his point.

incorrect use of redaction criticism by some practitioners is not the non-use or repudiation of the discipline but rather its correct application! The correct use of redaction criticism involves a proper understanding of what this discipline can and cannot do. What can redaction criticism do? Of what value is this discipline? There would appear to be several helpful insights and contributions that redaction criticism brings to the study of the Gospels.

The Evangelists as Interpreters of Tradition

When we speak today of the "theology" of Mark or a Lukan "emphasis," to a great degree we are indebted to the work of the redaction critics. In evaluating redaction criticism one must recall the view that dominated gospel studies until the rise of this discipline. Up to this time the Evangelists were considered faceless editors who simply gathered gospel traditions and assembled "tradition collections" that were valuable for studying the *Sitz im Leben* of the early church. Redaction criticism can be thanked for having restored the writers of the Gospels to their rightful place as authors. The gospel writers are Evangelists who wrote Gospels. They were not merely collectors of tradition; they were interpreters of these traditions. To be sure, many of the redaction critics did not attribute divine authority to the Evangelists or inspiration to their works, but this is not a property or attribute of the discipline itself but rather of the presuppositions one brings to its practice.[2] A lasting contribution of redaction criticism has been to emphasize the important role that the Evangelists played in the composition of the Gospels.

The Gospels as Wholes

Once the Evangelists were acknowledged as theological authors, a natural corollary was that their works were to be viewed as whole books and not just collections of isolated pericopes. Form criticism tended to focus its attention on the individual "trees" (pericopes) in the "forest" (the individual Gospels), and in so doing tended to lose sight of the forest itself. Even though redaction criticism at times focuses its attention on an individual pericope and how a particular Evangelist interpreted it, this is done in the context of how the redac-

2. G. B. Caird comments in this regard, "Redaction Criticism treat[s] the evangelists as interpreters, but all too often with the tacit assumption that to interpret is to misinterpret. Considering that they [redaction critics] are themselves professional interpreters, it might seem wiser to allow for the possibility that an interpreter should occasionally be right" ("The Study of the Gospels: III. Redaction Criticism, *ET* 87 [1976]:172).

tion fits into the whole Gospel. It always asks such questions as "Does this emphasis occur elsewhere in the Gospel? How does the redaction of the Evangelist here fit the entire Gospel?" Skillful redaction criticism never loses sight of the "forest," for it sees each Gospel as the work of an individual author and in so doing investigates the whole work in order to understand that author's theological emphasis. To use a slightly different analogy, whereas form criticism tended to focus all of its attention on the individual pieces of the puzzle and sought to learn all it could about what each piece revealed about the early church and the historical Jesus, redaction criticism focuses its study on the unique shades and hues that each Evangelist gave to these bits of tradition. Its ultimate concern is how these pieces fit together to make particular portraits that can truthfully be entitled: "The Gospel according to Matthew," "The Gospel according to Mark," "The Gospel according to Luke," and "The Gospel according to John."

The Meaning of the Gospels

Since the rise of redaction criticism we are better able than before to see what parts of the Gospels are due to the editorial work of the Evangelists and thus better able to perceive their emphases. This does not mean that up to this time no work had been done in this area. The analysis of the characteristic vocabulary and style of each Evangelist has always been part of any good commentary.[3] Source criticism was likewise concerned with this subject,[4] and some works deal specifically with this area of study.[5] Yet the interest in the theology of the gospel writers that redaction criticism brought about has led to a greater effort than ever before to discover the style, vocabulary, and editorial work of the Evangelists. Furthermore, with the added insights of form criticism as to the shape of the tradition before it was written down, we understand more clearly how the Evangelists ordered and arranged the materials that were available to them. Through all this we are better able to detect those elements, i.e., the editorial redaction, which serve as the raw materials for the production of a Matthean, Markan, and Lukan theology.

---

3. See, for instance, Willoughby C. Allen, *A Critical and Exegetical Commentary on the Gospel According to St. Matthew* (Edinburgh: T. & T. Clark, 1922), pp. xiii–lxii; Vincent Taylor, *The Gospel According to St. Mark* (London: Macmillan, 1959), pp. 44–54; Alfred Plummer, *A Critical and Exegetical Commentary on the Gospel According to St. Luke* (Edinburgh: T. & T. Clark, 1905), pp. xli–lxvii; etc.

4. See, for instance, John C. Hawkins, *Horae Synopticae* (Oxford: Clarendon, 1909).

5. See the series of articles on "Marcan Usage" by C. H. Turner, in *JTS* 25–29 (1924–28); H. J. Cadbury, *The Style and Literary Method of Luke* (Cambridge: Harvard University, 1920); etc.

With the investigation of an Evangelist's theology,[6] we have finally come to the place of examining the "meaning" of the text! The main concern of form criticism does not lie with the meaning of the text, i.e., the meaning of the Gospel of Matthew, the Gospel of Mark, and so on, but rather with the investigation of the subject matter found in the text. In other words, form criticism was not interested in the meaning of the Gospels themselves but with what it could learn from the "stuff" found in the Gospels concerning the history of the early church (the second *Sitz im Leben*) and about the historical Jesus (the first *Sitz im Leben*). Without denying the legitimacy of such study, it must be remembered that if Matthew, Mark, and Luke are not pericope collections but Gospels, we are not actually seeking the meaning of these "books" when we merely investigate the subject matter contained in them. We are seeking the meaning of these "books" only when we attempt to understand what the authors are trying to teach by their works. In redaction criticism we have passed beyond the investigation of the "stuff" contained in the Gospels to the investigation of *how* that "stuff" is used by the gospel writers and *how* it functions in the purpose of their Gospels. This pursuit after the meaning of the Gospels requires the careful delimitation of each author's contribution to his work, and this is better discerned today than it was before, thanks to the work of the redaction critics.

The Entire History of the Gospel Traditions

Redaction criticism has brought a more accurate description of the history of the tradition (*Traditionsgeschichte*). Marxsen has provided a most useful model for describing this history by his reference to the three separate *Sitz im Leben*(s), or life situations, found in the Gospels: the ministry and teachings of the historical Jesus (the first *Sitz im Leben*); the situation of the early church during the "oral period"[7] (the second *Sitz im Leben*); and the situation of the individual Evangelists (the third *Sitz im Leben*). This terminology has provided helpful handles for the discussion of the gospel materials, and their usage has helped to clarify and give a degree of precision to the discipline that was not

6. It should again be pointed out that the redaction critics' interest in the "theology" of the Evangelists is not an interest in their total theological beliefs but primarily a concern for their unique theological emphases.

7. By "oral period" we simply mean the period between the historical Jesus and the period when the Gospels were written down. There is no need to deny that during this period a little, or some, or much, or a great deal of the gospel traditions were being written down. It is also not necessary to deny that oral traditions continued to play a part in the life of the church after the Gospels were written.

previously possible. As a result, the student is better able to compre-
hend with greater accuracy what area of gospel research is being referred to when someone speaks of a gospel tradition in the first, second, or third *Sitz im Leben.*

The Quest of the Historical Jesus

Joachim Jeremias has argued that in the quest for the *ipsissima verba*
or *vox* of Jesus there are five helpful bulwarks that keep us from mod-
ernizing the historical Jesus and enable us to penetrate back to the first
Sitz im Leben. One of these is "the remarkable literary criticism," which
among other things has taught us "to recognize the style of composition of the evangelists, and hence to distinguish between tradition and
redaction."[8] This safeguard functions in both a positive and a negative
way. If a passage or saying in a Gospel betrays a terminology and style
that is typically "Matthean" (or "Markan" or "Lukan"), it functions
negatively and raises questions concerning its authenticity. This does
not mean, of course, that such passages are *de novo* creations of the
Evangelist. It may be that the gospel writer has retold the tradition in
his own vocabulary and style. Nevertheless, it does indicate that the
material has been "reworked" by the Evangelist, so that it is far more
difficult to establish the authenticity of such passages or sayings. On
the other hand, this bulwark can be used positively in the sense that if
a passage betrays a non-Matthean (or non-Markan or non-Lukan) terminology and style, then it is clearly traditional. Being "traditional"
does not, of course, prove that the material is authentic, since we have
simply proven that the material did not arise out of the third *Sitz im
Leben.* But we must certainly admit that since the second *Sitz im Leben* is
closer to the first *Sitz im Leben* than is the third, something that existed
in the second *Sitz im Leben* has a greater probability of being authentic
than something that arose in the third.

Another way in which redaction criticism is useful in this area involves the appearance within a Gospel of certain materials that, at first
glance at least, seem to oppose the main emphasis of the Evangelist.
For example, if we find in Matthew traditional material that contains
non-Matthean terminology and a non-Matthean style and that also
appears to diverge from the normal emphases of this Evangelist, this

8. Joachim Jeremias, *The Problem of the Historical Jesus,* trans. Norman Perrin (Philadelphia: Fortress, 1964), pp. 15–20. The other four bulwarks listed by Jeremias are the laws
form criticism has discovered which governed the shaping of the material; greater understanding of the religious climate and customs of Jesus' day; greater knowledge of Galil-
ean Aramaic which Jesus spoke; and the rediscovery of the eschatological character of
Jesus' message.

finding argues in favor of the tradition being so well-known that Matthew felt compelled to include it despite its lack of "fitting" into his particular theological emphasis. Such strong traditional material is quite likely to be traceable to the historical Jesus himself.[9]

Hermeneutical Insights

Redaction criticism has shown that the Evangelists were truly interpreters of the Jesus traditions. Present-day exegetes can gain a great deal of insight into the interpretation of the Gospels by investigating how the Evangelists dealt with the materials that lay before them. In so doing, we can observe how they understood the meaning that the texts possessed in the first and/or second *Sitz im Leben* and applied this to their own situation. This in turn provides insight as to how we today, upon understanding the meaning imparted by the Evangelists to the gospel materials, can apply them to our own situation in life. Wording this somewhat differently, we can say that observing the significance that the Evangelists gave to the meaning of the gospel materials enables us better to see how the Gospels can be significant today. Furthermore, if one attributes divine authority to the Evangelists, we often possess not only a divine Word from Jesus himself, but an authoritative interpretation of that Word.[10] We are doubly enriched in such instances. And, if we have in the triple tradition a threefold interpretation of a saying or deed of Jesus, are we not far richer as exegetes than if each of the Evangelists simply repeated in unison the *ipsissima verba* of Jesus? Rather than a single Word from the Lord repeated three times, we possess a trio of voices (or a quartet, if we are able to penetrate back to the actual words of the historical Jesus) that sing the divine message. As we seek to sing that message to our audiences today, we can be greatly helped by observing how the Evangelists orchestrated that message to meet the particular needs of their audiences.

We have already observed several examples of how this works. One of these involved Jesus' teaching on divorce. It was pointed out that the "exception clause" in Matthew 5:31–32 and 19:7–9 is redactional in nature.[11] If we assume that Matthew, like Paul, has "the Spirit of God" (1 Cor. 7:40), Matthew by his redaction helps us to understand that in

9. For a fuller discussion of this criterion for authenticity, see Robert H. Stein, "The 'Criteria' for Authenticity," in *Gospel Perspectives*, ed. R. T. France and David Wenham (Sheffield, England: JSOT, 1980), 1:247–48.

10. For a discussion of where one finds authority in the process of *Traditionsgeschichte*, see Robert H. Stein, *An Introduction to the Parables of Jesus* (Philadelphia: Westminster, 1981), p. 63.

11. See above pp. 151–53.

Mark 10:11–12 and Luke 16:18 Jesus was not seeking to give a universal law to cover every possible situation in life. On the contrary in rebuking the loose attitude certain Pharisees had toward divorce, Jesus emphasized the divine plan found in Genesis 1:27 and 2:24 by means of an overstatement. By his readaction Matthew helps us to interpret what Jesus meant by his saying on divorce, for Matthew understood it as an overstatement for effect. Jesus found divorce so contrary to the plan of God that he did not want to enter into the debate over "the good reasons for divorce" (Mark 10:2f.). As a result of his redaction, Matthew helps us to apply Jesus' teaching on divorce to our own situation.

Another example we looked at was Matthew 10:37.[12] Here we found an important parallel to Luke 14:26. Matthew by his redaction helps us to understand what the terms *love* and *hate* mean by his use of the words *loving more*. Matthew was aware that the love-hate imagery was an idiomatic expression for loving more or preferring someone over another. We have seen that Matthew provides insight as to how the parable of the lost sheep (Luke 15:4–7) which was addressed to the Pharisees and scribes (Luke 15:2–3) is applicable to the church (Matthew 18:10–14).[13] Matthew also by his placement of Matthew 10:34 ("Do not think that I have come to bring peace on earth; I have not come to bring peace, but a sword.") reveals that this verse should be interpreted in a nonpolitical sense because in the following two verses we read of family strife, not political conflict. Through such interpretative techniques the Evangelists enable us not only to see how they applied these teachings to their own situation in life but also provide insights as to how we can apply them to our situation as well.

Conclusion

In concluding this section on the value of redaction criticism, it needs to be pointed out once again that the aims of this discipline are limited. Redaction criticism does not seek to discover the total theology of the Evangelists but rather the particular emphases that they gave to the tradition. As a result the redactional theology of Matthew, Mark, and Luke will, by definition, tend to be different. What is "unique" to Matthew's theology, as evidenced by his redactional emphases, cannot be unique in Mark or Luke as well. Likewise, a unique Lukan emphasis in the triple tradition can hardly be a unique emphasis of Matthew and/or Mark. Redaction criticism clearly emphasizes the "disunity" or,

12. See above pp. 153–54.
13. See above pp. 247–51.

to use a better term, the "diversity" of the Gospels. To speak of the "diversity" found in the Gospels, however, does not require that these different emphases conflict with or contradict each other. We must keep in mind that in redaction criticism we are not investigating the total theology of the Evangelists. This has already been pointed out.[14] Yet the frequent error of equating the diversity of the Evangelists with their total theology must be called once again to our attention. The tremendous unity of Matthew, Mark, and Luke, which any non-Christian reading these books for the first time would immediately recognize, must not be forgotten or lost sight of in the pursuit of the unique emphasis of each Evangelist in his handling of the tradition. After all, the early church included *all four of the Gospels* in its canon of Scripture! This indicates that the great unity of these Gospels was apparent and that their diversity was interpreted in the context of this unity.

14. See above pp. 234–35.

Glossary

Apocryphal   An adjective used to designate noncanonical works written in the second to sixth centuries such as: the Gospel of Thomas, the Acts of Paul, the Epistle to the Laodecians, the Apocalypse of Peter.

Apologetics   A term coming from the Greek *apologia* and referring to a reasoned defense of one's faith. In gospel studies it is frequently used of attempts to demonstrate that the Gospels do not contradict one another or that the accounts in them correspond to what actually happened.

Authentic   When used with regard to the sayings of Jesus, a saying is "authentic" when the saying in its present form originated from Jesus himself.

Community (e.g. Markan)   The supposed church community whose practices and beliefs are reflected within the Gospel of Mark.

Docetism   An early Christian heresy associated with gnosticism which due to its view that matter was evil denied the incarnation (cf. 1 John 4:2-3). Docetism maintained that the Word was a pure Spirit, disguised as a man. It only "seemed" (*dokeo*) that the Word had become incarnate.

Double Tradition   The material common to both Matthew and Luke but not in Mark. For those who hold the two-source hypothesis, this is the Q material.

Form Criticism   The English equivalent of the German *Formgeschichte*. In gospel studies this refers to the investigation of the gospel traditions in order to learn about the situation in which they circulated during the oral period, i.e., the period between the resurrection of Jesus and the writing of the canonical Gospels. This period is sometimes referred to as the second *Sitz im Leben*.

Four-source Hypothesis   The theory that Matthew and Luke used four specific sources in composing their Gospels.

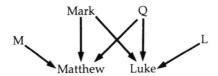

Fragmentary Hypothesis The theory that the synoptic Gospels arose out of numerous small remembrances (*memorabilia*) of Jesus' life and teachings rather than out of larger sources (such as Mark, Q, M, and L.)

Griesbach Hypothesis The theory that in the writing of the synoptic Gospels, Matthew was written first, Luke was second and used Matthew, and Mark was last and used both Matthew and Luke.

Harder Reading Used when comparing parallel accounts in the Gospels. This term refers to the account which appears to present the greater difficulty for the first-century reader. Since the tendency of the Gospel writers was to make the reading of an account easier, the harder reading possesses greater likelihood of being "authentic."

Harmony Used with regard to the synoptic Gospels when the main concern for placing the accounts in the three Gospels together in parallel form is the attempt to place the accounts of the synoptic Gospels in chronological order.

Hermeneutics The science by which one seeks to understand the meaning of a text and to explain that meaning and its implications to others.

Hermeneutical Circle The description of the interpretative process by which any part of a work is interpreted in the light of one's conception of the whole work, and the whole work is at the same time being interpreted in light of one's conception of the particular part.

Ipsissima verba Used with regard to the sayings of Jesus when one is convinced that he now possesses "the very words" of Jesus.

Ipsissima vox Used with regard to the sayings of Jesus when one is convinced that he now possesses "the very voice" of Jesus.

Kerygmatic Material dealing with the preaching (*kerygma*), or faith statements, of the early church. It is frequently understood as standing in contrast to the critical-historical reconstruction of the subject. For example, the kerygmatic Christ (the picture of Jesus Christ in the New Testament) versus the historical Jesus (the nonsupernatural Jesus of historical research).

Lachmann Fallacy The erroneous conclusion that Matthew's and Luke's never agreeing in order against Mark proves Markan priority. Lachmann himself was not guilty of this fallacy, but concluded that since Matthew and Luke never agree in order againt Mark *and* since there exist plausible reasons for Matthew and Luke having changed the order of Mark but not vice versa, this proves the priority of Mark.

Lachmann Hypothesis The theory that in the writing of the synoptic Gospels, Matthew and Luke used an earlier gospel which most resembles Mark, as well as another source. Frequently this theory is understood as arguing that Matthew and Luke used Mark and Q in writing their Gospels and is a synonym for the two-document (two-source) Hypothesis.

Literary Criticism Frequently used in two different ways. It can refer to the analysis of the Bible as literature. In this work it is used in its older sense to refer to the analysis of a document in order to discover the literary sources that underlie it, i.e., as a synonym for "source criticism."

Midrash Refers, in the narrow sense, to a Jewish homiletical commentary. In more general usage it refers to a literary genre dealing with an interpretation of Scripture.

Oral Period Generally used to define the period between the resurrection of Jesus and the writing of our Gospels (c. 30–65) when the transmission of the gospel materials was primarily oral.

Parallelismus membrorum Literally means "parallism of the members." It refers to a trait of Semitic poetry in which meter or rhythm plays a dominant role. Some of the more common forms are *synonymous parallelism,* in which the succeeding line(s) repeat the same thought; *antithetical parallelism,* in which the succeeding line gives the opposite thought; *chiastic parallelism,* in which we have the pattern of thought A - thought B - thought b - thought a; and *synthetic parallelism,* in which the second line continues or develops the thought of the first line.

Parousia A Greek term meaning "coming" which the New Testament uses to refer to the coming of the Son of man at the end of history, i.e., the second coming.

Patristic A term referring to the period of the early church fathers (from the end of the first to about the eighth century).

Pericope Used to describe a short section or passage of a writing. When used in gospel studies, it refers to a short, self-contained section of a Gospel.

Primitive When used with regard to the sayings of Jesus, a saying is "more primitive" when it has undergone less editorial modification and is therefore closer to what the historical Jesus uttered or to the actual historical circumstances.

Priority of Mark The theory that Mark was the first synoptic Gospel written and that it was the primary source used by Matthew and Luke.

Proto-Luke The earliest hypothetical form of the Gospel of Luke consisting essentially of Q and L material but not Mark.

Proto-Matthew The earliest hypothetical form of the Gospel of Matthew consisting essentially of Q and M material but not Mark.

Q Hypothesis The theory that Matthew and Luke used a common source of Jesus' sayings, most probably written, which consists essentially of the material common only to Matthew and Luke.

Redaction Criticism The English equivalent of the German *Redaktions-geschichte.* In gospel studies this refers to the investigation of the gospel traditions in order to learn about the situation in which they were written down into our canonical Gospels, i.e., the situation of the Evangelists. This is sometimes referred to as the third *Sitz im Leben.*

Seams The connections composed by the Evangelists to join together individual pieces of tradition. Assuming that Mark found most of the traditions that he incorporated into his Gospel as individual units, the Markan seams are the material that the Evangelist used to "sew together" these units to make the Gospel of Mark. Since such seams require more editorial works on the part of the Evangelist than his recounting various traditional materials, the Markan seams provide a rich source for ascertaining the Evangelist's redactional emphases.

Sitz im Leben   Literally means "situation in life." In gospel studies this refers to the different situations in life that can be investigated in the studies of the Gospels. The three *Sitz im Leben*(s) are: (1) the situation of the historical Jesus; (2) the situation of the early church during the oral period, i.e., between the first and third *Sitz im Leben*(s); and (3) the situation of the Evangelist when writing his Gospel.

Source Criticism   See "Literary Criticism."

Synopsis   Used with regard to the synoptic Gospels when the major emphasis in bringing the accounts of the three Gospels together is the attempt to place the accounts side by side in order to compare them. A horizontal parallel synopsis is one in which the parallel accounts are placed below each other.

Matthew ⸺⸺⸺⸺⸺⸺⸺⸺⸺⸺⸺⸺⸺⸺⸺⸺⸺⸺⸺⸺⸺⸺⸺⸺⸺

Mark ⸺⸺⸺⸺⸺⸺⸺⸺⸺⸺⸺⸺⸺⸺⸺⸺⸺⸺⸺⸺⸺⸺⸺⸺⸺⸺⸺

Luke ⸺⸺⸺⸺⸺⸺⸺⸺⸺⸺⸺⸺⸺⸺⸺⸺⸺⸺⸺⸺⸺⸺⸺⸺⸺⸺⸺

A vertical parallel synopsis is one in which the parallel accounts are placed side by side in vertical columns.

Matthew	Mark	Luke

Synoptic Problem   The "problem" as to why the Gospels of Matthew, Mark, and Luke look so much alike.

Tannaim   The Jewish rabbis of the first and second centuries.

Textual Criticism   The study of ancient manuscripts, whose autographs are unknown, in order to ascertain the most probable wording of the original texts.

Triple Tradition   The material common to Matthew, Mark, and Luke.

Two-Source Hypothesis   The hypothesis that Mark was the first Gospel written, and that Matthew and Luke used both Mark and another source (Q) in writing their Gospels.

Urevangelium   Generally used to refer to some hypothetical early gospel, usually understood to have been written in Aramaic, which underlies all three Synoptic Gospels.

Ur-gospel   See "Urevangelium."

Ur-markus (Ur-Mark)   Generally used to refer to some hypothetical early gospel which underlies the Gospel of Mark.

Scripture Index

Genesis

1:27—271
2:24—271
18:20-26—98
29:29—154
29:30-31—154

Exodus

31:31—98
32—259
34:7—98

Numbers

14:18-19—98

Deuteronomy

4:10—206
6:7—206
7:18—206
8:2—206
9:7—206
11:19—206

Psalms

22:1—58
118:25—55

Proverbs

3:9-10—226
10:3-4—226
13:21—226
15:1—226
17:2—226
22:6—226
22:16—226

Isaiah

35:5-6—249
53:4—98
53:12—63, 98
61:1—249

1QpHAB

2:7—164
7:2—164

Matthew

1:1—77, 190
1:16—190
1:17—190
1:20—77
1:22—80-81
1:22-23—247

2:1-12—102
2:4—190
2:13-23—102
2:15—80-81, 247
2:17—80-81
2:17-18—247
2:23—80-81, 247
3:3—84
3:7-10—90-91, 110
3:7-12—105
3:11-12—122
3:12—91, 110
3:13-16—73-74
3:15—143
3:16—75, 82
4:1-11—171
4:1—53
4:2-11—105
4:3-11—91, 110
4:4—81
4:6—81
4:10—81
4:12—240
4:14—80-81, 147
4:14-16—247
4:18—83, 155
4:20—82
4:22—75, 82

Index

Robert H. Stein (Ph.D., Princeton Theological Seminary) is the Mildred and Ernest Hogan Professor of New Testament Interpretation at The Southern Baptist Theological Seminary. He is the author of numerous books, including *A Basic Guide to Interpreting the Bible* and the commentary on Luke in the New American Commentary.